Attack and Die

CIVIL WAR MILITARY TACTICS AND THE SOUTHERN HERITAGE

Attack and Die

Civil War Military Tactics and the Southern Heritage

GRADY McWHINEY and
PERRY D. JAMIESON

The University of Alabama Press
University, Alabama

Library of Congress Cataloging in Publication Data

McWhiney, Grady.
  Attack and die.

  Bibliography: p.
  Includes index.
  1. Confederate States of America. Army—History.
2. United States—History—Civil War, 1861–1865—
Campaigns and battles. I. Jamieson, Perry D.
II. Title. III. Title: Civil War military tactics and
the Southern heritage.
E545.M38   973.7'3013   81-902
ISBN 0-8173-0073-2   AACR2

For
Harold Jamieson
and in memory of
E. B. "Pete" Long

"OUR CAUSE IN HISTORY. A land without ruins is a land without memories—a land without memories is a land without history. . . . The triumphs of might are transient—they pass and are forgotten—the sufferings of right are graven deepest on the chronicle of nations."—A toast at the Howitzer's Banquet, Richmond, Virginia, December 13, 1882.

"The muse of history will not turn traitor to your cause, . . . your fame shall not be forgotten. . . . England made the literature of her time—Scotland made none; England conquered—Scotland was overcome; and yet none remembers the victorious Edward—he has passed and is forgotten—but the names of William Wallace and Robert Bruce are graven ineffaceably upon the 'Chronicles of Nations' and the story of their deeds and their sufferings have been . . . intertwined with all that is noblest."—Response by the Reverend H. Melville Jackson.

Contents

Maps

Tables

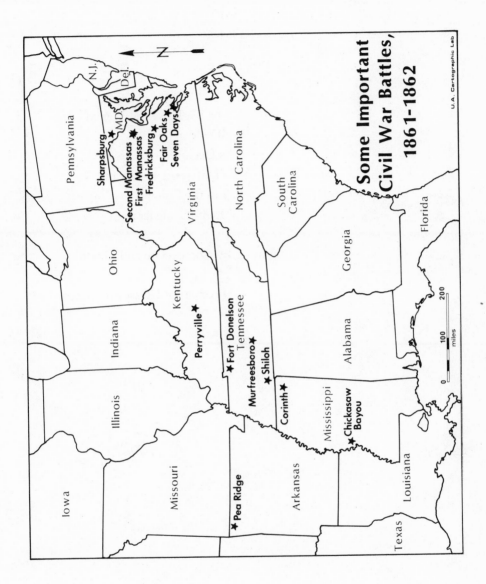

Some Important Civil War Battles, 1861-1862

N

Iowa

Missouri

Illinois

Indiana

Ohio

Pennsylvania

N.J.

Del.

MD.

★ Sharpsburg

Second Manassas
First Manassas
Fredricksburg ★
Fair Oaks ★
Seven Days ★

Virginia

Kentucky

★ Perryville

★ Fort Donelson

Tennessee

North Carolina

★ Murfreesboro
★ Shiloh

South Carolina

★ Pea Ridge

Arkansas

Corinth ★

Mississippi

★ Chickasaw
Bayou

Alabama

Georgia

Louisiana

Texas

Florida

0   100   200
miles

U.A. Cartographic Lab

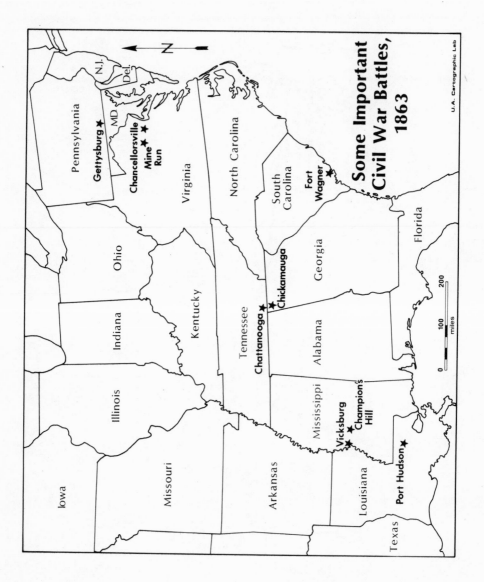

Some Important Civil War Battles, 1863

U.A. Cartographic Lab

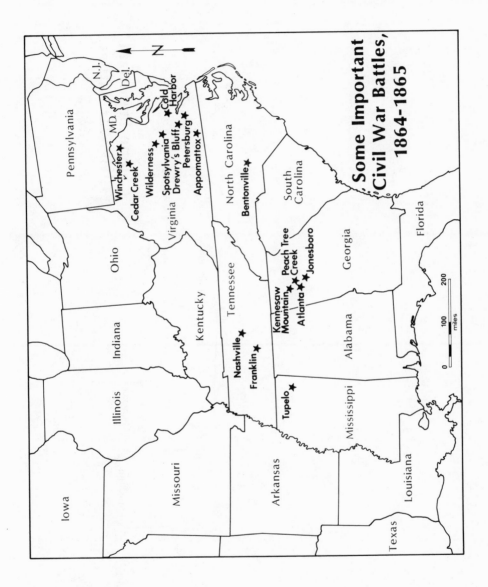

Some Important Civil War Battles, 1864-1865

N

Pennsylvania

N.J.

Del.

MD.

Winchester ★

Cedar Creek ★

Wilderness ★

Spotsylvania ★
Drewry's Bluff ★

Petersburg ★

Appomattox ★

Cold
Harbor ★

Virginia

North Carolina

Bentonville ★

South
Carolina

Georgia

Florida

Ohio

Kentucky

Tennessee

Peach Tree
Creek ★

Kennesaw
Mountain ★

Atlanta ★★

Jonesboro ★

Alabama

Indiana

Nashville ★

Franklin ★

Tupelo ★

Illinois

Missouri

Arkansas

Mississippi

Louisiana

Iowa

Texas

0   100   200
miles

Preface

There are nearly as many explanations of Confederate defeat as there are historians writing about the Civil War. They have blamed excessive southern localism, poor diplomacy, the blockade, financial problems, weak administration, an unsound political system, excessive democracy, inadequate resources, misuse of the black population, better northern leadership, loss of the will to fight, and a host of other things. Northerners often seem satisfied that the outcome was inevitable: sinful southern slaveholders had no chance against righteous Yankee freedom lovers. Southerners have tended to argue that the Confederacy faced overwhelming odds.

One historian claims that "in view of the disparity of resources, it would have taken a miracle, a direct intervention of the Lord on the other side, to enable the South to win. As usual," he insists, "God was on the side of the heaviest battalions."[1] But the side with "the heaviest battalions" has not always prevailed. Despite an almost two-to-one inferiority in numbers, Epaminondas decisively defeated the Spartans at Leuctra in 371 B.C. At Cannae in 216 B.C. Hannibal destroyed over 90 percent of a numerically superior Roman force. At Preston in 1648 Oliver Cromwell defeated an army more than twice the size of his own. At Rossbach in 1757 Frederick the Great outmaneuvered an army of over 64,000, twice his numbers; he lost 500 men while inflicting 7,700 casualties. At Buena Vista in 1847 Zachary Taylor, commanding fewer than 5,000 Americans, defeated over 15,000 Mexicans; indeed, throughout the Mexican War the Americans won every battle against much more numerous opponents. And in the twentieth century, of course, there were the French in Algeria and the Americans in Viet Nam.

The tragedy for the Confederates was that they rushed confidently and courageously against the more numerous Yankees but failed to defeat them. "Southern morale was exceedingly high at the beginning of the conflict,"

---

[1]Richard N. Current, "God and the Strongest Battalions," in *Why the North Won the Civil War*, ed. David Herbert Donald (Baton Rouge, 1960), 22.

noted Bell I. Wiley. "Indeed, it is doubtful that any people ever went to war with greater enthusiasm than did Confederates in 1861." As defeat followed defeat, however, this spirit faded. In his perceptive little book, *The Road to Appomattox*, Wiley included a most instructive chart that he called "Curve of Confederate Morale." It shows that from a high point after the Battle of First Manassas in July 1861, southern morale dropped sharply following the fall of Fort Henry, Fort Donelson, and Nashville in February 1862; it rose somewhat in the summer and early fall of 1862, as Confederate armies invaded Kentucky and Maryland, but dropped continually throughout the winter and spring of 1862–1863 to reach a low after the surrender of Vicksburg and the disaster at Gettysburg in July 1863. From that time on, except for brief periods of optimism associated with some limited Confederate successes, southern morale plunged downward.[2]

What Wiley demonstrated is the close correlation between military events and the will to resist. Confederate morale declined steadily after 1861 and was only partially and temporarily revived by incomplete military triumphs. "The victory of Chickamauga sent up the Confederate loan 5 pct.," announced Judah P. Benjamin, but by then another prominent Southerner had concluded that the "enemy in due time will penetrate the heart of the Confederacy . . . and the hearts of our people will quake & their spirits will yield to the force of overpowering numbers. . . . The enemy is superior to us in everything but courage & therefore it is quite certain if war is to go on, until exhaustion overtake the one side or the other side, that we shall be the first to be exhausted." But there were some Confederates, like one determined old Texan, who refused to give up hope of victory. "As to the fate of Lee's army," he wrote just after Appomattox, "we may . . . look upon it as one amongst our disasters, but we must mend it by renewed energy, and at last, if we cannot force the envading robbers from our soil, we can all die in the effort."[3]

A great many Confederates did just that. Charles P. Roland has pointed out that more than a fourth of the million men who served in the Confederate army died of wounds or disease, and that in relation to the southern white population "these service casualties were as great as those endured by major European participants in the wars of the twentieth century. If the North during the Civil War had suffered commensurately she would have lost more than 1,000,000 men instead of 360,000. The American Colonies in revolt against England would have lost 94,000 men instead of 12,000. The United States in World War II would have lost well over 6,000,000 men instead of

[2]Bell I. Wiley, *The Road to Appomattox* (Memphis, 1956), 43, unnumbered illustration between 34 and 35.

[3]Judah P. Benjamin Diary, October 17, 1863, Confederate States of America Records, Library of Congress; Wiley, *Road to Appomattox*, 59, 75.

somewhat more than 300,000. The Confederacy rendered the heaviest sacrifices in lives . . . ever made by Americans."[4]

How and why the Confederacy lost so many men is the burden of this book. We contend that the Confederates bled themselves nearly to death in the first three years of the war by making costly attacks more often than did the Federals. Offensive tactics, which had been used so successfully by Americans in the Mexican War, were much less effective in the 1860s because an improved weapon—the rifle—had vastly increased the strength of defenders. The Confederates could have offset their numerical disadvantage by remaining on the defensive and forcing the Federals to attack; one man in a trench armed with a rifle was equal to several outside it. But Southerners, imprisoned in a culture that rejected careful calculation and patience, often refused to learn from their mistakes. They continued to fight, despite mounting casualties, with the same courageous dash and reckless abandon that had characterized their Celtic ancestors for two thousand years. The Confederates favored offensive warfare because the Celtic charge was an integral part of their heritage.

---

[4]Charles P. Roland, *The Confederacy* (Chicago, 1960), 194–95.

Acknowledgments

Many people contributed in one way or another to this book. Although no attempt is made here to list everyone who aided us or influenced our thinking, we are nevertheless grateful to them all.

We are particularly indebted to Thomas L. Connelly of the University of South Carolina and to two anonymous readers of our manuscript for their advice and criticism; to archivists Richard J. Sommers of the United States Army Military History Institute, Marie T. Capps of the United States Military Academy Library, Michael P. Musick of the National Archives, Carolyn Wallace of the University of North Carolina at Chapel Hill, and Mattie U. Russell of Duke University for helping us locate valuable items; to The University of Alabama's Research Grants Committee for research support; to Malcolm M. MacDonald and everyone else at The University of Alabama Press who worked on this volume—especially our excellent copy editor Beverly T. Denbow—for their careful professionalism; to Linda M. DeVolin of the University of Texas at El Paso for checking references; and to Wanda G. Reece of The University of Alabama for typing the manuscript.

Finally, we owe Forrest and Ellen McDonald special thanks. Forrest generously allowed us to draw upon some of the ongoing research in which he and one of the authors of this volume are engaged on the Celticness of Southerners. An earlier version of this book's final chapter was prepared at the behest of Ellen for an issue of *Continuity* that she edited.

GM
PDJ

Part One

What Happened

1

It Was Not War—It Was Murder

On July 1, 1862, General George B. McClellan's Federal forces held a strong position on Malvern Hill, near the James River, a few miles southeast of Richmond, Virginia. "It was a fine afternoon," recalled a Union officer, "hot but tempered by a cooling breeze. The soldiers waited. . . . The ranks were full." Confederate observers noted that "all approaches" to the hill were protected by Union artillery and "guarded by swarms of infantry, securely sheltered by fences, ditches, and ravines."[1] The Yankees were ready.

So were the Confederates. General Robert E. Lee had decided to disregard the advice of a division commander and to assault this formidable Federal position. For the task he selected country boys and men from the Deep South—mostly from Georgia, Alabama, Mississippi, Louisiana, and South Carolina—together with regiments from North Carolina and Virginia. These were proud soldiers, even a bit cocky now because for nearly a week they had been pushing Yankees back, and the Southerners moved briskly when ordered forward late in the afternoon of July 1 after considerable delays, confusion, and misunderstood orders. Union General Fitz John Porter thought they came on with "a reckless disregard of life, . . . with a determination to capture our army, or destroy it."

But their courage was insufficient to bring them victory. "[R]egiment after regiment, and brigade after brigade [of Confederates] rushed at our batteries," Porter recalled, "but the artillery . . . mowed them down with shrapnel, grape, and canister; while our infantry, withholding their fire until the enemy were within short range, scattered the remnants of their columns." Fourteen Confederate brigades tried unsuccessfully to break the Union line before the slaughter ended. General Daniel H. Hill, whose division lost

---

[1]Fitz John Porter, "The Battle of Malvern Hill," in *Battles and Leaders of the Civil War*, ed. Robert U. Johnson and Clarence C. Buel (4 vols., reissue, New York, 1956), II, 417; Daniel H. Hill, "McClellan's Change of Base and Malvern Hill," ibid., 392.

2,000 of its 6,500 men in what he called these "grandly heroic" assaults, wrote afterward: "It was not war—it was murder."[2]

What Hill called murder became almost commonplace during the Civil War. Confederate attacks, whether or not they drove back the enemy, usually cost many southern lives. A Federal officer described the charges made by the troops of Stonewall Jackson at Chancellorsville: "It was dusk when his men swarmed out of the woods for a quarter of a mile in our front. . . . They came on in line five and six deep. . . . I gave the command to fire, and the whole line of artillery was discharged at once. It fairly swept them from the earth; before they could recover themselves the line of artillery had been loaded and was ready for a second attack. . . . [When it came] I poured in the canister for about twenty minutes, and the affair was over." Confederate General Samuel W. Ferguson stated that the Second Alabama once charged the famous Federal Lightning Brigade in "han[d]some style, routing the enemy, . . . chasing them for several miles and capturing about fifty of their white horses," but this victory cost the Confederates heavily and took the life of the Second's commander, Colonel R. G. Earle, who "was killed a considerable distance ahead of his regiment. His loss I felt greatly," Ferguson admitted.[3]

At Sharpsburg a Federal remembered that the advance of his unit was stopped by a "long and steady line of rebel gray . . . sweeping down through the woods." Another Northerner recounted the "invincible bravery" of the attacking Confederates and how his regiment "opened a withering, *literally* withering, fire on the rebels . . . , but they still advanced. A color-bearer came forward within fifteen yards of our line, and with the utmost desperation waved a rebel flag in front of him. Our men fairly roared, 'Shoot the man with the flag!' and he went down in a twinkling and the flag was not raised in sight again." Several charges at Sharpsburg cost the Twenty-seventh North Carolina Regiment 62 percent of its 325 men. One company lost all but 5 of its 30 men; two-thirds of the men and all of the officers in another company were killed or wounded.[4]

At Gaines's Mill a Texas regiment lost 380 of its 500 men in a single

[2]U.S. War Dept., *The War of the Rebellion: A Compilation of the Official Records of the Union and Confederate Armies* (128 vols., Washington, 1880–1901), Series 1, XI (pt. 2), 496 (hereinafter cited as *OR;* unless otherwise indicated, all references are to Series 1); Porter, "Battle of Malvern Hill," II, 417; Hill, "McClellan's Change of Base," II, 395, 394.

[3]Alfred Pleasonton, "The Successes and Failures of Chancellorsville," in *Battles and Leaders,* III, 179–80; Samuel W. Ferguson, "Memoirs of Samuel Wragg Ferguson of South Carolina, Brigadier General, C.S.A." (bound typescript written in 1900), 139, Samuel Wragg Ferguson Papers, Duke University.

[4]Rufus R. Dawes, *Service With the Sixth Wisconsin Volunteers* (Marietta, Ohio, 1890), 90; Thomas L. Livermore, *Days and Events, 1860–1866* (Boston, 1920), 137, 140–41; James A. Graham, "Twenty-Seventh Regiment," in *Histories of the Several Regiments and Battalions from North Carolina, in the Great War, 1861–'65,* ed. Walter Clark (5 vols., Raleigh, 1901), II, 437.

charge, and a member of a Louisiana regiment reported that when his unit charged "four of my companions fell dead, and four severely wounded, within ten steps of me, in the short space of fifteen minutes, while I escaped with a bullet hole in my hat. Strange to say, from the position in which our regiment was placed not a single one of the enemy was visible, being concealed behind a breastwork of logs."[5]

Confederate assaults on fortified positions produced the heaviest losses. General A. P. Hill lost 1,300 men from his corps in an attack on the Federal line at Bristoe Station, which the Confederate secretary of war described as "a gallant but over-hasty pressing of the enemy." In 1864 a Union soldier whose regiment was armed with repeating rifles wrote from City Point, Virginia: "The Rebs made 3 charges on us but we stood up to the rack with our 7 Shooters & repulsed them each time & we piled the Rebs in heaps in front of us. . . . We are as good as a Brigade." Of the disastrous Confederate assault against the strong Federal defenses at Franklin, a Tennessean reported: "O, my God! what did we see! It was a grand holocaust of death. Death had held high carnival. . . . The dead were piled the one on the other all over the ground. I never was so horrified and appalled in my life."[6]

The South lost 175,000 soldiers in the first twenty-seven months of combat. This number was more than the entire Confederate military service in the summer of 1861 and it far exceeded the strength of any army that Lee ever commanded. More than 80,000 Southerners fell in just five battles. At Gettysburg 3 out of every 10 Confederates present were hit; one brigade lost 65 percent of its men and 70 percent of its field officers in a single charge. A North Carolina regiment started the action with some 800 men; only 216 survived unhurt. Another unit lost two-thirds of its men as well as its commander in a brief assault.[7]

The announcement by President Jefferson Davis early in the war that "the Confederate Government is waging this war solely for self-defense" implied that the South would concentrate on warding off Federal attacks, but it is doubtful that Davis actually intended his words about "self-defense" to be more than a propaganda statement. He had long favored offensive over defensive warfare and he would continue to do so throughout the war. In July 1861 he informed General Joseph E. Johnston: "I could not permit you

----

[5]Bell I. Wiley, *The Life of Johnny Reb: The Common Soldier of the Confederacy* (Indianapolis, 1943), 32; Henry E. Handerson to his father, July 13, 1862, in *Yankee in Gray: The Civil War Memoirs of Henry E. Handerson, with a Selection of His Wartime Letters*, ed. Clyde Lottridge Cummer (Cleveland, 1962), 96.

[6]Douglas S. Freeman, *Lee's Lieutenants: A Study in Command* (3 vols., New York, 1942–1944), III, 240–47; Bell I. Wiley, "The Common Soldier of the Civil War," *Civil War Times Illustrated*, XII, No. 4 (July 1973), 42; Sam R. Watkins, *"Co. Aytch": A Side Show of the Big Show* (reissue, New York, 1962), 235.

[7]Thomas L. Livermore, *Numbers & Losses in the Civil War in America: 1861–65* (reissue, Bloomington, 1957), 140–41; *OR*, XXVII (pt. 2), 647, 645, 578.

to suppose that I had allowed any rule to stand in the way of the one great
object of giving to our columns capacity to take the offensive." In 1862 Davis
praised the Confederate survivors of the Seven Days' campaign. "You
marched to attack the enemy in his entrenchments with . . . daring valor," he
told them; "you charged upon him in his strong positions, drove him from
field to field . . . , compelling him to seek shelter under cover of his gunboats
where he now lies cowering before the army he so lately derided &
threatened with entire subjugation." The president's appeal to the army in
February 1864 revealed a continued commitment to offensive tactics. In this
speech Davis reminded the soldiers of their "glorious victories" over "vastly
more numerous hosts" that had been achieved by "desperate assault," and he
urged them to ever greater efforts. "Soldier! the coming spring campaign will
open under auspices well calculated to sustain your hopes," he promised.
"Your brave battlecry will ring loud and clear through the land of the
enemy." And, finally, in October 1864 the president told an audience in
Columbia, South Carolina, "I believe it is in the power of the men of the
Confederacy to plant our banners on the banks of the Ohio."[8]

Despite Davis's enthusiasm for offensive warfare, there were good reasons
why the South might have elected to remain on the defensive. The North
had greater resources and a three-to-two military manpower advantage over
the South. Offensive operations almost certainly would exhaust the Confederacy more quickly than the Union because invasions and tactical offensives
use up more men and resources than defenses. As a rule, defense is the most
economical form of warfare. Civil War defenders, as will be explained more
fully later, enjoyed even greater advantages than usual because tactics lagged
behind military technology in the 1860s. The rifled muzzleloader gave the
defense at least three times the strength of the offense; consequently, it
would have been possible *theoretically* for the Confederates using defensive
tactics to have remained in their entrenchments and to have killed every man
in the Union army before the South exhausted its own human resources. The
Confederacy only had to be defended to survive. As Federal General Henry
W. Halleck pointed out: "the North must conquer the South."[9]

But defensive tactics were not what the Confederates elected to use. From
the war's outset southern sentiment overwhelmingly favored an invasion of
the North. Confederate Secretary of State Robert Toombs announced in

---

[8]Jefferson Davis, *Jefferson Davis, Constitutionalist: His Letters, Papers and Speeches*, ed. Dunbar
Rowland (10 vols., Jackson, 1923), V, 338; Grady McWhiney, "Jefferson Davis and the Art of
War," *Civil War History*, XXI (1975), 101–12; *OR*, II, 977; Jefferson Davis to the Army in
Eastern Virginia, July 5, 1862, Jefferson Davis Papers, Duke University; *OR*, Series 4, III,
104–05; *Charleston Courier*, October 6, 1864.

[9]Henry W. Halleck to Francis Lieber, March 4, 1863, Francis Lieber Papers, Henry E.
Huntington Library, San Marino, California. Over two million men enlisted in the Union army,
but Livermore, *Numbers & Losses*, 63, estimated that only about 1,556,000 Northerners and
about 1,082,000 Southerners actually served as long as three years in either army.

May 1861 that he was for "taking the initiative, and carrying the war into the enemy's country." He opposed any delay. "We must invade or be invaded," he said. The famous Confederate war clerk, John B. Jones, feared that the government's military policy might be defensive. If so, he warned in June 1861, "it will be severely criticized, for a vast majority of our people are for 'carrying the war into Africa' without a moment's delay." When President Davis indicated in a public speech just after the Battle of First Manassas, in July 1861, that he was ready to take the offensive, Jones noted in his diary: "Never heard I more hearty cheering. . . . Every one believed our banners would wave in the streets of Washington in a few days; . . . that peace would be consummated on the banks of the Susquehanna or the Schuylkill. The President had pledged himself . . . to carry the war into the enemy's country. . . . Now . . . the people were well pleased with their President." Davis called his policy defensive-offensive, but as it was practiced, and as the president encouraged it to be practiced, it was offensive warfare.[10]

By taking the tactical offensive early in the war more often than their opponents, the Confederates hoped to crush or capture one or more large Union armies, but they were never able to achieve this goal. Instead, their attempts to take the war to the enemy, to attack and destroy him, ruined the Confederate army. "There is an insane desire on the part of the Southern people, & some of the Generals to assume the offensive," wrote Colonel Benjamin S. Ewell in 1864. "Our successes have consisted in driving back the enemy & in defeating their attempts to invade. Our failures in attempts to carry the war into their territory. There have been exceptions to this but the remark is generally correct."[11]

Confederate forces attacked in eight of the first twelve big battles of the war, and in these eight assaults 97,000 Confederates fell—20,000 more men than the Federals lost in these same battles. The first twelve major campaigns of the war, those in which the total casualties exceeded 6,000 men, were Shiloh, Fair Oaks or Seven Pines, Seven Days, Second Manassas, Sharpsburg, Perryville, Fredericksburg, Murfreesboro, Chancellorsville, Vicksburg, Gettysburg, and Chickamauga. The Confederates clearly assumed the tactical offensive in all of these battles except Sharpsburg, Fredericksburg, and Vicksburg. Both sides attacked for a time at Shiloh and at Second Manassas, so one is counted here as a Confederate attack and the other as a Union attack.[12] (See table 1.) The South simply bled itself to death in the first three years of the war by taking the tactical offensive in nearly 70 percent of the major actions.

---

[10]John B. Jones, *A Rebel War Clerk's Diary*, ed. Earl S. Miers (New York, 1958), 18, 27, 36; Davis, *Jefferson Davis*, V, 339.

[11]Benjamin S. Ewell to Elizabeth S. Ewell, April 4, 1864, Benjamin Stoddert Ewell Papers, William and Mary College.

[12]Livermore, *Numbers & Losses*, 140–41.

Table 1

THE FIRST TWELVE MAJOR CAMPAIGNS OR BATTLES OF THE WAR IN WHICH TOTAL CASUALTIES EXCEEDED 6,000 MEN

Battle or Campaign	Tactical Offensive	Number of Men Engaged		Losses & % Lost	
		US	CS	US	CS
Shiloh	US & CS	62,682	40,335	10,162 (16.2)	9,735 (24.1)
Fair Oaks	CS	41,797	41,816	4,384 (10.5)	5,729 (13.7)
Seven Days	CS	91,169	95,481	9,796 (10.7)	19,739 (20.7)
Second Manassas	US & CS	75,696	48,527	10,096 (13.3)	9,108 (18.8)
Sharpsburg	US	75,316	51,844	11,657 (15.5)	11,724 (22.6)
Perryville	CS	36,940	16,000	3,696 (10.0)	3,145 (19.7)
Fredericksburg	US	100,007	72,497	10,884 (10.9)	4,656 (6.4)
Murfreesboro	CS	41,400	34,732	9,220 (22.3)	9,239 (26.6)
Chancellorsville	CS	97,382	57,352	11,116 (11.4)	10,746 (18.7)
Vicksburg	US	45,556	22,301	3,052 (6.7)	29,396*(100.0)
Gettysburg	CS	83,289	75,054	17,684 (21.2)	22,638 (30.2)
Chickamauga	CS	58,222	66,326	11,413 (19.6)	16,986 (25.6)
TOTALS:		809,456	622,265	113,160	152,841

Total engaged in these twelve campaigns
US = 809,456
CS = 622,265
187,191 more US troops engaged

Total losses in these twelve campaigns
US = 113,160 (or 13.9% of those engaged)
CS = 152,841 (or 24.6% of those engaged)
39,681 more CS troops lost

*Captured

After 1863 the Confederates attacked less often. Unsuccessful offensives had spent too much of their limited manpower, and thus forced them to defend. Even so, Confederate commanders attacked in three of the last ten major campaigns of the war,[13] and they frequently met enemy advances with counterattacks. Southerners doubtless would have attacked more often if they could have replaced their losses. General Ulysses S. Grant appreciated this Confederate aggressiveness and developed a plan to neutralize it. "We ought not to make a single exchange nor release a prisoner on any pretext whatever until the war closes," he informed a high government official on August 19, 1864. "We have got to fight until the military power of the South is exhausted, and if we release or exchange prisoners captured it simply becomes a war of extermination." The day before, Grant explained his strategy more fully in a letter to another general: "It is hard on our men held in Southern prisons not to exchange them, but it is humanity to those left in the ranks to fight our battles. Every man we hold, when released on parole or otherwise, becomes an active soldier against us at once either directly or indirectly. If we commence a system of exchange which liberates all prisoners taken, we will have to fight on until the whole South is exterminated. If we hold those caught they amount to no more than dead men. At this particular time to release all rebel prisoners . . . would insure Sherman's defeat and would compromise our safety here."[14]

Casualty lists reveal that the Confederates destroyed themselves by making bold and repeated attacks. They took the tactical offensive in 91 percent of the battles in which they suffered their greatest percentage losses; they defended in 89 percent of the battles in which they suffered the lowest percentage of casualties. In ten of the eleven battles that cost them their highest percentage of casualties, the Confederates were on the tactical offensive, and in the other battle—Sharpsburg—they were compelled to defend their position with costly counterattacks. The Federals assumed the tactical offensive in five of the eight battles in which they suffered their highest percentage of casualties, and in the other three—Murfreesboro, Gettysburg, and Chickamauga—they made several counterattacks.[15] (See table 2.)

A close examination of two battles reveals how so many men were lost. Both Murfreesboro and Chickamauga are examples of sustained Confederate

---

[13]Ibid., 108–41. The last ten major campaigns in which the estimated total casualties in each exceeded 6,000 men were Chattanooga, the Wilderness and Spotsylvania, Johnston's Atlanta campaign (including the battles of Buzzard's Roost, Snake Creek Gap, New Hope Church, and Kennesaw Mountain), Hood's Atlanta campaign (including the battles of Peach Tree Creek; Atlanta, July 22 and 28; and Jonesboro, August 31 and September 1), Cold Harbor, Petersburg, Winchester, Cedar Creek, Franklin, and the Appomattox campaign. The Federals took the tactical offensive in all of these actions except Hood's Atlanta campaign, Cedar Creek, and Franklin.

[14]*OR*, Series 2, VII, 614–15, 607.

[15]Livermore, *Numbers & Losses*, 140–41.

attacks, and an analysis of regimental losses in each battle indicates a high degree of correlation between assaults and casualties. Because the Federals were on the defensive in both battles they suffered relatively fewer casualties, except for those units that were outflanked or surrounded. It is significant that half of the most battered Union regiments incurred their highest casualties when they attacked or counterattacked. At Murfreesboro the Fifteenth Indiana lost 130 of its 440 men in a single bayonet charge, and the Thirty-fourth Illinois and the Thirty-ninth Indiana each sustained 50 percent casualties in a counterattack. In still another attempt to check the Confederate advance a brigade of regulars charged into a dense cedar grove and lost 500 men in about twenty minutes. The Sixteenth and Eighteenth U.S. Infantry regiments, which formed the center of this assault group, lost 456 men from a combined total of 910.[16] At Chickamauga the Eighty-seventh Indiana suffered over 50 percent casualties in one charge across an open field, and three Illinois regiments—the Twenty-fifth, Thirty-fifth, and Thirty-eighth—together with the Twenty-sixth Ohio, tried to dislodge part of General Bushrod Johnson's Confederate Division from the crest of a hill. The attack failed, and it cost the Federal regiments 791 of their 1,296 men.[17]

Confederate losses in these two battles were even more exceptional. Of the eighty-eight Confederate regiments present at Murfreesboro, twenty-three suffered over 40 percent casualties. Moreover, 40 percent of the infantry regimental commanders were killed or wounded, and in several regiments every field officer was lost. Eight of the twenty Confederate brigades that fought at Murfreesboro sustained more than 35 percent casualties, and 25 percent of the infantry brigade commanders were killed or wounded.[18]

Table 2

BATTLES IN WHICH THE HEAVIEST LOSSES OCCURRED

For the Confederates:

Battle or Campaign	Men Engaged	Men Killed or Wounded	Percentage Lost
Gettysburg	75,054	22,638	30.2
Murfreesboro	34,732	9,239	26.6
Chickamauga	66,326	16,986	25.6
Shiloh	40,335	9,735	24.1

[16]*OR*, XX (pt. 1), 495–96, 305–06, 314–15, 319–21, 325–26, 394–95, 401–03.

[17]Ibid., XXX (pt. 1), 1058–59, 427–30, 529–31, 521–22, 654–58, 590, 839–40, 173, 174.

[18]Ibid., XX (pt. 1), 676–81, 693, 758, 780, 852, 855, 875, 900; unpublished reports in the William P. Palmer Collection of Braxton Bragg Papers, Western Reserve Historical Society, Cleveland.

Sharpsburg	51,844	11,724	22.6
Atlanta (July 28)	18,450	4,100	22.2
Seven Days	95,481	19,739	20.7
Franklin	26,897	5,550	20.6
Tupelo (July22)	6,600	1,326	20.1
Perryville	16,000	3,145	19.7
Atlanta (July 22)	36,934	7,000	19.0

For the Federals:

Battle or Campaign	Men Engaged	Men Killed or Wounded	Percentage Lost
Wilderness and Spotsylvania	88,892	26,302	29.6
Port Hudson (June 14)	6,000	1,604	26.7
Olustee	5,115	1,355	26.5
Murfreesboro	41,400	9,220	22.3
Cedar Mountain	8,030	1,759	21.9
Fort Wagner	5,264	1,126	21.4
Gettysburg	83,289	17,684	21.2
Chickamauga	58,222	11,413	19.6

Reckless charges accounted for most Confederate casualties. At Murfrees-boro the First Louisiana charged across an open field. "Our loss was very severe at this place," wrote the commander. The regiment lost 7 of its 21 officers and nearly 100 of its 231 men.[19] Attacks made by other Confederate units were just as costly. Colonel J. J. Scales, commander of the Thirtieth Mississippi, was ordered to charge and capture several Federal batteries. Five hundred yards of open ground "lay between us and those . . . batteries," wrote Scales. "As we entered [this field] a large body of [Union] infantry in addition to the Batteries on my flanks and front rained their leaden hail upon us. Men fell around on every side like autumn leaves and every foot of soil over which we passed seemed dyed with the life blood of some one or more of [my] gallant [men]. . . . Still no one faltered, but the whole line advanced boldly and swiftly to within seventy-five yds. of the battery when the storm of death increased to such fury that the regt. as if by instinct fell to the ground." This single charge cost the Thirtieth Mississippi half of its 400 men.[20] A young soldier in the Twenty-fourth Alabama recalled how his regiment made three desperate charges at Murfreesboro and that each time

---

[19]Report of Captain Taylor Beatty, First Louisiana Infantry, Palmer Collection.
[20]Report of Lieutenant Colonel J. J. Scales, Thirtieth Mississippi Infantry, ibid.

30 or 40 of his comrades fell.[21] The commander of the Twenty-sixth Alabama reported the Federal fire so heavy that 38 of his men defected during the first thrust.[22]

More characteristic was the courage shown by General James R. Chalmers's Brigade of Mississippians. This unit not only hit the strongest part of the Union line at Murfreesboro, but half the men in the Forty-fourth Mississippi Regiment went into battle armed only with sticks, and most of the Ninth Mississippi's rifles were still too wet from the previous night's rain to fire. Nevertheless, the men charged.[23]

As the Mississippians faltered, General Daniel S. Donelson's Brigade of Tennesseans came up. No unit on either side fought any harder than this brigade; it destroyed itself in attacks against the Union center in the Round Forest. One of Donelson's regiments lost half of its officers and 68 percent of its men; another lost 42 percent of its officers and over half of its men. The Eighth and Sixteenth Tennessee regiments spent several hours and 513 of their combined total of 821 men in brave but unsuccessful efforts to break the Federal line.[24]

Sometime in the early afternoon two fresh Confederate brigades tried where Chalmers's and Donelson's men had failed. Generals John K. Jackson and Daniel W. Adams led their men across a field thick with bodies. Both of Jackson's two furious assaults aborted. In an hour of combat he lost more than a third of his men, including all his regimental commanders. One of his regiments, the Eighth Mississippi, lost 133 of its 282 men. Adams had no more success than Jackson, though his men made what one Federal called "the most daring, courageous, and best-executed attack . . . on our line." Adams was wounded and his brigade, caught in a crossfire, retreated. One of his units, the Thirteenth and Twentieth Consolidated Louisiana Infantry, entering the fight with 620 men, lost 187 on the afternoon of December 31 and another 129 in an attack two days later.[25]

Confederate losses at Chickamauga were even more severe than at Mur-

---

[21]Charles T. Jones, Jr., "Five Confederates: The Sons of Bolling Hall in the Civil War," *Alabama Historical Quarterly*, XXIV (1962), 167.

[22]Report of Lieutenant Colonel N. N. Clements, Twenty-sixth Alabama Infantry, Palmer Collection.

[23]Report of Major J. O. Thompson, Forty-fourth (Blythe's) Mississippi Infantry, and Lieutenant Colonel T. H. Lyman, Ninth Mississippi Infantry, ibid. Thompson reported: "During the night of Friday [December] 26 all guns in the hands of Blythe's Regiment were taken from them and distributed among the regiments of Chalmers' Brigade. The Sunday morning following we were furnished with refuse guns that had been turned over to the Brigade ordnance officer. Many of these guns were worthless. . . . Even of these poor arms there was not a sufficiency and after every exertion on my part to procure arms, one half of the Regt. moved out with no other resemblance to a gun than such sticks as they could gather."

[24]*OR*, XX (pt. 1), 710–12, 714–18, 543–46.

[25]Ibid., 838–39, 841–42, 795–99; Alexander F. Stevenson, *The Battle of Stone's River* (Boston, 1884), 113.

freesboro. At least twenty-five of the thirty-three Confederate brigades present lost more than a third of their men, and incomplete returns indicate that at least forty-two infantry regiments suffered over 40 percent casualties. Nearly half of all regimental commanders and 25 percent of all brigade commanders were killed or wounded.[26]

Just as at Murfreesboro the heaviest losses at Chickamauga occurred when units assaulted strong Union positions. General Lucius E. Polk's Brigade of about 1,400 men attacked Kelly's field salient twice on September 20. The first attack, checked by heavy guns and musket fire, cost the Confederates 350 casualties in about ninety minutes. In the second attack the brigade lost 200 men. An assault against the Federal position on Horseshoe Ridge cost the Twenty-second Alabama 55 percent of its men, and two battalions of Hilliard's Legion lost nearly 60 percent of their effectives in an attack on Snodgrass Hill, where the Federals had thrown up breastworks.[27]

Throughout the war the side that attacked usually suffered the most casualties, both proportionally and often absolutely. In only four battles—each a relatively minor affair—were the Confederates able to inflict upon the Federals casualties that exceeded by 10 percent or more those suffered by the Confederates themselves, but what is important about these four battles is that in all of them the Federals attacked. At Cedar Mountain on August 9, 1862, Federal General Nathaniel P. Banks assailed Stonewall Jackson's Corps. Caught by surprise, the Confederates gave ground for a time but their counterattacks ultimately drove back the Federals. Banks lost 421 more men than Jackson did—1,759 to 1,338—yet this number represented a 14 percent greater loss than the Confederates sustained because the Federals were outnumbered 16,868 to 8,030. In 1863 the Federals made two disastrous attempts to drive the Confederates from strongly fortified positions. At Port Hudson on June 14 some 6,000 Union troops, again under the direction of Banks, attacked 3,487 Confederates. The defenders suffered only 47 casualties (1.3 percent); Federal losses were more than 25 percent greater—1,604. A month later, at Fort Wagner, 5,264 Federals sustained 1,126 casualties in an attack on 1,785 Confederates; only 169 of the defenders were killed or wounded. Finally, in June 1864, Federal General William T. Sherman, frustrated in his attempt to outmaneuver General Joseph E. Johnston, uncharacteristically attacked the prepared Confederate position at Kennesaw Mountain. After losing nearly 2,000 of the 16,225 Union troops engaged, Sherman withdrew and returned to his flanking movements. His frontal assault killed and wounded only 270 of the 17,733 Confederate defenders.[28]

What these four minor battles show, in conjunction with other data, is that the Federals made few sustained assaults against strong positions. When their

---

[26]*OR*, XXX (pt. 2), 11–532.

[27]Ibid., 176–78, 336–37, 424–29.

[28]Livermore, *Numbers & Losses*, 140–41.

attacks failed, they often learned not to try such tactics again. To have suffered in four years of combat only four relatively minor assaults in which their casualties exceeded their opponent's by 10 percent or more is quite remarkable for an army that was forced by the political nature of the conflict to invade and conquer. There were blunders aplenty by the Federals, and at least three of their attacks—Cold Harbor, Vicksburg, and Fredericksburg—were costly affairs.[29] They were saved from having to make other wasteful assaults, and perhaps from defeat, because the Confederates were so willing to take the initiative.

The Confederates were much slower than the Federals to learn how self-destructive attacks could be. In contrast to the four assaults in which the Federal attackers suffered casualties that exceeded by 10 percent or more those of their opponents, the Confederates sustained comparable casualties in five attacks. What is more significant, only 75,392 men were engaged—and a mere 8,312 were killed or wounded—in these four Federal assaults, but in those five by the Confederates 361,173 men fought and 51,917 of them fell. Put another way, in the five battles in which the Confederates had their most disproportionate losses, they sustained nearly six times as many casualties as the Federals did in the four battles in which their losses were the most incommensurate. During the Seven Days' campaign in 1862 General Lee lost 19,739 of his 95,481 men—9,943 more men than Union General McClellan lost—in daring assaults against 91,169 Union troops. Confederate General John Bell Hood wasted no fewer than 11,100 men in two attacks against Sherman's forces near Atlanta in July 1864, or a total of 8,552 more men than the Federals lost in these engagements. Again, in 1864 at Franklin, Hood's assaults cost 5,550 casualties; this was 4,328 more men killed and wounded than the Federals suffered. That same year at Tupelo, Mississippi, reckless charges by the forces of Confederate General Stephen D. Lee, directed on the battlefield by General Nathan B. Forrest, felled 1,326 of the 6,600 Confederates engaged, or nearly 16 percent more than the Federals lost.[30] (See table 3.)

These bloody Confederate offensives took the lives of the bravest southern officers and men. Relatively few combat officers went through the conflict without a single wound, and most of those who did could claim, as did General Reuben L. Walker, who participated in no less than sixty-three battles, that "it was not my fault." Only three of the eight men who commanded the famous Stonewall Brigade survived the war. What happened to the commanders of one regiment is told in a bare sketch penned by semiliterate Bartlett Yancey Malone, who "was attached to the 6th N. C. Regiment . . .

---

[29]Comparisons on relative losses are impossible for Cold Harbor and Vicksburg because Confederate losses are unknown, but at Fredericksburg the Federals lost 6,228 (or 4.5 percent) more men than the Confederates. Livermore, *Numbers & Losses*, 140–41.
[30]Ibid.

which was commanded by Colonel Fisher who got kild in the first Manassas Battel. . . . And then was commanded By Colonel W. D. Pender untell [his promotion; he was subsequently killed in battle]. . . . And then Captain I. E. Av[e]ry . . . was promoted to Colonel and . . . in command untell . . . the day the fite was at Gettysburg whar he was kild. And then Lieut. Colonel Webb taken command."[31]

Confederate generals not only led their forces into battle, they died with their men. Fifty-five percent of all Confederate generals (235 of 425) were killed or wounded in battle.[32] Thirty-one generals were hurt twice, eighteen were wounded three times, and a dozen were hit four or more times. Clement A. Evans, William ("Extra Billy") Smith, and William H. Young were wounded five times. Young was hit in the shoulder and had two horses shot from under him at Murfreesboro; he was hit in the leg at Jackson, in the chest at Chickamauga, in the neck and jaw at Kennesaw Mountain, and again in the leg at Allatoona, where another horse was shot from under him and he was captured. John R. Cooke, William R. Terry, and Thomas F. Toon were wounded seven times, but the record seems to have been set by William Ruffin Cox, who joined the Second North Carolina Infantry as a major in 1861 and fought through the war with the Army of Northern Virginia. He was wounded eleven times.

Twenty-one of the seventy-seven Confederate generals who were killed or mortally wounded in battle had been shot at least once before they received their fatal injuries. Some of them had been hit two or more times. William D. Pender survived three wounds before his leg was shattered and he died at Gettysburg. Stephen D. Ramseur recovered from wounds received at Malvern Hill, Chancellorsville, and Spotsylvania, only to die at Cedar Creek.

More generals lost their lives leading attacks than any other way. Seventy percent of the Confederate generals killed or mortally wounded in action fell in offensives.[33] In a single charge against Federal fortifications at Franklin in 1864, six Confederate generals—John Adams, John C. Carter, Patrick R. Cleburne, States Rights Gist, Hiram B. Granbury, and Otho F. Strahl— were killed or mortally wounded.

Throughout the war Confederate leaders seemed to ignore the casualty lists and to mutilate themselves and their armies. A northern observer

---

[31]James I. Robertson, Jr., *The Stonewall Brigade* (Baton Rouge, 1963), 243; Bartlett Yancey Malone, *Whipt 'Em Everytime: The Diary of Bartlett Yancey Malone*, ed. William Whatley Pierson, Jr. (Jackson, 1960), 28.

[32]These figures are based on data taken from Ezra J. Warner, *Generals in Gray: Lives of the Confederate Commanders* (Baton Rouge, 1959), and Mark Mayo Boatner III, *The Civil War Dictionary* (New York, 1959).

[33]Only 23 percent of these seventy-seven generals were killed while on defense. Seven percent died in ways that can be classified neither as offense nor defense. Stonewall Jackson and Micah Jenkins, for example, were accidently killed by their own men, and John Hunt Morgan was killed by Union cavalrymen after he was surprised while asleep in a private home.

Table 3

BATTLES WITH THE GREATEST PERCENTAGE DIFFERENCE IN LOSSES SUFFERED BETWEEN THE CONFEDERATES AND THE FEDERALS

Battles Favorable for the Confederates:

Battle	Forces		Losses	Confederate Advantage in	
				Actual Casualties	Percentage Lost
Port Hudson (6/14)	US	6,000	1,604	1,557	25.4
	CS	3,487	47		
Cedar Mountain	US	8,030	1,759	421	14.0
	CS	16,868	1,338		
Fort Wagner (7/18)	US	5,264	1,126	957	11.9
	CS	1,785	169		
Kennesaw Mountain	US	16,225	1,999	1,729	10.8
	CS	17,733	270		
TOTALS:	US	35,519	6,488	4,664	13.7
	CS	39,873	1,824		

Battles Favorable for the Federals:

Battle	Forces		Losses	Federal Advantage in	
				Actual Casualties	Percentage Lost
Atlanta (7/28)	US	13,226	559	3,541	18.0
	CS	18,450	4,100		
Franklin	US	27,939	1,222	4,328	16.2
	CS	26,897	5,550		
Tupelo	US	14,000	636	690	15.6
	CS	6,600	1,326		
Atlanta (7/22)	US	30,477	1,989	5,011	12.5
	CS	36,934	7,000		
Seven Days	US	91,169	9,796	9,943	10.0
	CS	95,481	19,739		
TOTALS:	US	176,811	14,202	23,513	12.5
	CS	184,362	37,715		

pointed out that "Southern leaders were, at least up to 1864, bolder in taking risks than their opponents, but also that they pushed their forces under fire very nearly to the limits of endurance." Such actions were justified, according to Confederate Colonel W. C. P. Breckinridge, because "it was the fate of the Southern armies to confront armies larger, better equipped, and admirably supplied. Unless we could by activity, audacity, aggressiveness, and skill overcome these advantages it was a mere matter of time as to the certain result. It was therefore the first requisite of a Confederate general that he should be willing to meet his antagonist on these unequal terms, and on such terms make fight. He must of necessity take great risks and assume grave responsibilities."[34]

Unfortunately for the Confederates, their willingness to "take great risks" brought them no decisive victories and unbearable losses. Perhaps this can be illustrated best by a comparison of casualties. In half of the twenty-two major battles or campaigns of the war the Federals attacked. They lost 119,000 men when they assaulted and 88,000 when they defended. The Confederates lost 117,000 men when they attacked, but only 61,000 when they defended. Every time the Confederates attacked they lost an average of ten more men out of every hundred engaged than the Federal defenders, but when the Confederates defended, they lost seven fewer men out of every hundred than the Union attackers. In the first dozen major campaigns, when the Confederacy was most often the aggressor, every southern general sustained greater average percentage losses than his opponents. Lee suffered an average loss in his first six big battles of 19.2 percent, or 6.0 percent greater than his opponents' losses; in the first three battles Braxton Bragg directed, his average loss per battle was 25.1 percent, or 7.3 percent greater than his opponents'; John C. Pemberton, in his one major campaign, surrendered his entire army, resulting in losses 93.3 percent greater than those he inflicted on the Federals; Albert Sidney Johnston and P. G. T. Beauregard, who shared command at Shiloh, suffered 24.1 percent losses, or 7.9 percent greater than Grant did in this battle; and in his first major action Joseph E. Johnston sustained 13.7 percent losses, or 3.2 percent greater than his opponents'.[35] (See tables 4 and 5.)

Bismarck is reputed to have said that fools learn from their own mistakes, but that he preferred to learn from the mistakes of others. The Confederacy failed because its leaders made the same mistakes time and again. "The rebls," observed a Union private in 1863, "fight as though a mans life was not worth one sent or in other words with desperation; or like Gen. Lafeyet said to Washington, there is more *dogs* where them came from." By 1865 the South's supply of soldiers had about run out. "It is a most sad and humiliat-

---

[34]Livermore, *Numbers & Losses*, 71; W. C. P. Breckinridge, "The Opening of the Atlanta Campaign," in *Battles and Leaders*, IV, 278.

[35]These computations are based on figures given in Livermore, *Numbers & Losses*, 140–41.

Table 4

COMPARISON OF LOSSES SUSTAINED BY EIGHT CONFEDERATE COMMANDERS

ROBERT E. LEE

Opponent	Campaign or Battle	Confederate Numbers	Confederate Losses	Confederate Percent	Union Numbers	Union Losses	Union Percent
McClellan	Seven Days	95,481	19,739	20.7	91,169	9,796	10.7
Pope	2d Manassas	48,527	9,108	18.8	75,696	10,096	13.3
McClellan	So. Mountain*	18,714	1,885	10.1	28,480	1,728	6.1
McClellan	Sharpsburg	51,844	11,724	22.6	75,316	11,657	15.5
Burnside	Fredericksburg	72,497	4,656	6.4	100,007	10,884	10.9
Hooker	Chancellorsville	57,352	10,746	18.7	97,382	11,116	11.4
Meade	Gettysburg	75,054	22,638	30.2	83,289	17,684	21.2
		(419,469)	(80,496)	(19.2)	(551,339)	(72,961)	(13.2)
Meade	Mine Run	44,426	680	1.5	69,643	1,272	1.8
Grant	Wilderness through						
	Cold Harbor	c. 70,000	c. 32,000	c. 45.7	c. 122,000	c. 50,000	c.41.0
Grant	Weldon Railroad	14,787	1,200	8.1	20,289	1,303	6.4
Grant	Appomattox	49,496	6,666	13.5	112,992	9,066	8.0
		c. 598,178	c. 121,042	c. 20.2	c. 876,263	c. 134,602	c. 15.4

JOSEPH E. JOHNSTON

Opponent	Campaign or Battle	Confederate Numbers	Confederate Losses	Confederate Percent	Union Numbers	Union Losses	Union Percent
McClellan	Fair Oaks	41,816	5,729	13.7	41,797	4,384	10.5
Sherman	Atlanta	66,089	9,187	13.9	110,123	10,528	9.6
Sherman	Bentonville	16,895	1,508	8.9	16,127	933	5.8
Sherman	Kennesaw Mt.	17,733	270	1.5	16,225	1,999	12.3
McClellan	Williamsburg	31,823	1,570	4.9	40,768	1,866	4.6
		174,356	18,264	10.5	225,040	19,710	8.8

* Counted in the text as part of the Sharpsburg campaign.

Table 4 (continued)

BRAXTON BRAGG

Buell	Perryville	16,000	3,145	19.7	36,940	3,696	10.0
Rosecrans	Murfreesboro	34,732	9,239	26.6	41,400	9,220	22.3
Rosecrans	Chickamauga	66,326	16,986	25.6	58,222	11,413	19.6
Grant	Chattanooga	46,165	2,521	5.5	56,359	5,475	9.7
		163,223	31,891	19.5	192,921	29,804	15.4

P. G. T. BEAUREGARD

McDowell	1st Manassas	32,232	1,969	6.1	28,452	1,492	5.2
Grant	Shiloh	40,335	9,735	24.1	62,682	10,162	16.2
		72,567	11,704	16.1	91,134	11,654	12.8

EARL VAN DORN

Curtis	Pea Ridge	14,000	600	4.3	11,250	1,183	10.5
Rosecrans	Corinth	22,000	2,470	11.2	21,147	2,196	10.4
		36,000	3,070	8.5	32,397	3,379	10.4

JUBAL EARLY

Sheridan	Winchester	17,103	2,103	12.3	37,711	4,680	12.4
Sheridan	Cedar Creek	18,410	1,860	10.1	30,829	4,074	13.2
		35,513	3,963	11.2	68,540	8,754	12.8

JOHN BELL HOOD

Sherman	Peach Tree Ck.	18,832	2,500	13.3	20,139	1,600	7.9
Sherman	Atlanta	36,934	7,000	19.0	30,477	1,989	6.5
Sherman	Atlanta	18,450	4,100	22.2	13,266	559	4.2
Sherman	Jonesboro	29,764	c. 4,458	c. 15.0	34,630	1,348	3.9
Thomas	Franklin	26,897	5,550	20.6	27,939	1,222	4.4
Thomas	Nashville	23,207	c. 6,000**	25.9	49,773	2,949	5.9
		154,084	c. 29,608	c.19.2	176,224	9,667	5.5

JOHN C. PEMBERTON

Sherman	Chickasaw Bayou	13,792	197	1.4	30,720	1,213	3.9
Grant	Champion's Hill	20,000	2,181	10.9	29,373	2,254	7.7
Grant	Vicksburg	29,396	29,396**	100.0	45,546	3,052	6.7
		63,188	31,774	50.3	105,649	6,519	6.2

** This figure includes troops captured.

Table 5

COMPARISON OF CASUALTIES SUFFERED BY CONFEDERATE AND UNION ARMY COMMANDERS

CONFEDERATE ARMY COMMANDERS

	Total Casualties Inflicted on the Enemy by His Troops in Major Battles or Campaigns	Total Casualties Suffered by His Troops in Major Battles or Campaigns	Difference	Average Percentage Loss of Men Engaged		Difference
				His Force	His Opponent	
Robert E. Lee	c. 134,602	c. 121,042	c. 13,560	c. 20.2	c. 15.4	(c. 4.8)
Jubal Early	8,754	3,963	4,791	11.2	12.8	1.6
Joseph E. Johnston	19,710	18,264	1,446	10.5	8.8	(1.7)
Braxton Bragg	29,804	31,891	(2,087)	19.5	15.4	(4.1)
Earl Van Dorn	3,379	3,070	309	8.5	10.4	1.9
P. G. T. Beauregard[1]	11,654[2]	11,704	(50)	16.1	12.8	(3.3)
John Bell Hood	9,667	c. 29,608	(c. 19,941)	c. 19.2	5.5	(c. 13.7)
John C. Pemberton	6,519	31,774[3]	(25,255)	50.3	6.2	(44.1)

NOTES: [1]Beauregard shared command with Joseph E. Johnston at First Manassas but actually Beauregard directed operations; he took command at Shiloh after the death of Albert Sidney Johnston.

[2]This figure does not include those Yankees killed or wounded at Petersburg (8,150 in four days) because returns for Beauregard's force are unavailable.

[3]This number includes 29,396 Confederate troops that Pemberton surrendered at Vicksburg.

UNION ARMY COMMANDERS

George B. McClellan	40,647	11,216	9.5	14.4	4.9
George H. Thomas	c. 11,550[4]	c. 7,379	5.0	c. 23.3	c. 18.3
William T. Sherman	c. 29,220	c. 9,051	7.4	c. 13.4	c. 6.0
William S. Rosecrans	28,695	5,866	17.4	21.1	3.7
George G. Meade	23,318	4,362	11.5	15.8	4.3
Ulysses S. Grant	c. 83,699[5]	c. 2,387[6]	18.1	c. 31.0	c. 12.9
Philip H. Sheridan	3,963	(4,791)	12.8	11.2	(1.6)
Ambrose E. Burnside	4,656	(6,228)	10.9	6.4	(4.5)
Joseph Hooker	10,746	(370)	11.4	18.7	7.3

NOTES: [4]This figure includes Confederates captured at Nashville.

[5]This number includes 29,396 Confederates captured at Vicksburg.

[6]Not included in this total are some of Grant's losses during the Petersburg campaign because Confederate losses in these actions are unknown and no comparisons can be made.

ing picture," a general reported to President Davis in March 1865. "You hear of victories, . . . I see disasters, disorderly retreats and utter confusion on our part, with combinations and numbers against us which must prevail." A few months before a distraught Southerner had exclaimed: "I do not see what can extricate us but God. The West Pointers have . . . generaled us to the verge of death itself."[36] He was right; by attacking instead of defending, the Confederates had murdered themselves.

---

[36]Quoted in L. Van Loan Naisawald, *Grape and Canister: The Story of the Field Artillery of the Army of the Potomac, 1861–1865* (New York, 1960), 536; Braxton Bragg to Jefferson Davis, March 26, 1865, Autograph File, Dearborn Collection, Harvard University; *OR*, LI (pt. 2), 1005.

Part Two
How It Happened

2

The Charge Decided the Victory

At least two writers believe that the Confederacy died in Mexico. Bernard DeVoto claimed that Jefferson Davis learned just enough about warfare "in exactly five days of action" during the Mexican War to guarantee the South's defeat in the 1860s. And Hamilton J. Eckenrode suggested that the Confederacy was doomed to defeat as early as 1847 when Davis formed his regiment of Mississippians into an obtuse angle and halted the attacking Mexicans at Buena Vista with converging rifle fire. "The applause [for this spectacular feat] was so great that he was deceived himself," wrote Eckenrode. "He was looked on in the South as a great soldier and he was firmly convinced of his own military talents. His war service was destined to be decisive of his future. It put him in the Senate and made him President of the Confederacy. When the Richmond *Examiner* near the close of the war said, 'If we are to perish, the verdict of posterity will be, Died of a V,' it was commenting bitterly on the consequences that had flowed from the famous obtuse angle of Buena Vista."[1]

Historical pathologists may consider the autopsy performed by DeVoto and Eckenrode to be hopelessly superficial, but there is no doubt that much can be learned about the nature and the course of the Confederacy's demise from a close examination of Mexican War military campaigns and how they influenced both the techniques of warfare as well as the young men who would lead armies against each other in the war for southern independence.

The tactics used by American commanders in the Mexican War were similar to those employed in early nineteenth-century warfare. Infantry marched in columns and deployed into lines to prepare for battle. Once deployed, a company or two advanced as skirmishers in front of each regiment. The infantry volleyed with the enemy, then advanced in closely ordered lines, hoping to get near enough to the defenders to break up their lines with a concentrated volley and then carry their position with the bayonet. Artil-

---

[1]Bernard DeVoto, *The Year of Decision, 1846* (Boston, 1943), 203, 284; Hamilton J. Eckenrode, *Jefferson Davis: President of the South* (New York, 1923), 45.

lery was a valuable defensive arm, able to shift from one threatened point of the line to another, and might also be used on the offensive. Cavalry patrolled the flanks and rear of the line, ready to saber charge the enemy infantry once it was out of formation and in retreat.[2]

Tactics usually are based on weaponry, and the main infantry weapon of the Mexican War was the smoothbore musket, with either flintlock or percussion ignition system. At least nine different models of smoothbore flintlocks were made at government armories after 1800 and most of these were used in Mexico; the Model 1822 was the most famous. During the war 38,000 smoothbore muskets were issued, while only about 10,000 .54-caliber rifles were issued in the same period.[3]

The musket of the Mexican War had many shortcomings. It was a clumsy weapon to handle. Lew Wallace, who served with the First Indiana Volunteers in Mexico, remembered his regiment's weapon as "a heavy muzzle-loading musket of Revolutionary pattern" that took twelve commands to load.[4] The musket was unreliable in damp weather and had no uniform ignition system. The flintlock system had been standard, but the percussion system was introduced in 1841 and both systems were seen in Mexico. General Winfield Scott preferred the old flintlock system because it had been more thoroughly tested and plenty of flints were on hand.[5]

The greatest limitation of the musket was its inaccuracy and short range. Smoothbores had no rifling, and even in the hands of good marksmen they were inaccurate weapons, with an effective range of only a few hundred yards.[6] Charles P. Kingsbury, a veteran of the Mexican War, wrote: "The fire of the musket becomes very uncertain beyond the distance of two hundred yards, as the vertical variations of the shots exceed the height of the enemy's lines." William Gilham thought the musket could be "made effective up to 300 yards" but admitted that "beyond 400 yards it is useless."[7] Ulysses

---

[2]The relationship of Mexican War tactics and early nineteenth-century tactics is considered in Grady McWhiney, "Who Whipped Whom? Confederate Defeat Reexamined," *Civil War History*, XI (1965), 7. The relationship of Mexican War tactics and Civil War tactics is discussed in the same article and in Grady McWhiney, *Braxton Bragg and Confederate Defeat* (New York, 1969), 72–73, 89, 227, 231, and also in Grady McWhiney, *Southerners and Other Americans* (New York, 1973), 61–71. A relationship between Mexican War strategy and Civil War strategy has been suggested by James W. Pohl, "The Influence of Antoine Henri de Jomini on Winfield Scott's Campaign in the Mexican War," *Southwestern Historical Quarterly*, LXXVII (1973), 85–110.

[3]George Winston Smith and Charles Judah, eds., *Chronicles of the Gringos: The U.S. Army in the Mexican War, 1846–1848; Accounts of Eyewitnesses & Combatants* (Albuquerque, 1968), 383; Justin H. Smith, *The War With Mexico* (2 vols., New York, 1919), I, 450.

[4]Lew Wallace, *Lew Wallace, An Autobiography* (2 vols., New York, 1906), I, 131.

[5]Smith and Judah, *Chronicles*, 382–84.

[6]Ibid., 382–83; Smith, *War With Mexico*, I, 450.

[7]Charles P. Kingsbury, *An Elementary Treatise on Artillery and Infantry, Adapted to the Service of the United States* (New York, 1856), 134; William Gilham, *Manual of Instruction for the Volunteers and Militia of the Confederate States* (Richmond, 1861), 46.

S. Grant remarked that a man with a musket at a range of a few hundred yards "might fire at you all day without you finding it out." Roswell Ripley chided some Mexican infantry at Churubusco for trying to use their muskets at a range of over 350 yards. Lieutenant Richard S. Ewell of the dragoons considered it a Mexican "fashion" to attempt musketry at exaggerated ranges. Candid American officers admitted that their own troops often tried to extend their musket fire beyond effective range. Major Luther Giddings said of his volunteer regiment at Monterey: "In vain did we caution our men not to fire until commanded. . . . [M]ost of them discharged their guns as they obtained a good aim, but when the enemy were too distant to secure the most satisfactory results."[8]

Rifles had greater accuracy and range than muskets. Several models of United States or Harpers Ferry rifles and some Hall's breech-loading rifles saw service in Mexico, but the most famous rifle of the war was the Model 1841 or Mississippi Rifle, the first general-issue rifle with the percussion system. This was the weapon used by Colonel Jefferson Davis's First Mississippi Rifles at Monterey and Buena Vista.[9]

The musket, however, was much more common in Mexico than the rifle, which was regarded as a special weapon with special uses. At the time of the Mexican War, the regulation tactical manual assumed that no more than one of a regiment's ten companies would be a rifle company.[10] Rifle companies from different units might be detached and put together to create a rifle battalion, as was done in General Joseph Lane's Indiana Brigade at Buena Vista.[11] Rifle units were used for skirmishing or to cover the flank of a larger unit.[12] For the most part, rifle fire was viewed as a support to musketry: rifles were expected to draw the enemy's fire; muskets and bayonets were to decide the issue. General John A. Quitman's Brigade at Monterey consisted of two regiments, one armed with rifles and the other with muskets. Quitman reported after the battle that his plan had been to give the enemy "the full fire of the rifle regiment" and then to have the musket regiment make its charge.[13]

In spite of its limited effective range and other shortcomings, the musket was well regarded in the 1840s. It was quicker in operation than the shorter and heavier rifle. George B. McClellan recalled in the 1870s that at the

[8]Ulysses S. Grant, *Personal Memoirs* . . . (2 vols., New York, 1885), I, 95; Roswell Ripley, *The War With Mexico* (2 vols., New York, 1849), II, 257; Smith and Judah, *Chronicles*, 239; Luther Giddings, *Sketches of the Campaign in Northern Mexico in Eighteen Hundred Forty-six and Seven* (New York, 1853), 181.

[9]Smith, *War With Mexico*, I, 450; Smith and Judah, *Chronicles*, 383–84.

[10]Winfield Scott, *Infantry-Tactics; Or, Rules for the Exercise and Manoeuvres of the United States Infantry* (3 vols., New York, 1846), I, 8.

[11]*House Executive Document*, 30 Cong., 1 sess., No. 8, 189, 191.

[12]Ibid., 322; Raphael Semmes, *The Campaign of General Scott, in the Valley of Mexico* (Cincinnati, 1852), 343.

[13]*House Executive Document*, 30 Cong., 1 sess., No. 17, 16.

beginning of the Mexican War the percussion system smoothbore musket "was regarded as the best possible weapon for infantry of the line."[14] Although individual musket fire was inaccurate, musket fire delivered in concentrated volleys could be powerful within its range. Roswell Ripley described Mexican musketry at Churubusco as being delivered "without accurate aim, it is true, but in heavy rolling volleys, and with deadly force." Captain John Gibbon's *The Artillerist's Manual* held that while musket fire was "uncertain" beyond 200 yards, "when troops are in compact masses, the fire is still very effective beyond that distance."[15]

American infantry in Mexico relied on the musket and the bayonet. General Zachary Taylor, the commander in the northern theater of the war, often expressed confidence in this accessory to the musket. Before the Battle of Palo Alto, Taylor instructed his men to rely on the bayonet. After the fighting at Resaca de la Palma Taylor said: "My orders was to make free use of the bayonet, which was done as far as it be, or as the enemy would permit." When he had captured Monterey, Taylor wrote Secretary of State James Buchanan: "I determined to carry the place pretty much with the bayonet, commencing with the out works."[16]

The bayonet could be an effective weapon in the Mexican War because the musket fire of defenders was sometimes so weak that determined attackers could get close enough for bayonet fighting. The Americans attacked at Resaca de la Palma, charging through chaparral and winning the battle after some close combat. Lieutenant Edmund Kirby Smith, a member of the Fifth United States Infantry, said of this engagement: ". . . it was hand to hand conflict—a trial of personal strength in many instances, where the bayonet failed, the fist even was used." Another American officer recalled men being killed by sword, bayonet, and lance.[17] Bayonet fighting also occurred at Cerro Gordo and elsewhere.[18]

Bayonet charges sometimes were successful even against defenders protected by field entrenchments. The *tête de pont* on the Churubusco River, a strong point of the Mexican position at Churubusco, was taken by the Americans with a shock bayonet charge at double-quick time. Engineer Isaac I. Stevens summarized what happened: "This was the terrible and decisive

[14]Smith, *War With Mexico*, II, 450; George B. McClellan, "Army Organization," *Harper's New Monthly Magazine*, XLIX (1874), 408.

[15]Ripley, *War With Mexico*, II, 258; John Gibbon, *The Artillerist's Manual* (New York, 1860), 248–49.

[16]Smith, *War With Mexico*, I, 165–66; Zachary Taylor to Dr. R. C. Wood, May 9, 1846, *Letters of Zachary Taylor from the Battlefields of the Mexican War*, ed. William K. Bixby (Rochester, 1908), 2; Zachary Taylor to James Buchanan, August 29, 1847, ibid., 178.

[17]Smith and Judah, *Chronicles*, 71, 83. See also James Longstreet, *From Manassas to Appomattox: Memoirs of the Civil War in America*, ed. James I. Robertson, Jr. (reissue, Bloomington, 1960), 27.

[18]*House Executive Document*, 30 Cong., 1 sess., No. 8, 281; Smith and Judah, *Chronicles*, 212; Semmes, *Campaign of General Scott*, 69.

conflict of the war, and was a case of a combined movement of all the divisions. The enemy's intrenched works were carried at the point of the bayonet."[19] Lieutenant Colonel Ethan Allan Hitchcock said of the same action: "Our troops plunged into a wet ditch surrounding the enemy's works and, floundering through it, passed over the parapet of a regularly constructed work and at the point of the bayonet drove the enemy off."[20]

The musket and the bayonet also were the basis of tactical theory of the period. The authorized tactical manual at the outbreak of the Mexican War was a musket and bayonet tactics, Winfield Scott's three-volume *Infantry-Tactics*. This highly regarded manual followed French tactical theory and represented the work of the greatest American military leader of the early nineteenth century. At least six editions of Scott's *Infantry-Tactics* appeared between 1835 and 1848, and at least four more between the Mexican and Civil wars, but the original work was never revised.[21]

Tactical theory recognized that individual musket fire was inaccurate and tried to compensate for this by keeping infantrymen in close-ordered lines to concentrate their firepower. Attack tactics were designed to compress men together, keep them well ordered during an advance, and bring them to the opposing line ready for a concentrated volley and bayonet charge. Scott's *Tactics* stressed close-order formations, forming regiments in tightly ordered lines of either two or three ranks. (Scott assumed that the three-rank formation would be the more common, but it was suspended by the War Department in 1835.) Scott dictated that ranks form only thirteen inches apart. Related units, regiments of the same brigade or brigades of the same division, were to form with an interval between units of only twenty-two paces.[22] The men in the ranks were expected to keep in close order, dressing their line by maintaining an elbow-to-elbow touch during an advance. Scott's *Tactics* insisted that "the alignment can only be preserved, in marching, by the regularity of the step, the touch of the elbow, and the maintainance of the shoulders in a square with the line of direction."[23] Scott warned that if the men "do not strictly observe the touch of elbows, it would be impossible for

---

[19]Semmes, *Campaign of General Scott*, 287–88; Hazard Stevens, *The Life of Isaac Ingalls Stevens* (2 vols., Boston, 1900), I, 183.

[20]Ethan A. Hitchcock, *Fifty Years in Camp and Field; Diary of Major-General Ethan Allan Hitchcock, U.S.A.*, ed. W. A. Croffut (New York, 1909), 283.

[21]Scott, *Infantry-Tactics*, editions of 1835, 1840, 1842, 1846, 1847, 1848, 1852, 1857, 1860, and 1861. Scott also presided over a board of officers that produced a similar, though not identical, tactical manual for militia troops. U.S. War Dept., *Abstract of Infantry Tactics; Including Exercises and Manoeuvres of Light-Infantry and Riflemen; for the use of the Militia of the United States* (Boston, 1830). Several editions were published (1847, 1853, 1861), but the work was never revised. On the militia tactics see also Winfield Scott, *Memoirs of Lieut.-General Scott, LL.D. Written by Himself* (2 vols., New York, 1864), I, 207–08.

[22]Scott, *Infantry-Tactics*, I, endorsement on unnumbered page, 5, 7, 9, 10.

[23]Ibid., 80–81.

an individual to judge whether he marches abreast with his neighbour, or not, and whether there be not an interval between them."[24]

Scott's *Tactics* were more concerned with maintaining order than with creating élan. If an attack was to end in a successful bayonet charge, élan was desirable, and Scott recognized that. He directed, for example, that a line begin its advance "with life."[25]

Scott's first concern, however, was that an advance be close, steady, and orderly. He did not want attackers to make a rapid advance, which was unnecessary because the musketry of a defending line was ineffective until the attackers reached short range. Moreover, a rapid advance was undesirable because it would disorder the ranks and destroy the close order necessary for effective firepower. Following Scott's manual, men advanced with a "direct step" of twenty-eight inches at a "common time" rate of 90 steps per minute. Scott also allowed the "direct step" to be used at a "quick time" rate of 110 steps per minute. Scott's *Tactics* discouraged the use of any step rate faster than "quick time" and stated that troops were to be "habitually exercised" at nothing more rapid than "quick time." Scott believed that "double quick time" and the "run" were unnecessary for line infantry in ordinary circumstances, though he acknowledged that there were exceptional cases. In the last "eight or ten paces preceding the shock of a charge," for example, "quick time" might be accelerated to 140 steps per minute or even a "run" might be used. Scott refused, however, to recognize the "double quick time" as a standard step rate. He discouraged its use because "ranks of men cannot march any length of time at so swift a rate, without breaking or confusion."[26]

Scott's *Tactics* sought a disciplined close order and allowed loose order only in skirmisher tactics, which were common in the early nineteenth century. (The French infantry of the Napoleonic era had fought "under cover of swarms of skirmishers."[27]) Skirmishers were deployed in very loose formation in advance of the main lines to cover their own troops and to develop the enemy's fire. Scott's *Tactics*, which included a section of tactical instructions for skirmishers, assumed that each regiment would have one company of rifles or light infantry that would do the skirmishing for the remainder of the regiment. Scott's manual equated skirmish tactics with rifle tactics, and it did not expect more than two companies per regiment to deploy as skirmishers.[28]

Skirmishers were a feature of the Mexican War, but they were usually deployed in the small numbers called for in Scott's *Tactics*, two companies or less per regiment. General David E. Twigg's Division at Monterey used only

---

[24]Ibid., 81.

[25]Ibid., 124.

[26]Ibid., 29, 82, 132.

[27]J. F. C. Fuller, *A Military History of the Western World* (3 vols., New York, 1954–1956), II, 419.

[28]Scott, *Infantry-Tactics*, II, 188–89.

two companies as skirmishers.[29] At Cerro Gordo, the same division again deployed two companies as skirmishers, reinforcing them later with two more. These four companies did the skirmishing for a division of about 2,600 men.[30]

When the Americans did adopt skirmish tactics in Mexico, they were not complying with tactical theory but were reacting to terrain and circumstance. At Resaca de la Palma, where the Americans charged through dense chaparral to attack the Mexicans, skirmish tactics were necessary. Captain C. F. Smith, who commanded four companies in this attack, said afterward that it was "impossible" for a regular line of battle to get through the chaparral, so he deployed his men as skirmishers.[31] The street fighting and firm Mexican resistance at Monterey forced the Americans to again adopt skirmish tactics. Lieutenant Colonel Thomas Childs, for example, commanded a picked force of about eight companies that was deployed as skirmishers.[32]

Mexican War commanders did not want to use skirmish tactics and loose-order formations because effective musket fire required the concentration of firepower in close-order formations. Loose-order formations weakened a unit's firepower and made troops harder to control. When the Americans were forced to use loose order at Resaca de la Palma, officers complained that the chaparral terrain and loose formations made their units difficult to handle. Captain L. N. Norris deployed his regiment as skirmishers and reported that it "became very much scattered." The major commanding the Fifth United States Infantry Regiment, which also advanced in skirmish order, said that his men "became much separated and extended, rendering it impossible to advance with much regularity."[33]

Close-order line formations delivered the most effective musketry and were the most common infantry formations of the Mexican War. At the opening of the war, Taylor formed virtually all of his infantry at Palo Alto into one long line.[34] The line formation dominated subsequent battlefields of the war and was used in every major engagement of both Taylor's and Scott's campaigns. The deployment of Twigg's Division at Monterey may be considered typical. The division deployed from column to line, covered by two companies of skirmishers. Lieutenant Colonel Henry Wilson reported: "After passing through some corn fields, the column was halted, and the command of the whole [division] was assumed by Lieutenant Colonel [John] Garland, 4th infantry, and a company of the 3d brigade thrown out as

[29]*House Executive Document*, 30 Cong., 1 sess., No. 17, 6.

[30]Ibid., No. 8, 275, 292; Smith, *War With Mexico*, II, 45.

[31]*House Document*, 29 Cong., 1 sess., No. 209, 29–30. See also Longstreet, *From Manassas to Appomattox*, 27.

[32]*Senate Document*, 29 Cong., 2 sess., No. 1, 104; Ripley, *War With Mexico*, I, 234.

[33]*House Document*, 29 Cong., 1 sess., No. 209, 19, 20.

[34]Grant, *Memoirs*, I, 94–95; Smith, *War With Mexico*, I, 164–66.

skirmishers, when the line resumed its forward movement. A second company of skirmishers (Captain John Scott's 1st infantry) was then deployed to cover the front of the 1st infantry battalion. After clearing the corn fields and obtaining the plain, the line advanced with steadiness and rapidity."[35]

The alternative to the line formation was the column, which was intended to deliver an attack with decisive impact at the point where the head of the column struck the defending line. Line attacks relied on concentration of musketry; column attacks relied on shock tactics. Line attacks were more common, but column attacks occasionally were used. General Bennet Riley's Brigade made a decisive attack at Contreras, deploying in two columns to charge the Mexican defenders.[36] An officer in this charge later recounted: "We marched towards them still under heavy fire of musketry, for some twenty or thirty yards, then halted, and deployed column. During all this time we had not fired a shot and men were dropping in our ranks at every moment. I admire the coolness of our men during this trying time even more than their head long impetuosity after the word *charge* was given."[37] Near the defending line, the Americans redeployed into line, entered the Mexican position "almost in a body," and the charge succeeded.[38]

The use of the column formation was sometimes dictated by terrain. General William J. Worth attacked at Churubusco with the two brigades of his division, using both line and column formations. Colonel Newman S. Clarke's Brigade advanced in line through the lava beds south of Churubusco. On the main road to Churubusco, Lieutenant Colonel John Garland's Brigade was ordered "to advance rapidly in column, and attempt a direct assault." Garland's column formation was dictated by the road; once his brigade left the road, it deployed into a line formation.[39]

The column formation was useful in Mexico because Mexican War units were small enough that columns could maintain mobility. Small columns were especially suitable for storming-party tactics, which the Americans used at both Molino del Rey and Chapultepec. The center of the American attack at Molino del Rey was an assaulting column of 500 picked men under Major George Wright.[40] In the Chapultepec assault, the Americans used two storming parties, "little columns"[41] of 250 men each, one commanded by Captain Samuel Mackenzie and the other by Captain Silas Casey.

[35]*House Executive Document*, 30 Cong., 1 sess., No. 17, 6.

[36]Ibid., No. 8, 328; Smith and Judah, *Chronicles*, 242; Ripley, *War With Mexico*, II, 242.

[37]Smith and Judah, *Chronicles*, 244.

[38]Ripley, *War With Mexico*, II, 243.

[39]*House Executive Document*, 30 Cong., 1 sess., No. 8, 316; "Map of Genl. Worth's Operations" to accompany his report on Churubusco, ibid., 317.

[40]*House Executive Document*, 30 Cong., 1 sess., No. 8, 362–63; Semmes, *Campaign of General Scott*, 325; Smith, *War With Mexico*, II, 143–45.

[41]*House Executive Document*, 30 Cong., 1 sess., No. 8, 377–78. See also Smith and Judah, *Chronicles*, 263; Grant, *Memoirs*, I, 154; Hitchcock, *Fifty Years*, 301–02.

The square formation, primarily a defense against cavalry, was used successfully in Mexico in many different situations. The Fifth United States Regiment formed a square and stopped an attack by Mexican lancers against Taylor's right flank at Palo Alto. The Mexican horsemen came within about fifty yards of the square before the American musket fire defeated their attack.[42] During its march to Monterey, the Second Ohio was harassed by Mexican cavalry and formed a square. The regiment's colonel then ordered it to march in square rather than column, the usual marching formation. The Mexican cavalry made several unsuccessful attacks, both mounted and dismounted, against all sides of the square and eventually withdrew; the Second Ohio went on with its march.[43] One regiment of General Thomas L. Hamer's Brigade used the square formation to help protect a mortar threatened by Mexican lancers at Monterey.[44]

Although the square formation was used successfully in Mexico, there were indications that the formation was not indispensable, because infantry commanders often made a line defense against cavalry. The most famous defense against cavalry in the Mexican War was the well-known "V" defense of Taylor's left and rear at Buena Vista, in which Colonel Jefferson Davis's First Mississippi Rifles and parts of General Joseph Lane's Brigade repulsed the Mexican cavalry sent against them. Lane said of this defense: "Instead of throwing my command into squares to resist the charge, the enemy were received in line of two ranks, my force reserving its fire until the enemy were within about seventy yards."[45] One of Lane's regimental commanders argued that because his regiment had its left flank secured on a ravine and its line could not be turned, he did not need to have his regiment form a square.[46]

All of these formations—line, column, and square—were used successfully in Mexico, and American soldiers gained confidence in them. The formations of Scott's *Tactics* were compatible with musket and bayonet weaponry, but Lew Wallace complained that Scott's *Tactics* were "smothered by details" and that only "a student with positive aptitude could master [Scott]."[47] Most of these details were made necessary, however, by the limitations of the musket and the need for precise, close-order tactical formations. In the major engagements of both Taylor's and Scott's campaigns, the Americans used these tactics, took the offensive, and were successful, even when they encountered field entrenchments.

The Americans successfully attacked field works at Monterey, Cerro

---

[42]*House Document*, 29 Cong., 1 sess., No. 209, 14, 19; Smith and Judah, *Chronicles*, 66.

[43]*House Executive Document*, 30 Cong., 1 sess., No. 8, 211–12.

[44]Ibid., No. 17, 10.

[45]Ibid., No. 8, 183.

[46]Ibid., 187.

[47]Wallace, *Lew Wallace*, I, 131.

Gordo, and elsewhere, leaving some American soldiers without much regard for entrenchments. Isaac I. Stevens and Raphael Semmes both regarded Churubusco as a case where the bayonet was successful over entrenched works.[48] Roswell Ripley published a history of the Mexican War just after it ended in which he was skeptical of the value of field entrenchments. He believed an attack by good troops would overcome field works. "Napoleon never failed in carrying any lines which he attacked," Ripley argued, "and other high authorities admit that [entrenchments] may, in general, prevent the passage of undiscipline[d] soldiers but seldom when the assailants are superiors in hardihood and discipline." Ripley considered the Mexican field works at Cerro Gordo an example of both the "efficiency" and the "uselessness" of entrenchments. The field works on the Mexican right were held successfully against the Americans. They were strong works, and the attackers were volunteers. The entrenchments on the Mexican left were attacked by better troops and were quickly carried. "The lines of abattis and the fort on the summit of Cerro Gordo," Ripley said, "retarded the progress of the veterans of the second division scarcely one instant after the attack commenced."[49] Henry W. Halleck, who reviewed in the late 1850s the tactics of the main engagements of the Mexican War, thought that the war might have demonstrated the value of field works if the Mexican works had been better constructed and defended.[50]

The belief that the current weaponry and tactics could overcome entrenchments and other battlefield problems was not limited to the infantry arm; Americans were equally confident of the weaponry and tactics of their artillery. At the outbreak of the Mexican War, the Americans had five batteries of field artillery. Each battery consisted of four or six bronze guns, which included two or more six-pounders and usually one or two twelve-pound howitzers. American artillery ordnance was better than that of the Mexicans. "The Mexicans were armed about as we were so far as their infantry was concerned," Ulysses S. Grant recalled, "but their artillery fired only solid shot. We had greatly the advantage in this arm."[51]

The tactical manual for field artillery during the Mexican War was based on the work of Captain Robert Anderson, later the defender of Fort Sumter. In 1839 Anderson published *Instruction for Field Artillery, Horse and Foot*, a translation of a French artillery drill manual. The following year the War Department made Anderson's translation the authorized artillery tactics.[52] In 1843 a board of officers convened to prepare an artillery tactics, with

[48]Stevens, *Life of Isaac Ingalls Stevens*, I, 183; Semmes, *Campaign of General Scott*, 287–88.
[49]Ripley, *War With Mexico*, II, 78.
[50]Henry W. Halleck, *Elements of Military Art and Science* (New York, 1862), 438.
[51]Smith, *War With Mexico*, I, 450–51; Grant, *Memoirs*, I, 95.
[52]Robert Anderson, *Instruction for Field Artillery, Horse and Foot* (Philadelphia, 1839), endorsement on unnumbered page.

Brevet Major Samuel Ringgold as the senior officer of this board and Anderson as a member. The Ringgold board produced a manual that was essentially the same as Anderson's and gave it the same title. Ringgold changed the method of serving the gun to a British system, but he retained the French system of battery maneuvers and most other details from Anderson's translation. The work of the Ringgold board was authorized by the War Department and published in 1845. *Instruction for Field Artillery* was a drill manual for artillery, including schools of the piece, the driver, and the battery. It taught artillerymen how to maneuver their guns and batteries on the march and in battle, but it did not advise them when or where they ought to use their pieces or how their arm could best cooperate with infantry. It was a drill manual, not a work of tactical theory.[53]

The confidence American soldiers had in their artillery was not based on tactical theory but on the performance of the arm in the field. In the earliest battles of the Mexican War, the artillery played a major role and won praise. The day after Palo Alto, Taylor said that he had fought the battle "principally with artillery." When Henry W. Halleck reviewed the tactics of the Mexican War, he regarded Palo Alto as "virtually a cannonade." Major Luther Giddings of the First Ohio Regiment said that Palo Alto "demonstrated, in the practical operations of war, the wonderful perfections of our light field-batteries." Lieutenant Jeremiah Mason Scarrit of Taylor's staff wrote after the American victories at Palo Alto and Resaca de la Palma: "There was a great deal of personal gallantry shown and the most enthusiastic and determined spirit both in officers and men. But the light artillery was the back bone of our success."[54]

The artillery lived up to its early reputation as the war went on, distinguishing itself in both Taylor's and Scott's campaigns. The best-known artillery action of the Mexican War took place at Buena Vista, where the American field guns were the decisive factor in Taylor's successful defense. The batteries of Braxton Bragg, Thomas W. Sherman, and John M. Washington demonstrated at Buena Vista the great mobility and power of field artillery on the tactical defensive. Taylor and his second in command, General John E. Wool, both praised the artillery in their reports. Wool thought the Americans could not have held the position an hour without their artillery. Taylor said of his artillery at Buena Vista: "Moving rapidly

---

[53]Henry J. Hunt, "Artillery," in *Papers of the Military Historical Society of Massachusetts* (14 vols., Boston, 1913), XIII, 103; "Tactics for Field Artillery," ii, Proceedings and Report of the Barry Board, in the Papers of the Barry Board, Record Group 94, Adjutant General's Office, Navy and Old Army Branch, National Archives. This document incorrectly identifies Captain James Monroe as the senior member of the Ringgold board. Board of Artillery Officers, *Instruction for Field Artillery, Horse and Foot* (Baltimore, 1845).

[54]Zachary Taylor to Dr. R. C. Wood, May 9, 1846, in Taylor, *Letters of Zachary Taylor*, 1; Halleck, *Elements of Military Art* (1862 edition), 414; Giddings, *Sketches of the Campaign*, 41; Smith and Judah, *Chronicles*, 71.

over the roughest ground, it was always in action at the right place and the right time, and its well-directed fire dealt destruction in the masses of the enemy."[55]

Taylor's remark underscored the strong point of American artillery in Mexico—its mobility. On the defensive, artillery could be shifted rapidly to support any threatened point of a main line. A staff officer from Massachusetts said of the field batteries: "They move over the ground like lightning, and with great accuracy too. They are the strongest arm of our service." Artillery was mobile and rapid enough that it could undertake pursuit. Captain Thomas W. Sherman, with one gun of his battery, pursued Mexican cavalry after Buena Vista until it was out of range.[56]

The limited range of the musket and the close-order line formations that it necessitated made it possible for artillery to be used effectively on the offensive. Artillery could advance close to a defending infantry line before entering effective musket range. Infantry massed in close-order line formations was vulnerable to the fire of field guns, so artillery sometimes took the offensive and advanced in front of its own infantry. At Palo Alto, James Duncan's Battery advanced beyond the main line of infantry and covered Taylor's left flank.[57] The next day at Resaca de la Palma, S. G. Ridgely's Battery preceded the attacking American infantry, firing grape and canister, and advancing during every slackening of the enemy's fire.[58] At Contreras, General Persifor F. Smith committed an artillery battery in front of his infantry. He sent John B. Magruder's Battery forward to a position partly covered by a rock ledge and then later advanced his brigade of infantry as a support to Magruder.[59]

Mobility and offensive effectiveness were also expected of the mounted arm. At the outbreak of the Mexican War, the Americans had two regiments of dragoons, armed with musketoons, Prussian dragoon-style sabers, and horse pistols. The Mounted Rifles carried percussion rifles and Colt's army revolvers but not sabers.[60] The tactical manual of the mounted arm was *Cavalry Tactics*, a three-volume translation of French tactics authorized by the War Department in 1841 that provided for a close-order line tactics with a two-rank formation. A ten-squadron regiment would form in two ranks of five squadrons each, with only a twelve-pace interval between squadrons.[61]

American mounted troops in Mexico had many tactical duties. They often were used to skirmish, to cover the flanks of infantry, to serve as couriers, or

[55]*House Executive Document*, 30 Cong., 1 sess., No. 8, 150; also 138–39.

[56]Smith and Judah, *Chronicles*, 290; *House Executive Document*, 30 Cong., 1 sess., No. 8, 194.

[57]*House Document*, 29 Cong., 1 sess., No. 209, 2.

[58]Ibid., 15, 20.

[59]*House Executive Document*, 30 Cong., 1 sess., No. 8, 326.

[60]Smith, *War With Mexico*, I, 139, 450.

[61]U.S. War Dept., *Cavalry Tactics* (3 parts, Washington, 1841), I, endorsement on unnumbered page, 13; Smith, *War With Mexico*, I, 139.

to stand in reserve, ready to pursue the enemy when his ranks were broken.[62] Mounted units also did some reconnaissance work in Mexico, although the most famous scouting of the war was done by engineers. Engineer Isaac I. Stevens was critical of the failure to use the dragoons to find routes to turn the Mexican position at Cerro Gordo. Before the Battle of Cerro Gordo, Stevens complained in his diary: "The dragoons are admirable for extensive reconnoissances, yet no attempt has been made to determine the practicability and even the existence of certain routes, on both the right and left."[63] The reconnaissance that found the turning route at Cerro Gordo was not made by dragoons, but—like many other reconnaissances of the Mexican War—was made by engineers, Lieutenant P. G. T. Beauregard and Captain Robert E. Lee.[64]

When used in main combat actions, the American mounted units of the Mexican War often fought dismounted. A Texas cavalry regiment dismounted at Monterey to support Colonel Jefferson Davis's Mississippi Rifles.[65] Parts of Colonel Archibald Yell's Arkansas cavalry, parts of Colonel Humphrey Marshall's Kentucky cavalry, and other mounted units were deployed dismounted at Buena Vista.[66] During the siege of Vera Cruz, Colonel William S. Harney used his dragoons in both mounted and dismounted formations.[67]

The supreme action for mounted troops was the mounted charge, the saber charge. There were few successful mounted charges in the Mexican War, but they were memorable actions. One of the most famous was a saber charge made by Captain Philip Kearny's Troop of the First Dragoons during the pursuit after Churubusco. Dragoons from Kearny's and three other troops sabered Mexicans retreating from Churubusco to Mexico City.[68] The mounted charge was a viable tactic in pursuit operations; infantry in retreat and out of formation was vulnerable to saber charges. In another well-known operation of the war, Captain C. A. May of the Second Dragoons led a column of fours in a charge at Resaca de la Palma that overrode a Mexican battery and captured General Rómulo Díaz de la Vega.[69] K. Jack Bauer, a careful historian of the Mexican War, contended that May's charge was "poorly executed." Bauer noted that "May was a colorful figure who became one of the heroes of the war as a result of this mishandled charge. Nothing in

---

[62]For examples, see George H. Gordon, "The Battles of Contreras and Churubusco," in *Papers of the Military Historical Society of Massachusetts*, XIII, 576; *House Executive Document*, 30 Cong., 1 sess., No. 8, 363, 373; *House Document*, 29 Cong., 1 sess., No. 209, 27; *House Executive Document*, 30 Cong., 1 sess., No. 8, 421.

[63]Stevens, *Life of Isaac Ingalls Stevens*, I, 123.

[64]*House Executive Document*, 30 Cong., 1 sess., No. 8, 261.

[65]Smith and Judah, *Chronicles*, 83.

[66]*House Executive Document*, 30 Cong., 1 sess., No. 8, 145, 164–65, 181.

[67]Ibid., 251–52.

[68]Ibid., 341, 347; Semmes, *Campaign of General Scott*, 291.

[69]*House Document*, 29 Cong., 1 sess., No. 209, 15–16, 21.

his performance at Resaca de la Palma or later in the war dispells the notion
that he was one of the least deserving heroes of the conflict."[70] Resaca de la
Palma was won by the infantry and artillery, not by May's charge. Saber
charges such as Kearny's and May's were uncommon. They did not decide
any major action of the war. Whenever they occurred, however, they
strengthened confidence in the mounted attack and the saber.

All three arms were used on the tactical offensive and all three fought
aggressively in Mexico, yet American combat losses were low. Taylor's small
army took the tactical offensive at both Palo Alto and Resaca de la Palma.
Taylor reported that he lost 55 of the 2,288 men and officers at Palo Alto, or
2 percent of his force. For Resaca de la Palma he reported a loss of 6
percent.[71] Scott's army attacked at Cerro Gordo, in some places assaulting
field works. The Americans won the battle at a cost of about 5 percent of
their numbers.[72] Even in the bloodiest attacks of the Mexican War, American losses were fairly light. The combined American losses in the attacks at
Contreras, Churubusco, Molino del Rey, and Chapultepec total about 2,700,
less than the loss of the Federal Twelfth Corps at Chancellorsville.[73]

Time and again in Mexico the Americans took the tactical offensive, suffered fairly light losses, and were successful. Close-order musket and
bayonet tactics succeeded for the Americans in every major engagement of
the war. Whether or not the Mexican defenders were behind field works
seemed to make little difference. Every arm of the service shared in the
successes on the tactical offensive. In 1859 Henry W. Halleck summarized
the American victory at Resaca de la Palma: "The Americans attacked the
whole line with skirmishers, and with dragoons supported by light artillery,
and the charge of a heavy column of infantry decided the victory."[74]

Mexican War tactics were not significantly different from early nineteenth-
century tactics. Infantry fought in lines and relied on disciplined close-order
formations, concentrated musketry, and the bayonet. Artillery was used on
both the defensive and offensive. Cavalry was held ready to saber charge
enemy troops once they were put out of formation and into retreat. Little
tactical innovation was attempted in Mexico because the standard tactics
proved successful. In the decade after the Mexican War, these tactics were
undone by changes in weaponry.

---

[70]K. Jack Bauer, *The Mexican War, 1846–1848* (New York, 1974), 60–62, 65n.

[71]*House Document*, 29 Cong., 1 sess., No. 209, 4–6, 10–11. There are arithmetical errors in
Taylor's table of losses for Resaca de la Palma.

[72]*House Executive Document*, 30 Cong., 1 sess., No. 8, 264, 265–74.

[73]Ibid., 384. Earlier, Scott reported his loss for Contreras and Churubusco as one man higher.
Ibid., 314. Worth gave virtually the same loss figures for Molino del Rey as Scott. Ibid., 367,
371. The Twelfth Corps at Chancellorsville lost 2,822. U.S. War Dept., *The War of the Rebellion:
A Compilation of the Official Records of the Union and Confederate Armies* (128 vols., Washington,
1880–1901), Series I, XXV (pt. 1), 185.

[74]Halleck, *Elements of Military Art* (1862 edition), 414.

3

The Weapon of the Brave

Many of the tactical lessons that Americans learned in the Mexican War were reinforced by tactical theory, which emphasized the offensive over the defensive and preached that vigorous assaults usually would overcome entrenchments. Tactical theoreticians before the conflict of the 1860s favored bayonet attacks and traditional close-order formations. The Napoleonic historian and military theorist Antoine Henri Jomini argued strongly for the tactical offensive in his 1838 *Summary of the Art of War*. "A general who waits for the enemy like an automaton," said Jomini, "without taking any other part than that of fighting valiantly, will always succumb when he shall be well attacked."[1] The most important military theorist in America from the 1830s to the 1860s, West Point Professor Dennis Hart Mahan, was also an advocate of the tactical offensive. Mahan's most influential work was *An Elementary Treatise on Advanced-Guard, Out-Post, and Detachment Service of Troops, and the Manner of Posting and Handling Them in Presence of an Enemy*. In this book Mahan offered his general plan for the tactical offensive, dividing the attacking force into an advanced guard, main body, and reserve. The advanced guard, or skirmishers, would clear the way for the attack. The main body and the reserve would follow in columns. When the advanced guard was checked, it would fall back on the main body, which would then either deploy into line and open fire or make "a vigorous charge with the

---

[1] Antoine Henri Jomini, *Summary of the Art of War*, trans. O. F. Winship and E. E. McLean (New York, 1854), 207. The extent and limitations of Jomini's influence on Civil War tactics and strategy has been variously evaluated. David Herbert Donald, "Refighting the Civil War," in *Lincoln Reconsidered: Essays on the Civil War Era* (New York, 1956), 82–102; T. Harry Williams, "The Military Leadership of North and South," in *Why the North Won the Civil War*, ed. David Herbert Donald (Baton Rouge, 1960), 23–47; Frank E. Vandiver, *Their Tattered Flags* (New York, 1970), 88, 94; Thomas L. Connelly and Archer Jones, *The Politics of Command: Factions and Ideas in Confederate Strategy* (Baton Rouge, 1973), 6–30, 174–76; Grady McWhiney, "Ulysses S. Grant's Pre–Civil War Military Education," in *Southerners and Other Americans* (New York, 1973), 61–71, and "Jefferson Davis and the Art of War," *Civil War History*, XXI (1975), 101–12.

bayonet."[2] Mahan's offensive system was incorporated into army regulations.[3] Another example of the importance given to offensive tactics is *Camp and Outpost Duty for Infantry*, primarily a camp and picket manual with a sprinkling of tactical advice, written by General Daniel Butterfield and published in 1862. Butterfield's book contended that infantry always should take the offensive against enemy "infantry or positions" and that élan and shock would carry the day. "If the enemy awaits, or marches also to meet you," one maxim advised, "surpass your adversary in ardor, and enter head foremost into the opposed mass; once the shock is given, re-establish order by quickly rallying at a few paces in front; lastly, renew the shock, or pursue . . . with a few skirmishers, according as the enemy resists or runs away."[4]

When theorists discussed the tactical defensive, they emphasized the importance of regaining the offensive. Jomini insisted that "the best of all for an army which awaits the enemy defensively, is to know how to retake the initiative when the moment has arrived for doing so with success." Mahan advocated using the bayonet to regain the initiative from an attacking enemy. Under Mahan's system, if the advanced guard were attacked, the main body would come to its support and "will usually attack with the bayonet." If the advanced guard were driven away, the main body would deploy into line and defend itself by fire. If the enemy continued to advance, Mahan suggested the defenders form columns and charge. "A charge by a column, when the enemy is within 50 paces," said Mahan, "will prove effective, if resolutely made." Mahan's student, Henry W. Halleck, borrowed much of his *Elements of Military Art and Science* from Jomini. Halleck adopted Jomini's idea that a defending commander should always try to regain the offensive, even if he were defending an entrenched position. Halleck praised entrenched lines with intervals in the works because these intervals "allowed the assailed to act on the offensive, by charging the enemy at the opportune moment."[5]

At the same time that the tactical offensive was being emphasized, field entrenchment received considerable attention. The teaching and writing of Dennis Hart Mahan, particularly *A Complete Treatise on Field Fortification*

---

[2]Dennis Hart Mahan, *An Elementary Treatise on Advanced-Guard, Out-Post, and Detachment Service of Troops, and the Manner of Posting and Handling Them in Presence of an Enemy* (New York, 1847), 51. Mahan's influence also has been variously evaluated. Stephen E. Ambrose, *Duty, Honor, Country: A History of West Point* (Baltimore, 1966), 99–102; Edward Hagerman, "From Jomini to Dennis Hart Mahan: The Evolution of Trench Warfare and the American Civil War," *Civil War History*, XIII (1967), 197–220, and "The Professionalization of George B. McClellan and Early Civil War Field Command: An Institutional Perspective," *Civil War History*, XXI (1975), 113–35; Grady McWhiney, *Braxton Bragg and Confederate Defeat* (New York, 1969), 16–20.

[3]U.S. War Dept., *Regulations for the Army of the United States, 1857* (New York, 1857), 90–93.

[4]Daniel Butterfield, *Camp and Outpost Duty for Infantry* (New York, 1862), 110–11.

[5]Jomini, *Art of War*, 204, 205; Mahan, *Advanced-Guard*, 12; Henry W. Halleck, *Elements of Military Art and Science* (New York, 1846), 110–11.

(1836), made him the foremost American exponent of field works before the Civil War. In his preface to *Field Fortification*, he argued that field entrenchments were in the best interest of a society that relied on volunteer soldiers because they would help save the lives of men and would help militia gain equality with regulars.[6] Mahan warned his West Point cadets against relying solely on their choice of battle plan to compensate for the weaknesses of a position, and he advised them to use field works to improve poor positions.[7]

Tactical theorists respected field entrenchments but believed that a vigorous offensive would overcome them. Confronted with strong entrenchments, Jomini preferred a turning movement to a "doubtful attack," but he was not afraid to attack entrenched lines on either a flank or in the center, depending on the specific circumstances.[8] When a commander attacked field works, Jomini recommended an artillery barrage and a main attack by three small columns, supported by skirmishers and reserves. He emphasized the role of élan in such attacks. "After these recommendations," said Jomini, "there is only one thing to do, this is to launch one's troops with all the vivacity possible upon the works . . . for the least hesitation is worse in such a case than the most audacious temerity." Mahan suggested that entrenchments be attacked either by bayonet alone or by a combined action of artillery and the bayonet. He did not believe that musketry alone could carry field works.[9]

The bayonet also was recommended for defending entrenchments. Mahan said of defending field works: "The results of innumerable actions proved that the defence with the bayonet is the surest method of repelling the enemy." Henry D. Grafton, an 1839 graduate of West Point, agreed with Mahan. In his 1854 work, *A Treatise on the Camp and March*, Grafton contended: "All intrenchments should be defended to the last extremity; and the assailed should mount the parapet, and rely chiefly on the bayonet to repel the assault, when the enemy commences to get upon the berm."[10]

The bayonet was highly regarded after the Mexican War, and several bayonet manuals appeared between the 1840s and the 1860s. In 1852 George B. McClellan published his *Manual of Bayonet Exercise*, a translation of French bayonet tactics. McClellan admitted that there would not be much bayonet fencing done by infantry in line formations, but he argued that learning the skill was good for morale. McClellan maintained that "the men will surely be more steady and composed, from the consciousness of the fact that they can

---

[6] Dennis Hart Mahan, *A Complete Treatise on Field Fortification* (New York, 1836), vii–viii.

[7] Dennis Hart Mahan, lithographed United States Military Academy textbook, "Advanced guard, outpost & detachment service of troops," 15, United States Military Academy Library. This textbook is not related to the Mahan work published under a similar title.

[8] Jomini, *Art of War*, 232.

[9] Ibid., 230; Mahan, *Field Fortification*, 95.

[10] Mahan, *Field Fortification*, 8; Henry D. Grafton, *A Treatise on the Camp and March* (Boston, 1854), 35.

make good use of their bayonets, and easily protect their persons against everything but balls." John C. Kelton prepared a bayonet manual that was used for cadet instruction at West Point, and R. Milton Cary offered Confederate soldiers a *Skirmishers' Drill and Bayonet Exercise* that he borrowed from French theory. Cary's title page carried the motto: "The bayonet is the weapon of the brave."[11]

The musket remained the companion of the bayonet after the Mexican War. Until the middle of the 1850s, the rifle continued to be what it was in Mexico, a special weapon with special uses. Mahan regarded riflemen as sharpshooters, a "lurking and often invisible foe," best used to intimidate the enemy. John Gibbon's *The Artillerist's Manual*, a compendium that was first published several years after the rifle replaced the musket, still retained the notion that the rifle was a special weapon. *The Artillerist's Manual* stated: "The effective range of the rifled spherical ball, is over 400 yards. The oblong rifle ball [Minié bullet] is effective at 1000 yards; but these arms exhibit their marked superiority when used by isolated marksmen."[12]

As long as the musket and bayonet were the main weapons of infantry, tactical theory recommended close-order formations. Before and after the Mexican War, tactical theorists objected to the use of loose order and minimized the role of skirmishers. Jomini opposed the use of loose order or skirmish order for anything other than the traditional duties of skirmishers. "The skirmishers are an accessory," said Jomini, "for they ought only to cover the line properly so called by favor of the ground, to protect the march of the columns, to fill up the intervals, or defend the approaches of a post." When Halleck's *Elements of Military Art and Science* discussed the standard two-line formation, it warned that too loose an order meant the lines could only advance slowly. If the lines try to move quickly, the formation "breaks and exhibits great and dangerous undulations."[13] Mahan also was skeptical of loose order. "A very extended order is necessarily without consistence," Mahan said, "and in the slightest change of position the line wavers, and not unfrequently, breaks." He also warned commanders against detaching too many skirmishers.[14]

The basic infantry formation for both assault and defense was the two-line formation. Jomini favored the two-line formation with a reserve, "for the order upon two lines besides the reserves, appearing to suffice for solidity, and giving more forces fighting at a time, seems also the most suitable." Ma-

---

[11]George B. McClellan, *Manual of Bayonet Exercise* (Philadelphia, 1852), 7–8; John C. Kelton, *A New Manual of the Bayonet, for the Army and Militia of the United States* (New York, 1861), iii; R. Milton Cary, *Skirmishers' Drill and Bayonet Exercise* (Richmond, 1861), unnumbered title page.

[12]Mahan, *Advanced-Guard*, 42; John Gibbon, *The Artillerist's Manual* (New York, 1860), 249.

[13]Jomini, *Art of War*, 295; Halleck, *Elements of Military Art*, 122. Halleck adopted Jomini's view of skirmishers.

[14]Mahan, "Advanced guard," 12; Mahan, *Advanced-Guard*, 144.

han said the two-line formation had become standard because it was compatible with the small size of American units and it allowed every musket "to tell effectively."[15] Theorists found it hard to determine what distance should be left between the two lines. Mahan made the general recommendation that the distance between the two lines be greater than the range of small arms fire.[16]

Tactical theory was unequivocal about columns: small columns were endorsed and heavy columns were rejected. Jomini favored small columns for attacking entrenchments, testifying, "I have seen these little columns succeed."[17] He was skeptical of heavy columns and doubted that a defending line could be carried even by the best troops if the attackers used a formation that deprived them of so much of their firepower. Jomini also was critical of heavy columns because they required troops to cover their flanks. Mahan warned his students against heavy columns: "In a very deep order, the troops readily become huddled by an inequality of motion; the head alone fights; disorder easily creeps into the mass; and a fire of artillery on it causes the most frightful ravages." Halleck characterized the heavy column as a dangerous formation because "it exposes large masses of men to the ravages of artillery, and diminishes the mobility and impulsion of an attack without adding greatly to its force."[18]

Tactical theory never endorsed any single formation, but the combination of lines and small columns often was praised. Jomini said that the "skilfull mixture of deployed lines and of columns, acting alternately according to circumstances, will ever be a good system." Mahan also favored a mixture of line and small columns. His general recommendation was that a commander use a two-line formation with reserves. The first line would be a deployed line, but the second line would consist of small columns, columns of battalions by divisions.[19] Mahan also suggested that reserves be held in small columns, a standard idea in nineteenth-century tactics. Reserves in column could march rapidly to the point where they were needed and then deploy into line. Halleck reviewed the various infantry formations and concluded that small columns generally would be the most decisive offensive formation. For the defensive, Halleck endorsed Mahan's two-line combination of line and small columns.[20]

The square formation was recommended as "always good against cavalry."

---

[15]Jomini, *Art of War*, 291; Mahan, *Advanced-Guard*, 34.

[16]Mahan, "Advanced guard," 12.

[17]Jomini, *Art of War*, 299–300.

[18]Ibid., 298–99; Mahan, "Advanced guard," 12; Halleck, *Elements of Military Art*, 123–24, 125.

[19]Jomini, *Art of War*, 219; Mahan, "Advanced guard," 12. "Division" had two meanings. A division was a large infantry unit made up of two or more brigades; it also meant, as it is used here, two companies of the same battalion. For a complaint about this double meaning, see H., "A Tactical Suggestion," *Army and Navy Journal*, VII (June 4, 1870), 659.

[20]Mahan, "Advanced guard," 12; Halleck, *Elements of Military Art*, 125.

Mahan's *Advanced-Guard* endorsed the square formation and argued that the use of more than one square would have the advantage that the squares could give mutual support.[21]

Military theorists before the Civil War stressed the tactical offensive and favored close-order musket and bayonet tactics, but they often generalized their principles and shaded their advice with exceptional cases. Jomini sometimes qualified a main idea with a list of exceptions.[22] Mahan's teachings were flexible, though his students often ignored his qualifications and subtleties.[23] Mahan was concerned about minimizing casualties, and he did not believe in reckless assaults. In *Field Fortification*, he suggested attacking entrenchments by surprise, though he acknowledged that this could not always be done. The attacker would then be forced to use either the bayonet alone or a combination of artillery and the bayonet. "The first is the most expeditious method," Mahan counseled. "But it is attended with great destruction of life." Later, in *Advanced-Guard*, Mahan recommended without any reservations that artillery preparation should precede assaults on entrenchments. He also reduced his opposition to loose order and suggested that the initial advance against entrenchments be made in skirmish order. *Advanced-Guard* advised: "When the enemy occupies strong artificial obstacles, . . . an attempt should be made to dislodge him by shells from howitzers; the troops for the assault may then be advanced as skirmishers, and when within about two hundred paces, should clear the intervening ground at full speed, in closing."[24]

It is difficult to estimate the influence that these recommendations about tactics and formations had on the soldiers who fought the Civil War. Some officers paid little attention to Jomini and Mahan. Jomini's *Summary of the Art of War* was not used as a textbook in tactics at West Point until 1859. Ulysses S. Grant said that he never read any of Jomini's writings. William J. Hardee, on the other hand, while he was commandant of cadets at West Point, read three works by Jomini. General Jacob D. Cox, a volunteer soldier, said that he read "the whole of Jomini's works," but Cox seemed more impressed by Jomini's military history than by his theory. Cox recalled that at the beginning of the war the officers at Camp Dennison, Ohio, read Mahan and the authorized tactics, but he also observed that most regular army officers studied little tactical theory after they left West Point. Cox said that in 1861 he asked Gordon Granger, a regular army officer, about this observation. " 'What would you expect,' [Granger] said in his sweeping way, 'of men who

---

[21]Halleck, *Elements of Military Art*, 125; Mahan, *Advanced-Guard*, 54, 55.

[22]Jomini, for example, opposed sending cavalry alone against infantry but then gave several exceptions to his rule. Jomini, *Art of War*, 306–07.

[23]McWhiney, *Braxton Bragg*, 20.

[24]Mahan, *Field Fortification*, 93, 95; Mahan, *Advanced-Guard*, 147.

have had to spend their lives at a two-company post, where there was nothing to do when off duty but play draw-poker and drink whiskey at the sutler's shop?' " Cox thought Granger's comments "picturesquely extravagant, but [they] hit the nail on the head, after all."[25]

Whether or not Civil War commanders were much influenced by the advice of the theorists, the advice itself was inappropriate for the battlefields of the 1860s. After the middle of the 1850s, many of the major ideas of the theorists became dangerous: the emphasis on the tactical offensive, the idea that vigorous assaults would overcome entrenchments, the high regard for the bayonet, and the reliance on traditional, close-order formations.

[25]McWhiney, "Grant's Pre–Civil War Military Education," 63; Nathaniel C. Hughes, Jr., *General William J. Hardee: Old Reliable* (Baton Rouge, 1965), 63–64; Jacob D. Cox, *Military Reminiscences of the Civil War* (2 vols., New York, 1900), I, 30, 175.

4

The New Rifle Can Stop the Advance

Theory about infantry formations and tactics became dated when a new shoulder arm was introduced. In the middle of the 1850s the rifle replaced the musket as the principle infantry weapon. The superior accuracy of small arms with rifled barrels was well known, but the rifle had always been clumsy and slow to load. Rifle bullets were made slightly larger than the bore and had to be hammered home. This ordnance problem was solved by developing an oblong bullet small enough in diameter that it could easily be dropped into the barrel, but with a hollow base that expanded on firing to fit the rifling of the barrel. This bullet was named after Captain Claude Étienne Minié of the Chasseurs d'Orleans, though Minié probably was not the sole, or even the first, person to suggest the principle.[1] Both accuracy and efficient loading were now possible with the rifle.[2]

The 1854 annual report of Secretary of War Jefferson Davis included data on ordnance tests of the rifle and the new rifle bullets. The tests were not finished, but Davis could announce: "they confirm the great superiority claimed for . . . [the rifle] abroad. They show that the new weapon, while it can be loaded as readily as the ordinary musket, is at least equally effective at three times the distance." Davis predicted that the rifle was almost certain to supersede the smoothbore musket, but he did not fully commit himself to conversion to the rifle. Davis urged "great caution" in adopting the rifle, "for

---

[1]Jac Weller, "Imported Confederate Shoulder Weapons," *Civil War History*, V (1959), 168.

[2]On the development of the rifle and its impact on tactics, see three works by J. F. C. Fuller: *The Generalship of Ulysses S. Grant* (New York, 1929), 57–62; "The Place of the American Civil War in the Evolution of War," *Army Quarterly*, XXVI (1933), 316–25; *A Military History of the Western World* (3 vols., New York, 1954–1956), III, 17–18; see also Bruce Catton, *America Goes to War* (Middletown, 1958), 14–20; John K. Mahon, "Civil War Infantry Assault Tactics," *Military Affairs*, XXV (1961), 57–68; Grady McWhiney, "Who Whipped Whom? Confederate Defeat Reexamined," *Civil War History*, XI (1965), 5–26.

the waste of public money is not the greatest of evils resulting from the adoption of an erroneous system."[3]

The next year, however, the government committed itself to conversion to the rifle. In his annual report for 1855, Davis announced that the national armories had ended all manufacture of smoothbores, that the production of rifles would begin before the end of the year, and that arrangements had been made to convert some of the old muskets to rifles. Some troops armed with rifles had already been issued the new rifle bullets. Davis credited the new bullets for "the increased range recently obtained by small-arms" and said that their "use in actual service has fully realized all the advantages that were anticipated."[4]

The new bullet made the rifle an effective weapon, extending the range and increasing the accuracy of shoulder arms fire. The maximum effective range of the musket was only a few hundred yards; rifle range was much greater. Cadmus M. Wilcox, who reviewed the status of the rifle in the late 1850s, said that well-directed rifle fire was "irresistible" at 600 yards and still destructive at 1,000 or 1,200 yards.[5] The basic infantry weapon of Federal troops during the Civil War, the Model 1861 Springfield rifle, had an effective range of between 300 and 400 yards and could kill at 1,000 yards. During most of the Civil War, Confederate troops carried rifles that were equally as good.[6]

The new infantry weapon required a new tactical manual. Scott's *Infantry-Tactics* was republished in 1852, 1857, 1860, and 1861, but it was never revised.[7] In his annual report for 1854, Secretary of War Davis said that he directed that a manual of rifle tactics be prepared to replace Scott's musket tactics, and the next year he reported that distribution of the new tactical manual had begun. The new manual was the two-volume work of Major William J. Hardee, *Rifle and Light Infantry Tactics*. Hardee prepared his *Tactics* after Davis ordered a study of the rifle tactics of foreign countries, and the work was chiefly a translation of French infantry tactics. Davis worked closely with Hardee on the preparation of the new manual, which was endorsed by the War Department and first published in 1855. It was repub-

---

[3]U.S. War Dept., *Report of the Secretary of War and accompanying documents for the year 1854* (Washington, 1854), 20.

[4]U.S. War Dept., *Report of the Secretary of War and accompanying documents for the year 1855* (Washington, 1855), 11, 12.

[5]Cadmus M. Wilcox, *Rifles and Rifle Practice* (New York, 1859), 243.

[6]Fuller, *Generalship of Grant*, 51, 52; Francis A. Lord, "Strong Right Arm of the Infantry: The '61 Springfield Rifle Musket," *Civil War Times Illustrated*, I (1962), 43–44; Weller, "Imported Confederate Shoulder Weapons," 158.

[7]Winfield Scott, *Infantry-Tactics; Or, Rules for the Exercise and Manoeuvres of the United States Infantry* (3 vols., New York, 1852). No revision was done in the editions of 1857, 1860, and 1861.

lished in 1860 and 1861 and in at least two Confederate editions, but only minor changes of the original edition were ever made.[8]

To compensate for the increased firepower that the rifle gave to infantry, Hardee made significant changes in Scott's tactical system—the greatest single change being in the rate of advance. Hardee's *Tactics* preserved Scott's basic rates of advance, but it also provided for more rapid ones. The rifle gave defenders greater range and accuracy of fire than the musket, and Hardee tried to compensate attackers for this by allowing them to advance more rapidly than Scott had permitted. Hardee retained Scott's "direct step" of twenty-eight inches, his "common time" rate of 90 steps per minute, and his "quick time" rate of 110 steps per minute. Scott did not recognize any step rate more rapid than these, permitting an accelerated "quick time" of 140 steps per minute only in exceptional circumstances. Hardee introduced a "double quick time" and the "run" as standard step rates. For his "double quick time," he introduced a thirty-three-inch step and executed it at 165 steps per minute. Thus Hardee's *Tactics* gave attackers a longer stride and a standard step rate more rapid than any step Scott permitted, even in emergencies.[9] For "urgent circumstances" Hardee's *Tactics* also provided that "double quick time" could be increased to 180 steps per minute. "At this rate," Hardee calculated, "a distance of four thousand yards would be passed over in about twenty-five minutes." Although Hardee thought that the "run" rarely would be used, he advocated that troops be "exercised" at running.[10] Hardee's *Tactics* advised that while the men practiced the "double quick time" or the "run," they should "breathe as much as possible through the nose, keeping the mouth closed. Experience has proved that, by conforming to this principle, a man can pass over a much longer distance, and with less fatigue."[11]

The combination of the long "double quick step" and the rapid "double quick time" was the most striking feature of the new tactics. The thirty-three-inch stride and the rapid gait were a challenge for infantrymen accustomed to Scott's "direct step" and "common time." Soldiers nicknamed the new tactics the "Shanghai Drill." After the new "double quick" gait had been

---

[8]War Dept., *Report of the Secretary of War 1854*, 26; War Dept., *Report of the Secretary of War 1855*, 12; Nathaniel C. Hughes, Jr., *General William J. Hardee: Old Reliable* (Baton Rouge, 1965), 44; William J. Hardee, *Rifle and Light Infantry Tactics; for the Exercise and Manoeuvres of Troops when acting as Light Infantry or Riflemen* (2 vols., Philadelphia, 1855). There were also editions of 1860 and 1861 and Confederate editions of 1861 and 1863. War Dept., *Report of the Secretary of War 1854*, 26; "Modified Infantry Tactics," *Army and Navy Journal*, II (January 7, 1865), 307; Astoria, "Army Sketches: Infantry Tactics," *Army and Navy Journal*, VI (August 22, 1868), 2.
   Hardee's biographer argued that Hardee made modifications in the French tactics that he followed, and that his manual was more detailed than its source. Hughes, *Hardee*, 46–48.
[9]Hardee, *Tactics*, I, 24, 25–26, 28.
[10]Ibid., 28, 87.
[11]Ibid., 28.

practiced at West Point, Cadet George William Cushing sent his family a cartoon sketch that he titled "Shanghae drill." Cushing's drawing depicted a line of cadets taking a long, running stride to keep up with their instructor. And, after the Civil War, one soldier recalled that Hardee's *Tactics*, "from the peculiar *pas gymnastique* used for the double quick step, was familiarly known as the 'Shanghai Drill.' "[12]

The new tactics were first practiced by West Point cadets in the fall of 1854. Experimenting with the new step rates was a memorable experience for the cadets. George D. Bayard, class of 1856, wrote in October 1854: "They are now drilling the Batallion by squads at the new system of Tactics, which has [been] translated from the French by Col. Hardee, & which it is proposed to substitute for the system at present employed by Skirmishers or Light Infantry. The object is to make the movements much more rapid." In the spring of 1856, Bayard correctly predicted that Hardee, as commandant of cadets, would substitute his tactical manual for Scott's.[13]

The longer stride and faster rate of Hardee's "double quick time" meant harder work for the cadets. After practicing the new tactics, George William Cushing wrote to his family: ". . . the drills are stopped, and [we are] mighty glad of it." Contrasting Hardee's system with Scott's, Cushing said: "[Hardee's] is much different from the old system of tactics—instead of marching about like so many animated pokers,—the men carry their pieces at a trail or right shoulder shift—and run at a kind of trot,—keeping dressed—though—and it is a very pretty drill to look at."[14]

Hardee's *Tactics* made other provisions to compensate attackers for the rifle fire of defenders. Hardee's system made it possible for troops to deploy from column to line more quickly than Scott's had permitted. Hardee's *Tactics* allowed commanders to deploy a column by platoon into line of battle either while at a halt or while still marching. With Scott's system, a halt was required.[15] After the Civil War, one soldier praised Hardee's system: "The principles upon which [Hardee's] formations were made were the same as in 'Scott's Tactics,' but a great improvement was introduced by providing for passing from one formation to another while in march, without that delay arising from halts and preparatory movements, and when these manoeuvres were made at double-quick, the least possible time was occupied in their execution. To those accustomed to the old stately system this celerity appeared impracticable, and that it would be impossible to avoid confusion.

---

[12]Sketch accompanying George William Cushing to Dear Folks, November 5, 1854, George William Cushing Letters, United States Military Academy; Astoria, "Army Sketches: Infantry Tactics," 2.

[13]George D. Bayard to Ester, October 7, 1854, May 30, 1856, George D. Bayard Papers, United States Military Academy.

[14]Cushing to Dear Folks, November 5, 1854, Cushing Letters.

[15]Hardee, *Tactics*, I, 140–46; Scott, *Infantry-Tactics*, I, 155.

Such, however, was not the case, but on the contrary, the general accuracy was better preserved." Ulysses S. Grant said of Hardee's *Tactics:* "The commands were abbreviated and the movement expedited. Under the old tactics almost every change in the order of march was preceded by a 'halt,' then came the change, and then the 'forward march.' With the new tactics all these changes could be made while in motion."[16]

Hardee made other changes in Scott's system. "The old method of obliquing," one soldier noted dryly, "adapted only to men with one leg shorter than the other, was changed to the more rational half-face method. The right-about while marching was introduced, as was also firing by ranks."[17] Moreover, Hardee introduced a unit that he called "comrades in battle," groups of four men adjacent to each other in rank and file. Comrades in battle were used in Hardee's skirmisher tactics and when a company faced to a flank.[18]

Hardee's skirmisher tactics provided for loose-order tactics in which skirmishers were granted considerable freedom of movement. The comrades in battle were created primarily to skirmish together. When a company deployed as skirmishers, Hardee said, "the comrades in battle, forming groups of four men, will be careful to know and to sustain each other." Hardee's *Tactics* assumed that a company deployed as skirmishers would occupy the same front as a regiment in line. If several companies of a battalion were deployed as skirmishers, each might occupy a front of about one hundred paces. "The interval between skirmishers depends on the extent of the ground to be covered," said Hardee, "but in general, it is not proper that the groups of four men [comrades in battle] should be removed more than forty paces from each other. The habitual distance between men of the same group in open grounds will be five paces; in no case will they lose sight of each other."[19] Hardee did not expect the movements of skirmishers to be "executed with the same precision as in closed ranks, nor is it desirable, as such exactness would materially interfere with their prompt execution."[20]

Hardee's skirmisher tactics were similar to Scott's, but there were important differences. Scott's musket tactics assumed that the left flank company of a battalion would always be a light infantry or rifle company and would skirmish for the battalion. Hardee's tactics assumed that all companies would be armed with rifles and that any company might provide skirmishers.[21] As

---

[16]Astoria, "Army Sketches: Infantry Tactics," 2–3; Ulysses S. Grant, *Personal Memoirs . . .* (2 vols., New York, 1885), I, 253.

[17]Astoria, "Army Sketches: Infantry Tactics," 3. For these changes, see Hardee, *Tactics*, I, 61–62, 72, 74.

[18]Hardee, *Tactics*, I, 6, 174–75; Astoria, "Army Sketches: Infantry Tactics," 2.

[19]Hardee, *Tactics*, I, 174–75.

[20]Ibid., 171.

[21]Scott, *Infantry-Tactics*, II, 188; Hardee, *Tactics*, I, 171–213.

in their line tactics, the greatest difference between Scott's and Hardee's skirmisher tactics was rate of movement. Scott expected skirmishers to advance at "quick time," 110 steps per minute. Hardee permitted skirmishers to use either "quick time" or "double quick time," 165 steps per minute, a rate Scott did not acknowledge as standard. He allowed skirmishers, "for cases of absolute necessity" only, a "double quick" rate of 140 steps per minute.[22]

In spite of these differences, Hardee's tactical system was much the same as Scott's. Ulysses S. Grant described Hardee's *Tactics* as "nothing more than common sense and the progress of the age applied to Scott's system." The range and accuracy of the rifle made loose-order tactics advisable, but Hardee's rifle tactics were as much a close-order tactics as Scott's musket tactics. Hardee assumed that battalions and companies would form in two ranks, thirteen inches apart, the same distance proposed by Scott.[23] Hardee used Scott's method of aligning by the touch of elbows, and he retained Scott's notion that to promote élan a line should begin an advance "with life." Hardee followed Scott on positioning battalion officers and most other such details.[24]

Hardee's work was thought to be so compatible with Scott's that the War Department attempted to use the two systems together. Hardee's manual was only two volumes, the second volume ending with a school of the battalion. The government believed that commanders could use Hardee's *Tactics* to drill units smaller than a brigade and could use Scott's third volume for brigade and larger units.[25]

The attempt to use Scott's third volume as a third volume for Hardee's work failed when the outbreak of the Civil War made massive drilling and training necessary. Scott's third volume confused commanders because it occasionally referred to Scott's first two volumes, which were now obsolete. In 1862 William W. Duffield, a volunteer soldier, published *School of the Brigade, and Evolutions of the Line*, which provided northern commanders with a brigade and larger unit tactics consistent with the Hardee system.[26] The Confederate Army wanted a substitute for Scott's third volume, to avoid using a manual that carried the name of a famous Federal general, and ultimately replaced it with John H. Richardson's *Infantry Tactics, or, Rules for the Excercise and Manoeuvres of the Confederate States Infantry*.[27]

[22]Scott, *Infantry-Tactics*, II, 189; Hardee, *Tactics*, I, 172.

[23]Grant, *Memoirs*, I, 253; Scott, *Infantry-Tactics*, I, 10; Hardee, *Tactics*, I, 6.

[24]Scott, *Infantry-Tactics*, I, 125, 124, 13; Hardee, *Tactics*, I, 67–68, 109, 8.

[25]Hardee, *Tactics*, II, 224; Astoria, "Army Sketches: Infantry Tactics," 2.

[26]William W. Duffield, *School of the Brigade, and Evolutions of the Line* . . . (Philadelphia, 1862). The "new system of infantry tactics" mentioned by Duffield in his preface, page 3, referred to the War Department's *U.S. Infantry Tactics* . . . (Philadelphia, 1861), which was taken directly from Hardee's work.

[27]John H. Richardson, *Infantry Tactics, or, Rules for the Exercise and Manoeuvres of the Confederate States Infantry* (Richmond, 1862).

Hardee's rifle tactics were well regarded and influential and in the 1860s were widely used in both the North and South. Large volunteer armies had to be trained in a few months, and Hardee's manual was used to drill both regulars and volunteers. Jacob D. Cox recalled that at Camp Dennison in the first weeks of the war: "Schools were established in each regiment for field and staff as well as for company officers, and Hardee's 'Tactics' was in the hands of everybody who could procure a copy. One of the proofs of the unprecedented scale of our war preparations is found in the fact that the supply of the authorized 'Tactics' was soon exhausted, making it difficult to get the means of instruction in the company schools." John Beatty, a bank clerk who became a brigadier general of volunteers, said that he mastered Hardee's manual after struggling with it during the first summer of the war. "Hardee for a month or so was a book of impenetrable mysteries," said Beatty. "The words conveyed no idea to my mind, and the movements described were utterly beyond my comprehension; but now [August 1, 1861] the whole thing comes almost without study."[28] Abridgments and pirates of Hardee were common throughout the war in both North and South. Three years after the Civil War, one soldier still had praise for Hardee's *Tactics:* "With active and intelligent troops [Hardee's] is a system well adapted, not alone to the parade-ground, but to all the varying circumstances of campaign service; and the habitual use of the double-quick gives to troops a celerity and an endurance advantageous to either the march, the battle, the skirmish, or the skedaddle."[29]

The most important successor to Hardee's manual was General Silas Casey's *Infantry Tactics,* which was based on the same French source as Hardee's and added very little to tactical theory. When Casey's work first appeared in 1862 it was not intended to be a revision of Hardee's *Tactics,* but rather was intended to make the Hardee system widely available in the North without crediting that system to a soldier who had become a Confederate general. Casey's work also was expected to fill the need for a brigade and larger unit tactics, and it included a third volume that treated these larger units because the attempt to use Scott's third volume for this purpose had failed. Casey said in his preface: "Since the introduction into our service of [Hardee's] drill, in connection with the tactics of General Scott, I have seen the necessity of a uniform system for the manoeuvres of all the infantry arm of service."[30]

[28]Jacob D. Cox, "War Preparations in the North," in *Battles and Leaders of the Civil War,* ed. Robert U. Johnson and Clarence C. Buel (4 vols., reissue, New York, 1956), I, 95; John Beatty, *The Citizen-Soldier; or, Memoirs of a Volunteer* (Cincinnati, 1879), 41.

[29]Astoria, "Army Sketches: Infantry Tactics," 3.

[30]Silas Casey, *Infantry Tactics, for the Instruction, Exercise, and Manoeuvers of the Soldier, a Company, Line of Skirmishers, Battalion, Brigade, or Corps D'Armee* (3 vols., New York, 1862), I, 5. Casey's manual was republished without revision in 1865.

Casey's manual displayed some awareness of the need for tactical change. In his preface Casey acknowledged several of the recent changes in infantry tactics, including the adoption of the two-rank formation in place of three and the decision "to increase the rapidity of the gait." He retained Hardee's step rates and virtually all of his system, but he did make a few changes. A more efficient deployment from column to line would help attackers overcome some of the advantage that the rifle gave defenders, and Casey offered a system of deploying a battalion from column to line that was somewhat simpler than Hardee's.[31] Casey also gave the division column, a small column of two companies, more emphasis than Hardee had.[32]

Casey's *Tactics* was not an innovative work. Thoroughly familiar with Hardee's *Tactics*, because he had presided over a board of officers that had reviewed it for the War Department in 1854–1855, Casey used the same close-order formations in his manual as had Scott and Hardee. Following them, Casey deployed ranks at a distance of thirteen inches.[33] He extended the interval between brigades from Scott's 22 paces to 150 paces, but he retained the old 22-pace interval for battalions. When a brigade used the two-line formation during tactical instruction, Casey said that he would post the second line 150 paces behind the first. For battlefield conditions, Casey would not fix a distance between the two lines and offered only a general observation: "In the presence of the enemy, the distance between the lines will depend upon circumstances; in general the second line should not be much exposed to the enemy's fire."[34]

Casey's ideas about skirmisher tactics were traditional. He borrowed from the old musket tactics the system of having two fixed companies that would do the skirmishing for a battalion. He assumed that all companies would be armed with rifles, but, he said, "It is intended that these [skirmisher] companies shall be composed of picked men, possessing the highest physical qualifications, marksmen as well, and that they shall be used as skirmishers."[35] When the War Department endorsed Casey's *Tactics* in August 1862, it suspended his skirmisher system, either omitting or changing the paragraphs on the fixed companies skirmisher system.[36] Casey replaced

---

[31] Ibid., 6, 30, 32; II, 113–48; Hardee, *Tactics*, II, 94–132.

[32] Casey, *Tactics*, II, 202–09, 210–15, 224. Hardee used the division column formation but gave it less emphasis than Casey. Hardee, *Tactics*, II, 29–37, 90–91.

[33] George W. Cullum, ed., *Biographical Registrar of the Officers and Graduates of the United States Military Academy, at West Point* (2 vols., New York, 1868), I, 306; Casey, *Tactics*, I, 5, 6, 12; Scott, *Infantry-Tactics*, I, 10; Hardee, *Tactics*, I, 6.

[34] Casey, *Tactics*, I, 9, 10.

[35] Ibid., 6.

[36] Ibid., endorsement on unnumbered page, 8, 11; II, 3. For an example of paragraphs that were changed rather than suspended, see paragraphs 785–87 in volume II, 177–78. The two fixed skirmisher companies were left in some of the plates that accompany Casey's *Tactics*, I, plate 1; II, plates 4 and 12.

his system of two fixed companies of skirmishers with a skirmisher system "applicable to any skirmishers from the battalion."[37]

Hardee's and Casey's manuals made only modest changes in Scott's system in order to compensate for the introduction of the rifle, but Scott complained that his system had been "pirated" and "abridged and emasculated down to utter uselessness." In his *Memoirs*, published during the Civil War, Scott was critical of Jefferson Davis and of both Hardee and Casey, whom he regarded as "pets" of Davis. *"It is extremely perilous to change systems of tactics in an army in the midst of a war,"* Scott warned, *"and highly inconvenient even at the beginning of one."*[38]

The new tactical manuals were introduced in response to the rifle, but tactical theory never fully appreciated the impact of the new shoulder weapon. One work that considered the problem was Cadmus M. Wilcox's *Rifles and Rifle Practice*, published in 1859. Wilcox had only general ideas about how the rifle would influence tactics. He noted that changes in infantry arms had always had a "preponderating influence upon [infantry's] formation for battle," and he predicted that the introduction of the rifle would make battlefields more extended than in the past. Wilcox never expressed concern that the rifle would increase attacker casualties, but he urged commanders to be cautious for another reason. The greater range of the rifle meant that battles could start more easily, and Wilcox predicted that commanders would have more trouble controlling their troops. He warned that a commander would have to begin a battle cautiously or "he may lose control of his men and their movements." Commanders would have to be careful "to prevent the fire of skirmishers from degenerating into a mere waste of ammunition." Unless a general were alert, Wilcox said, "his whole lines may become exposed at once to a destructive fire." As a result, Wilcox predicted, more tactical authority would have to be given to commanders of small units.[39]

Another work that considered the impact the rifle would have on tactics was John Gibbon's 1860 compilation, *The Artillerist's Manual*. It was devoted to the artillery arm, but at one point it touched on the question of the firepower of the rifle, arguing that the introduction of the rifle meant that firepower would dominate the bayonet. Gibbon's *Manual* contended that, although the bayonet had "great advantages" in battle, "the fact is now incontestible that the efficiency of a body of infantry resides essentially in its accuracy of fire; and this is made only the more apparent from the recent improvements in fire-arms." *The Artillerist's Manual* maintained that fire-

---

[37]Ibid., II, 3–4. For a postwar discussion of Casey's skirmisher system, see A Lover of Truth, "Casey's Companies of Skirmishers," *Army and Navy Journal*, VIII (October 1, 1870), 107.

[38]Winfield Scott, *Memoirs of Lieut.-General Scott, LL.D. Written by Himself* (2 vols., New York, 1864), I, 258–59.

[39]Wilcox, *Rifles*, 241–44.

power, not the bayonet, made the square a successful formation against cavalry: "In the successful and oft-repeated repulse of cavalry charges by squares of infantry, the main dependence is not in the use of the bayonet, but in close, well-directed fire, delivered as the horsemen approach." In spite of such observations, Gibbon's *Manual* underestimated the strength of the rifle. It predicted that infantrymen would waste much of their new firepower: "A *cool, well-directed* fire from a body of men armed with the new rifle or rifle musket is sufficient to stop the advance of almost any kind of troops. But the very best disciplined men will, in time of battle, fire with precipitancy and at too great a distance; from which results a great loss of ammunition and of effect upon the enemy."[40]

The great strength that the rifle would bring to field entrenchments was probably not fully understood in the 1850s. George B. McClellan's Crimean War report, which was sent to the Senate in 1857, included some observations about the entrenchments used in that European rifle war. In McClellan's report the importance of field works themselves was balanced with McClellan's appreciation for the quality of the troops defending them. McClellan said that the Russian works at Sebastopol had been reported as being of "stupendous dimensions," using "new systems of fortification." "The plain truth is that these defences were simple temporary fortifications of rather greater dimensions than usual," stated McClellan, and he then praised the artillery and infantry that had held the works. McClellan criticized the "popular fallacy" that the siege of Sebastopol had proved that temporary field works were better than permanent ones. It "proved nothing of the kind," McClellan said, but rather demonstrated that good troops could hold temporary works longer than was thought. Although McClellan credited the length of the siege of Sebastopol partly to the Russians' "just appreciation of the true use of field works" and "the employment of rifle pits on an extensive scale," he also praised the Russian artillery for its "fine practice" and the Russian infantrymen for their courageous defense, "standing to their works to repel assaults at the point of the bayonet."[41]

Cadmus M. Wilcox discussed the rifle and entrenchment briefly in *Rifles and Rifle Practice*. He did not foresee that the rifle would strengthen the entrenched defensive so much as it would simplify it. Entrenchments would not change much, Wilcox predicted, but satisfactory entrenchment would become easier because simple works defended by the rifle would be stronger than more elaborate works defended by the musket.[42]

After the introduction of the rifle, tactical theory continued to recommend the same formations that had been favored before the rifle. Wilcox's *Rifles and*

[40]John Gibbon, *The Artillerist's Manual* (New York, 1860), 220, 221–22.

[41]*Senate Executive Document*, 35 Cong., special sess., No. 1, 16, 22.

[42]Wilcox, *Rifles*, 249.

Rifle Practice, for example, endorsed in 1859 the same formations that Jomini and Mahan had—the two-rank line, small columns, and the square against cavalry. With the two-line formation, the problem of recommending a distance between the lines remained. Wilcox realized that the greater range of the rifle made the problem more difficult, but he offered only a general solution: "To shelter troops from the enemy's fire as long as possible without being too far distant, and to hold them well in hand, will probably be the best rule to observe." Wilcox favored small columns and was as critical of heavy columns as Jomini and Mahan had been. He warned that the great firepower of the rifle would be ruinous to heavy columns. Citing English experiments that had been conducted with the Enfield rifle in June 1855, Wilcox contended: *"The fire of grape-shot at its most effective distance is not so destructive to infantry columns as the fire of the present rifles."*[43]

The introduction of the rifle had produced changes in tactical thinking, but the changes were not extensive enough to compensate for the firepower of the new weapon. A manual of rifle tactics was introduced, replacing the manual of musket tactics. Step rates were increased and attacker movements were speeded up in an effort to overcome the firepower advantage that the rifle gave defenders. Few other changes were made, and the new rifle manual followed largely the old musket manual. Tactical theory after the middle of the 1850s did not fully comprehend the impact that the rifle would have on the strength of the tactical defensive, the value of field entrenchment, and the dangers of using close-order formations. Tactical manuals and theory continued to recommend traditional, close-order formations.

[43]Ibid., 243–44.

5

A Change of Tactics Is Absolutely Necessary

In the period between the Mexican War and the Civil War the rifling principle was adopted by the artillery as well as the infantry, but rifled cannon failed to gain the status of rifled shoulder arms. In 1860, years after rifling had been adopted for shoulder arms, the United States Ordnance Board recommended that half the bronze cannon then in service be rifled. The results were poor; the bronze guns could not stand the strain of rifling. At the outbreak of fighting in 1861, the basic smoothbore cannon was the twelve-pounder Napoleon that had been introduced in 1856. The most common rifles during the war were the ten-pounder Parrott and the three-inch ordnance rifle. Rifled cannon had greater range and accuracy than smoothbores, but infantry feared the smoothbores more: rifles had smaller bores and could not fire as large rounds of canister as the smoothbores.[1]

Rifled guns also caused an ordnance problem. After the Civil War Henry J. Hunt, chief of artillery of the Army of the Potomac, explained why he was not enthused when the three-inch rifle was adopted in 1861. He noted that "the complication from which the Napoleon gun had relieved us—a great variety of ammunition—was brought back with the rifle-gun, for which different systems of experimental projectiles, Parrott, James, Schenkl, Hotchkiss, and 'Ordnance,' were supplied, which gave different ranges with the same charges of powder. These systems would get mixed in the same battery, and affected its accuracy of fire."[2]

Hunt recalled that some artillery officers regarded the three-inch rifle as an improvement, and that the Ordnance Department wanted its adoption and the exclusion of the smoothbores. The smoothbores were favored, however,

---

[1] L. Van Loan Naisawald, *Grape and Canister: The Story of the Field Artillery of the Army of the Potomac, 1861–1865* (New York, 1960), 36–39; "Tactics for Field Artillery," 8, Proceedings and Report of the Barry Board, Papers of the Barry Board, Record Group 94, Adjutant General's Office, Navy and Old Army Branch, National Archives.

[2] Henry J. Hunt, "Artillery," in *Papers of the Military Historical Society of Massachusetts* (14 vols., Boston, 1913), XIII, 115.

by George B. McClellan, the first commander of the Army of the Potomac, who believed that the wooded terrain of Virginia would limit the effectiveness of the long-range rifles. He intended to keep two-thirds of his field guns smoothbores, a ratio that could not be met at first but was approached by the time of the Sharpsburg campaign. The smoothbores maintained their popularity, and at the end of the war about half the field artillery pieces of the Army of the Potomac were twelve-pounder smoothbores.[3]

Rifling was much more beneficial to infantry than to artillery. After the introduction of rifling, artillery lost strength relative to infantry. In 1859, after rifling had been applied to shoulder arms but before it had been applied to cannon, Cadmus M. Wilcox made this assessment: "It is clear that field artillery, with its present range, cannot with any chances of success remain in action in front of infantry; its comparative efficacy is lessened, and even by extending the range by increase of calibre, or by a successful application of the principle of rifling, cannot restore it to its former comparative condition." After the Civil War, Henry J. Hunt recalled that when infantry had been armed with muskets, artillery had been able to take position beyond infantry's range and work freely. When infantry adopted the rifle, artillery then often had to work under both artillery and infantry fire. L. Van Loan Naisawald, historian of the artillery of the Army of the Potomac, made this evaluation of the tactical situation after the introduction of rifled shoulder arms: "Field artillery could no longer unlimber within easy canister range of the enemy's ranks and at the same time be outside the effective range of the enemy's muskets. . . . The simple fact was that by 1861 the rifled musket had relegated the artillery to a defensive role."[4]

Tactical theory before the Civil War expected artillery to be used both offensively and defensively. "The artillery is at the same time an offensive and defensive arm," said Jomini, "equally formidable." Artillery theory stressed that when cannons were used on the offensive, their first target should be infantry, not works or batteries. Jomini suggested that about one-third of a commander's available guns should occupy the enemy's artillery, leaving the other two-thirds to fire on infantry and cavalry.[5]

Jomini liked the idea of an offensive cannonade. He suggested that it would be "advantageous to concentrate a very strong artillery mass upon a point where we should wish to direct a decisive effort, to the end of making a breach in the hostile line, which would facilitate the grand attack upon which

[3]Ibid.; George B. McClellan, *McClellan's Own Story* (New York, 1887), 117.

[4]Cadmus M. Wilcox, *Rifles and Rifle Practice* (New York, 1859), 247; Hunt, "Artillery," XIII, 111; Naisawald, *Grape and Canister*, 179.

[5]Antoine Henri Jomini, *Summary of the Art of War*, trans. O. F. Winship and E. E. McLean (New York, 1854), 317, 319. Halleck borrowed these ratios, and other main ideas on artillery theory, from Jomini. Henry W. Halleck, *Elements of Military Art and Science* (New York, 1846), 128–29; Jomini, *Art of War*, 318–19.

might depend the success of battle." Jomini urged that a cannonade on a defending line or an entrenched position was good fire tactics and also good for weakening the morale of the defenders. Offensive rushes by artillery was another, and more dangerous, undertaking. Mahan's *Advanced-Guard*, which first appeared during the Mexican War, noted that the artillery "has of late years begun to infuse a dash of the dare-devil spirit of the cavalier into its ranks. If it has not yet taken to charging literally, it has, on some occasions in our service, shown a well-considered recklessness of obstacles and dangers, fully borne out by justly deserved success." Gibbon's *Artillerist's Manual* admired the aggressiveness that artillery commanders had shown in Mexico, but it advised that such dash be balanced with calmness and intelligence: "It is of the first importance that the fire of a battery be delivered at a good range with calmness and intelligence, those impetuous exhibitions of dashing bravery encouraged in other arms being more out of place in this. There are circumstances, however, where several pieces, well-harnessed, may advance to within 300 yards of an enemy, and overwhelm him with a storm of grape or canister shot; but these cases are very rare, and require much tact and resolution to know how to profit by them." It was much safer for artillery to take the offensive with infantry. Mahan suggested that if artillery advanced with infantry, the guns should be in battery on the flanks of the infantry's line or near the heads of its columns.[6]

Tactical theory also made general suggestions about the defensive deployment of artillery. Jomini warned against scattering artillery too much along a defensive line. He thought an equal distribution along the line would be best, but he acknowledged other factors such as terrain and anticipation of where the enemy was most likely to attack. Mahan suggested that batteries on the defensive be posted within 600 paces of each other. He made other general suggestions such as that artillery not be posted where it would fire over friendly infantry, or where it would attract enemy artillery fire toward friendly infantry. Gibbon's *Artillerist's Manual* recommended posting batteries on the flanks of infantry and at least 60 yards in front of the intervals between regiments and brigades.[7]

The artillery tactical manual of the Mexican War period was replaced in the years before the Civil War, but the new manual retained much of the old

---

[6]Jomini, *Art of War*, 293, 230, 232, 318; Dennis Hart Mahan, *An Elementary Treatise on Advanced-Guard, Out-Post, and Detachment Service of Troops, and the Manner of Posting and Handling Them in Presence of an Enemy* (New York, 1847), 45; John Gibbon, *The Artillerist's Manual* (New York, 1860), 388–89; Mahan, *Advanced-Guard*, 62.

[7]Jomini, *Art of War*, 292, 293, 318–19; Mahan, *Advanced-Guard*, 60; Dennis Hart Mahan, lithographed United States Military Academy textbook, "Advanced guard, outpost & detachment service of troops," 12, United States Military Academy Library (as noted earlier, this textbook is unrelated to Mahan's work published under a similar title); Gibbon, *Artillerist's Manual*, 402.

one. In the late 1850s a board of officers was authorized by the War Department to prepare a new artillery tactics to replace the manual of 1845. Captain
William H. French was the senior officer of this board. Its other members
were Henry J. Hunt and William F. Barry, both of whom became Civil War
artillery commanders. The French board completed its report in 1859, and
its *Instruction for Field Artillery* was published the following year.[8] This
manual retained much of the old Ringgold board tactics, including the same
principles of battery tactics.[9] The French board added a school of the section
and made changes in the artillery foot drill, but most of the new manual was
based on the earlier tactics.[10]

A few other manuals were available to Civil War artillerists, but they did
nothing to advance tactical theory. George Patten's 1861 *Artillery Drill* was
an abridgment of the French board tactics and was published to help meet
the demand for tactical manuals early in the war. *The Hand-Book of Artillery*,
compiled by Joseph Roberts, used a question-and-answer format. Roberts
took his answers from Gibbon and from the authorized ordnance and tactical
manuals of the War Department.[11]

The 1850s witnessed changes for the mounted arm just as it did for other
branches of the army. The Mexican War had been fought by dragoon,
volunteer cavalry, and mounted rifle units. The United States Cavalry was
created in the 1850s. In March 1855, Congress authorized the raising of two
regiments of cavalry: the First United States Cavalry was organized that
summer at Fort Leavenworth, the Second at Jefferson Barracks. The new
cavalry regiments were armed with sabers, rifle-carbines, and Colt's navy
revolvers. In August 1861, all mounted units—dragoons, mounted riflemen,
and cavalry—were organized into a single arm, "to be called cavalry."[12]

Cavalry theory, like infantry theory, emphasized the tactical offensive over
the tactical defensive. Jomini's *Art of War* devoted little attention to cavalry
on the tactical defensive. Jomini believed that cavalry could not stand on the
defensive against infantry and artillery. Mahan agreed. "The defensive qual-

[8]Board of Artillery Officers, *Instruction for Field Artillery* (Philadelphia, 1860), v. This manual
was republished without revision in 1861 and 1863. After it was published, Robert Anderson
translated a French battery tactics, *Evolutions of Field Batteries of Artillery* (New York, 1860).
Anderson's entire manual was included as a new chapter, "Evolutions of Batteries," in the 1864
edition of *Instruction* and was retained in the 1867 edition.

[9]Compare, for example, Board of Artillery Officers, *Instruction for Field Artillery, Horse and
Foot* (Baltimore, 1845), 77–83, with the 1860 *Instruction*, 275–80.

[10]Board of Artillery Officers, *Instruction* (1860), 206–73, 79–83, 87–97; Hunt, "Artillery,"
XIII, 113–14; Barry Board, "Tactics for Field Artillery," ii; Astoria, "Army Sketches: Infantry
Tactics," *Army and Navy Journal*, VI (August 22, 1868), 3.

[11]George Patten, *Artillery Drill* (New York, 1861); Joseph Roberts, *The Hand-Book of Artillery
for the Service of the United States (Army and Militia)* (New York, 1860). Editions of this work
appeared in 1861, 1863, 1865, and 1875.

[12]Albert G. Brackett, *History of the United States Cavalry, From the Formation of the Federal
Government to the 1st of June, 1863* (New York, 1865), 140, 152, 160, 218–19.

ities of cavalry lie in the offensive," he wrote. "A body of cavalry which awaits to receive a charge of cavalry, or is exposed to a fire of infantry, or artillery, must either retire or be destroyed." Philip St. George Cooke published a tactical manual for cavalry in 1861 that declared, "The charge is the decisive action of cavalry." Cooke believed that successful cavalry charges depended on timing and élan. "[Cavalry's] opportunities pass in moments," he said. "Its successful commander must have a *cavalry eye* and rapid decision; once launched, its bravery is successful."[13]

Tactical theorists showed some caution about cavalry offensives against infantry. Jomini was wary of sending cavalry against infantry when the infantry line was "in good order," but he believed there were exceptional cases when a cavalry charge against infantry could succeed. Mahan thought it best to let infantry and artillery weaken the enemy's infantry before sending cavalry against it, but he was willing to suggest tactics that cavalry could use to attack either artillery or squares of infantry. Cooke took the position that cavalry should always be ready to support friendly infantry and artillery, and that if this required attacking infantry then the cavalry should do so. Cooke said: "At the moment of the enemy's first success—he has perhaps broken the first line, and makes a disorderly pursuit—the cavalry seizes the moment to overthrow his battalions."[14]

There were no such reservations about having cavalry take the offensive against cavalry. "Cavalry charges the enemy's cavalry to drive him from the field, to return against his battalions with more liberty," said Cooke. "Meeting an enemy by surprise, the cavalry should instantly charge his. This decision will give the advantage." Jomini thought that when cavalry attacked cavalry, the victor ordinarily would be the commander who had the last squadrons in reserve to throw on his enemy's flank.[15]

Theory about cavalry formations was similar to theory on infantry formations. Most theorists regarded the two-line formation as standard for cavalry as well as infantry. Except for reserves and echelon formations, Jomini opposed forming cavalry in more than two lines. Mahan believed that the purpose of the two-line formation was to deliver shock and make use of the saber. "The efficiency of this arm resides in the power of its shock," Mahan said, "and, as in a charge, the first rank alone is brought into actual combat with the enemy, the only reason for placing a second line is to close up gaps in the front, by casualties whilst charging; and also in the mêlée that succeeds the charge, to have a sufficient number of sabers in hand to do good service."

---

[13]Jomini, *Art of War*, 307, 315–16; Mahan, *Advanced-Guard*, 57; Philip St. George Cooke, *Cavalry Tactics or Regulations for the Instruction, Formations, and Movements of the Cavalry of the Army and Volunteers of the United States* (2 parts, Washington, 1861), II, 60, 61.

[14]Jomini, *Art of War*, 306–07; Mahan, *Advanced-Guard*, 58-59; Cooke, *Cavalry Tactics*, II, 61.

[15]Cooke, *Cavalry Tactics*, II, 61; Jomini, *Art of War*, 312. Halleck adopted this and other cavalry principles from Jomini. Halleck, *Elements of Military Art*, 127.

Cavalry, like infantry, was advised to use close-order formations, with enough space left in columns for wheeling. George B. McClellan's 1861 cavalry manual advised that cavalry form in columns "with wheeling distance, and closed in mass." McClellan said that "against civilized antagonists the compact charge in line should be used, in preference to that as foragers."[16] Jomini believed that most principles of infantry formation could be applied to cavalry, but one of his modifications was that cavalry columns would have to be loose enough to allow an efficient charge: "The column of attack should never be compact like that of infantry, but at full or half squadron distance, with a view to having ground for separating and charging."[17]

Cavalry theory emphasized the saber. Mahan believed that, except for a few cavalrymen used as flankers or skirmishers, most cavalrymen would seldom need to use firearms. McClellan's cavalry manual contended that "the strength of cavalry is in the 'spurs and saber.' " Henry W. Halleck maintained that cavalry would find pistols and carbines useless in a charge and that it should rely on lances and sabers. "In a regular charge in line the lance offers great advantages," said Halleck, "in the mêlée the saber is the best weapon; hence some military writers have proposed arming the front rank with lances, and the second with sabers."[18]

Cavalry theory favored the tactical offensive and at the same time recognized its difficulties. One problem for attacking cavalry was that a strong charge required that speed be balanced with order. "Although rapidity in the approach to the enemy is generally important," said Cooke's *Cavalry Tactics*, "very important too it is that the horses should not arrive exhausted, or even distressed or blown." Cooke wanted horsemen to charge as rapidly as possible without losing too much order or exhausting their horses. He suggested that the attackers trot to within 200 paces of the enemy's line, then gallop "with increasing speed," and charge when 50 to 60 yards from the enemy's line. Another difficulty for attacking cavalry was that in a two-line charge the first line usually became disordered. Jomini recommended that the first line always be recalled and reformed, no matter how successful its attack. If it were not recalled, the enemy would throw fresh units against it and defeat it.[19]

This and other problems with the two-line cavalry formation led to the

---

[16]Jomini, *Art of War*, 313; Mahan, *Advanced-Guard*, 34–35, 57; George B. McClellan, *Regulations and Instructions for the Field Service of the U.S. Cavalry in Time of War* (Philadelphia, 1861), 13.

[17]Jomini, *Art of War*, 310, 311. Joseph Wheeler took the same position in his Confederate cavalry tactics. Joseph Wheeler, *A Revised System of Cavalry Tactics, for the use of the Cavalry and Mounted Infantry, CSA* (3 parts, Mobile, 1863), III, 26.

[18]Mahan, *Advanced-Guard*, 57; McClellan, *Regulations and Instructions*, 13; Halleck, *Elements of Military Art*, 127–28.

[19]Cooke, *Cavalry Tactics*, II, 62; Jomini, *Art of War*, 312. See also Halleck, *Elements of Military Art*, 127.

appearance of an alternative system, the single-rank tactics. The two-rank Tactics of 1841, endorsed and first published by the War Department in that year, was reorganized and republished several times, but it was not revised until after the Civil War. The War Department's *Cavalry Tactics* taught the same two-rank system in 1864 that it had in 1841.[20] Although it did not revise the Tactics of 1841, the War Department in 1861 authorized another system of cavalry tactics, Philip St. George Cooke's *Cavalry Tactics*.[21] Some of Cooke's manual was borrowed and paraphrased from the War Department's Tactics of 1841.[22] Cooke, however, made a fundamental change in his tactics, the adoption of the single-rank formation. In the War Department tactics, a cavalry regiment would deploy in two ranks of five squadrons each; in Cooke's tactics, the regiment would deploy in a single rank of ten squadrons.[23]

Several advantages were claimed for the single-rank cavalry tactics. Cooke believed that his single-rank tactics would solve the problem of first-line disorder. In Cooke's system, the first line of a regiment would consist of only four squadrons deployed in line, with two others covering its flanks. The remaining four squadrons of the regiment would remain in reserve, in columns 300 or 400 paces in the rear of the front line. The second line, actually four squadrons in columns, "will be screened from much of the enemy's fire; will be reserved from the confusion which even success throws into the front rank; but that rank *defeated*, it not only escapes being involved, but is close at hand to profit by the impression which may have been made on the enemy."[24]

---

[20]U.S. War Dept., *Cavalry Tactics* (3 parts, Washington, 1841). There were editions of 1855, 1856, 1861, 1862, 1863, and 1864. The War Department tactics were the basis of several cavalry manuals. George B. McClellan's *Regulations and Instructions* followed the War Department's system precisely. Compare McClellan, *Regulations and Instructions*, 123–70, with War Dept., *Cavalry Tactics*, I, 13–92. George Patten, *Cavalry Drill and Sabre Exercise* (New York, 1862) was a one-volume version of the War Department tactics. J. Lucius Davis's *The Trooper's Manual: Or, Tactics for Light Dragoons and Mounted Riflemen* (Richmond, 1861) was the work of the colonel of the Tenth Virginia Cavalry. It endorsed the single-rank tactical system but included drills from both single- and double-rank systems, and its organization followed more closely the War Department's *Cavalry Tactics* than it did Cooke's *Cavalry Tactics*. William Gilham, *Authorized Cavalry Tactics, U.S.A., Manual of Instruction for the Volunteers and Militia of the United States* (Philadelphia, 1861), combined both the War Department and Cooke systems with tactical theory from Mahan and Halleck.

[21]Cooke, *Cavalry Tactics*, I, endorsement on unnumbered page. There were also editions of 1862 and 1864. Other cavalry manuals were influenced by Cooke's. Wheeler's *Revised System* was a Confederate single-rank tactics. *Cooper's Cavalry Tactics, For the Use of Volunteers* (New Orleans and Jackson, 1861), 41, taught a skirmishing system that was a simplification of Cooke's.

[22]Compare, for example, Cooke, *Cavalry Tactics*, I, 38, with War Dept., *Cavalry Tactics*, I, 75–76.

[23]Cooke, *Cavalry Tactics*, I, 3; War Dept., *Cavalry Tactics*, I, 13.

[24]Cooke, *Cavalry Tactics*, I, 10 and accompanying plate; II, 62, 93; I, 1.

Joseph Wheeler, chief of cavalry of the Army of Tennessee, offered Confederates a single-rank cavalry manual, *A Revised System of Cavalry Tactics*. Wheeler shared Cooke's belief that single-rank tactics would reduce the confusion produced by a charge in two ranks. "Another advantage in single rank," Wheeler asserted, "is the greater facility with which troops can be handled and reformed, after the confusion of a charge, and what is of more importance, disorder or confusion are less liable to be incurred." Wheeler also contended that the single-rank system would give attacking cavalry greater shock force. "We will suppose a Cavalry Brigade of four regiments to be drawn up to charge the enemy," argued Wheeler. "With the single rank formation the Brigade will be formed in four lines and inflict upon the enemy four successive shocks, each of which would be nearly as severe as a charge in two ranks, and the number of shocks being double, the amount of execution would certainly be much greater." Wheeler also praised the single-rank system's flanking squadrons, which he thought could be used to cover the attacking lines and prevent the enemy from seeing whether he was to be struck by one line or two, thereby giving a single-line charge the same "moral effect" as a two-line attack.[25] It was also claimed that the single-rank tactics would be easier to teach to volunteers.[26]

Cooke's single-rank system gained official approval, but it never replaced the two-rank tactics; Cooke's system and the War Department's system coexisted. The single-rank tactics were seen more often in the western theater than the eastern. In both theaters, the War Department's two-rank tactics remained the more common of the two systems. One problem with Cooke's single-rank system was that it was incompatible with the regimental organization of ten squadrons forming a regiment. To keep an even number of squadrons in each line, Cooke's system required that two squadrons always be deployed as flankers, whether or not they were needed. Another problem with Cooke's system was that it was introduced in the first year of the war. Confronted with the task of training masses of volunteers in 1861, commanders were reluctant to adopt a new tactical system, particularly one that required a change in regimental organization to make it effective. Consequently, the War Department's *Cavalry Tactics* remained the more common manual.[27]

---

[25]Wheeler, *Revised System*, I, i, ii.

[26]Cooke, *Cavalry Tactics*, I, 1. Cooke also claimed that his single-rank system had been recommended by George B. McClellan. One section of McClellan's Crimean War report did argue for single-rank tactics but also said that two-rank instruction "should be provided." *Senate Executive Document*, 35 Cong., special sess., No. 1, 278, 280. Further, McClellan's own cavalry manual, *Regulations and Instructions*, was a two-rank tactics, taken directly from the War Department system.

[27]"Cavalry Tactics," *Army and Navy Journal*, VI (February 6, 1869), 390; Cooke, *Cavalry Tactics*, I, 10 and accompanying plate; "The New Cavalry Tactics," *Army and Navy Journal*, XI (June 27, 1874), 730.

The period between the Mexican War and the Civil War was a difficult one for both artillery and cavalry theory. The introduction of rifling made artillery primarily a defensive arm, but artillery theory did not recognize this. The authorized artillery manual was replaced, but the new manual retained much of the old one. A few other manuals were available to artillerymen, but they did little to further artillery theory. Cavalry theory emphasized the tactical offensive and the saber. The War Department replaced the Tactics of 1841 with a similar two-rank system. After Cooke's single-rank tactics was introduced in 1861, there was no uniform tactical system for cavalry, but two competing schools.

Tactical manuals were primarily drill books and not works of tactical theory. They sometimes offered common sense advice that was not of great tactical value. Cooke's *Cavalry Tactics* warned troopers about jittery horses: "Rearing is a bad and dangerous habit." Cooke also gave instructors such advice as, "Explain to the men that the horse's head and neck must always be bent the way he is to go." The *Instruction for Field Artillery* advised artillery officers about procuring horses for their batteries: "Long-legged, loose-jointed, long-bodied, or narrow-chested horses should be at once rejected, as also those which are restive, vicious, or *too free* in harness." The same manual warned officers to keep their men off their caissons when within enemy artillery range: "The explosion of a caisson when the cannoneers are mounted might destroy many men."[28]

Just how many Civil War soldiers read any tactical manuals, even the one authorized for their arm, is questionable. L. Van Loan Naisawald found that few works were available to Union artillerymen other than their manual. In the early months of the Civil War, "Congress appropriated funds for the purchase of books of tactics and instruction for Volunteers, but the 'books' appear to have been limited to a few copies of the artillery manual." In his *Elements of Military Art and Science*, Henry W. Halleck observed: "There are innumerable works in almost every language on elementary tactics; very few persons, however, care to read any thing further than the manuals used in our own service." General Orlando M. Poe, an 1856 graduate of West Point, advised Jacob D. Cox, a volunteer soldier, to give his first attention to the *Army Regulations*. Cox concluded that the *Regulations* were more valuable than tactical works, because an officer with "a fair knowledge of tactics" could rely on "common sense for guidance in an action on the field," but army administration could only be learned by studying the *Regulations*.[29]

In the period between the Mexican War and the Civil War, there were

---

[28]Cooke, *Cavalry Tactics*, I, 26, 32; Board of Artillery Officers, *Instruction* (1860), 46, 73. The caisson advice also appeared in Gibbon, *Artillerist's Manual*, 400.

[29]Naisawald, *Grape and Canister*, 40; Halleck, *Elements of Military Art*, 134n; Jacob D. Cox, *Military Reminiscences of the Civil War* (2 vols., New York, 1900), I, 20.

greater changes in weaponry than in tactical theory and manuals. "The introduction of the rifled Parrott field-pieces, and the rifled muskets," wrote one soldier after the Civil War, "made a change of tactics absolutely necessary; and the text-books passed into obsoleteness."[30] Tactical theory underestimated the firepower of the rifle. New tactical manuals were prepared, but the new manuals retained much of the old ones. Changes were made, but the changes were to prove inadequate.

---

[30]Veteran, "Change of Tactics," *Army and Navy Journal*, III (September 23, 1865), 75.

6

Fieldworks Were Assaulted but Rarely Carried

American commanders had been successful on the tactical offensive in the Mexican War, and tactical theory of the 1850s emphasized the tactical offensive. Most Civil War commanders, especially Southerners, favored the tactical offensive; only a few made reputations for fighting on the tactical defensive. George G. Meade became famous for his defensive stand at Gettysburg, and he conducted the pursuit after Gettysburg and the Bristoe and Mine Run campaigns cautiously. Francis A. Walker, who served as a staff officer in the Army of the Potomac, thought Meade received less credit than he deserved for his defensive victory at Gettysburg. "The sword," said Walker, "is ever the higher honor than the shield."[1] George B. McClellan fought the Seven Days' battles on the tactical defensive, and he was never quick to take the offensive in any of his campaigns.[2] George H. Thomas became known as the "Rock of Chickamauga" for his defensive stand at that battle, but Thomas won his greatest victory on the tactical offensive at Nashville. Of the Confederate commanders, only Joseph E. Johnston won a reputation for defensive fighting. His biographers have praised him for understanding a "different valor," the valor of the strategic and tactical defensive.[3]

Many Civil War commanders sought the tactical offensive and made their reputations with it. Ulysses S. Grant was a strong advocate of the offensive.

---

[1]Francis A. Walker, "Meade at Gettysburg," in *Battles and Leaders of the Civil War*, ed. Robert U. Johnson and Clarence C. Buel (4 vols., reissue, New York, 1956), III, 406.

[2]McClellan often has been criticized for his slowness and caution. See, for example, Bruce Catton, *Mr. Lincoln's Army* (Garden City, 1951), 137–39, 150–51, 154–55, 228–29, 319–21, 327, 330–33; T. Harry Williams, *Lincoln and His Generals* (New York, 1952), 145–46, 168–69, 172–78. For studies more sympathetic to McClellan, see Warren W. Hassler, Jr., *General George B. McClellan, Shield of the Union* (Baton Rouge, 1957) and Edward Hagerman, "The Professionalization of George B. McClellan and Early Civil War Field Command: An Institutional Perspective," *Civil War History*, XXI (1975), 113–35.

[3]Gilbert E. Govan and James W. Livingood, *A Different Valor: The Story of General Joseph E. Johnston, C.S.A.* (Indianapolis, 1956).

"The art of war is simple enough," Grant believed. "Find out where your enemy is. Get at him as soon as you can. Strike at him as hard as you can and as often as you can, and keep moving on."[4] Grant said that when he was attacked by the Confederates at Shiloh, it was the first time in his career, which then included the Mexican War, Belmont, and Fort Donelson, that he had been put on the tactical defensive.[5] Grant also said that at the end of the first day at Shiloh he visited his division commanders and told them to retake the offensive the next day. "To [William T.] Sherman I told the story of the assault at Fort Donelson," Grant wrote, "and said that the same tactics would win at Shiloh."[6]

Grant fought vigorous tactical offensives during the Vicksburg and Chattanooga campaigns, and when he came to the eastern theater in 1864 his aggressive reputation preceded him. General E. M. Law of the Army of Northern Virginia, however, said that Robert E. Lee's soldiers found Grant to be even more aggressive than they anticipated. Law said that the Army of Northern Virginia expected Grant to be forceful, "but we were not prepared for the unparalleled stubbornness and tenacity with which he persisted in his attacks under the fearful losses which his army sustained at the Wilderness and at Spotsylvania." After the Virginia campaign began, Grant rarely fought on the defensive. In one of his official reports, Grant explained why he regarded his offensive tactics a success. "The battles of the Wilderness, Spotsylvania, North Anna, and Cold Harbor, bloody and terrible as they were on our side," Grant said, "were even more damaging to the enemy, and so crippled him as to make him wary ever after of taking the offensive."[7]

Robert E. Lee liked the tactical offensive and assumed it whenever he could. Lee won great victories on the tactical offensive at Second Manassas and Chancellorsville but also suffered terrible defeats while attacking at Malvern Hill and Gettysburg. Lee's fondness for the tactical offensive was perhaps best shown during one of his defensive battles, at Sharpsburg, September 17, 1862, where he was forced to fight on the tactical defensive while badly outnumbered and with his back to the Potomac River. In the bloodiest single day's fighting of the war, Lee's lines were battered by a series of piecemeal attacks. Lee shifted units to successively threatened parts of his line, made some counterattacks, and barely held his position. At the end of the day, he had no reserves whatsoever. In the middle of this battle, while

---

[4]This is quoted in T. Harry Williams, "The Military Leadership of North and South," in *Why the North Won the Civil War,* ed. David Herbert Donald (Baton Rouge, 1960), 43.

[5]Ulysses S. Grant, "The Battle of Shiloh," in *Battles and Leaders,* I, 480.

[6]Ibid., 476.

[7]E. M. Law, "From the Wilderness to Cold Harbor," in *Battles and Leaders,* IV, 142; U.S. War Dept., *The War of the Rebellion: A Compilation of the Official Records of the Union and Confederate Armies* (128 vols., Washington, 1880–1901), Series 1, XLVI (pt. 1), 22 (hereinafter cited as *OR;* all references are to Series 1).

the center of his line at the Sunken Road was being driven in, Lee considered taking the tactical offensive against the Federal right.[8] The battle ended with an attack by Confederate General A. P. Hill's Division on the Federal left. Four days after his bloody stand at Sharpsburg, Lee still wanted to take the offensive. On September 21 he wrote: ". . . it is still my desire to threaten a passage into Maryland, to occupy the enemy on this frontier, and, if my purpose cannot be accomplished, to draw them into the Valley, where I can attack them to advantage."[9]

Several of Lee's opponents attempted tactical offensives against him but were unsuccessful. Ambrose E. Burnside's attacks at Fredericksburg, December 13, 1862, ended in disaster. Joseph Hooker began the Battle of Chancellorsville on the offensive but soon surrendered the initiative to Lee. When John Pope arrived in the eastern theater, he bragged that he had fought successfully on the offensive in the West and that he intended to do the same against Lee's forces. In his well-known address to the Army of Virginia, Pope boasted: "I have come to you from the West, . . . from an army . . . whose policy has been attack and not defense. In but one instance [Shiloh] has the enemy been able to place our Western armies in defensive attitude. I presume that I have been called here to pursue the same system and to lead you against the enemy."[10]

Several western commanders earned reputations for taking the tactical offensive. The Confederate cavalryman Joseph Wheeler praised Braxton Bragg and Edmund Kirby Smith for their understanding of the tactical offensive: "Both fully appreciated the fact that, when an adversary is not intrenched, a determined attack is the beginning of victory." After the war, a corps commander of the Army of the Cumberland remembered that Bragg was always eager to take the offensive. "The battle [of Murfreesboro] was fought according to the plan of General Bragg," said Thomas L. Crittenden. "Indeed, our uniform experience was—at Perryville, at Stone's River, at Chickamauga—that whenever we went to attack Bragg we were attacked by him, and so our plan had to be extemporized." At Murfreesboro, Bragg took the initiative by striking the Union right, but his opponent, William S. Rosecrans, had also wanted to attack. In his orders to the Army of the Cumberland for December 31, 1862, Rosecrans said, "Close steadily in upon the enemy, and, when you get within charging distance, rush on him with the bayonet."[11]

---

[8]*OR*, XIX (pt. 1), 151. J. E. B. Stuart said the attack was considered on September 18 (ibid., 820) but the evidence for September 17 is overwhelming (ibid., 840, 915, 916, 920, 956–57); John G. Walker, "Sharpsburg," in *Battles and Leaders*, II, 679–80.

[9]*OR*, XIX (pt. 1), 143.

[10]Ibid., XII (pt. 3), 474.

[11]Joseph Wheeler, "Bragg's Invasion of Kentucky," in *Battles and Leaders*, III, 23; Thomas L. Crittenden, "The Union Left at Stone's River," ibid., 633; *OR*, XX (pt. 1), 183.

William T. Sherman believed that a commander should be willing to take the tactical offensive even against difficult positions. In his report on the Atlanta campaign, Sherman explained why he ordered the unsuccessful attacks against the Confederate entrenchments at Kennesaw Mountain. "An army to be efficient must not settle down to a single mode of offense," Sherman contended, "but must be prepared to execute any plan which promises success." Sherman argued that the Kennesaw Mountain defeat had some virtue, "as it demonstrated to General [Joseph E.] Johnston that I would assault and that boldly."[12]

Many other Civil War commanders made their reputations on the tactical offensive. Philip H. Sheridan won his victories at Winchester, Fisher's Hill, Waynesboro, and Five Forks on the tactical offensive. At Cedar Creek, Sheridan's forces were attacked while he was away from the battlefield. When Sheridan returned, he took the offensive and carried the field. Thomas Jonathan "Stonewall" Jackson became most famous for his attacks in the Shenandoah Valley and for his flank attack at Chancellorsville. John Bell Hood was among the most aggressive of the Confederate commanders. When Hood replaced Joseph E. Johnston as commander of the Army of Tennessee, he gave President Jefferson Davis the offensive style of fighting Davis wanted, both around Atlanta and later in the Tennessee campaign.

The tactical offensive proved a costly undertaking against defenders armed with accurate-firing rifled weapons. McClellan's piecemeal attacks against Lee at Sharpsburg cost the Army of the Potomac nearly 12,000 soldiers, and Burnside's Fredericksburg attacks were almost as costly. During his Vicksburg campaign, Ulysses S. Grant lost over 3,000 troops in his unsuccessful May 22 assaults before he went over to siege operations. After the Battle of the Wilderness, Grant fought most of the Virginia campaign on the tactical offensive. He lost over 18,000 troops at Spotsylvania Court House and about 12,000 at Cold Harbor.[13]

The tactical offensive was even more costly for the Confederates, who did not have the numbers to withstand high losses. Braxton Bragg, who liked close-order assault tactics, fought three major battles on the tactical offensive, losing over 3,000 men at Perryville, over 9,000 at Murfreesboro, and nearly

---

[12]*OR*, XXXVIII (pt. 1), 68, 69.

[13]Thomas L. Livermore, *Numbers & Losses in the Civil War in America: 1861–65* (reissue, Bloomington, 1957), 92, 96, 100; *OR*, XXXVI (pt. 1), 188. On the impact of the rifle on tactics, see J. F. C. Fuller, *The Generalship of Ulysses S. Grant* (New York, 1929), 57–62, and "The Place of the American Civil War in the Evolution of War," *Army Quarterly*, XXVI (1933), 316–25, and *A Military History of the Western World* (3 vols., New York, 1954–1956), III, 17–18; Bruce Catton, *America Goes to War* (Middletown, 1958), 14–20; John K. Mahon, "Civil War Infantry Assault Tactics," *Military Affairs*, XXV (1961), 57–68; Grady McWhiney, "Who Whipped Whom? Confederate Defeat Reexamined," *Civil War History*, XI (1965), 5–26.

17,000 at Chickamauga.[14] John Bell Hood's aggressive tactics used up the remaining strength of the Army of Tennessee. In his sorties around Atlanta and in the fighting at Jonesboro, Hood lost over 15,000 troops. In the Tennessee campaign, Hood shattered his forces in the attack at Franklin, which cost 5,500 casualties.[15] Robert E. Lee suffered his worst defeats, Malvern Hill and Gettysburg, on the tactical offensive. During the Seven Days' battles, Lee drove McClellan away from Richmond, but the Confederates lost almost 20,000 troops. Gettysburg cost the Confederate attackers nearly 23,000 troops. The southern loss in General George E. Pickett's famous charge has been estimated at 6,467, about 62 percent of the men who made the advance.[16]

The strength of the tactical defensive was further increased by the use of field entrenchments. The Mexican War had given American soldiers no great regard for field works. Tactical theory in the years before the Civil War considered entrenchment important but emphasized the tactical offensive and taught that a vigorous assault by good troops would overcome field works. The Civil War was the first American war in which field entrenchments were used extensively.[17]

Entrenchments were used in some early Civil War campaigns, but troops were not entrenched at every opportunity in the campaigns of 1861 and 1862. Lee did not entrench his lines at Sharpsburg in September 1862, although McClellan gave him time to do so. Ulysses S. Grant's men were not en-

---

[14]The Confederate loss at Perryville is given in *OR*, XVI (pt. 1), 1112. The Confederate losses at Murfreesboro and Chickamauga are difficult to determine from official reports. The 9,865 figure given in *OR*, XX (pt. 1), 681, is incomplete and low. Bragg's Murfreesboro losses are estimated at 10,314 in Grady McWhiney, *Braxton Bragg and Confederate Defeat* (New York, 1969), 372n. The Confederate loss at Chickamauga is estimated at nearly 17,000 by Livermore, *Numbers & Losses*, 106.

[15]Livermore, *Numbers & Losses*, 122–26, 132.

[16]Ibid., 86, 103; George R. Stewart, *Pickett's Charge* (Boston, 1959), 263. When the percentages lost by small units on the tactical offensive are examined, they are often high. For example, the Federal regiments that attacked the stone wall front at Fredericksburg lost heavily. The remarkably complete report of General Winfield S. Hancock, a division commander in this assault, includes both the numbers and the losses of his regiments, showing many regiments with high percentage losses. *OR*, XXI, 129–30, 226–32. Many examples of high loss percentages suffered by Confederate units on the offensive at Murfreesboro and Chickamauga are given in Chapter 1.

[17]For some differing viewpoints on the development of field entrenchments in the Civil War see "Field Intrenchments," *Army and Navy Journal*, VI (November 7, 1868), 184–85; Arthur L. Wagner, *Organization and Tactics* (Kansas City, 1894), 95, 102–03, and "Hasty Entrenchments in the War of Secession," in *Papers of the Military Historical Society of Massachusetts* (14 vols., Boston, 1913), XIII, 129–53; Fuller, *Generalship of Grant*, 57; Mahon, "Infantry Assault Tactics," 59, 65–66; Edward Hagerman, "From Jomini to Dennis Hart Mahan: The Evolution of Trench Warfare and the American Civil War," *Civil War History*, XIII (1967), 197–220.

trenched when the Confederates attacked them at Shiloh in April 1862. In an article written after the war, Grant offered several reasons for this, the first of which was that "up to that time the pick and spade had been but little resorted to at the West."[18]

In 1863 strong field entrenchments were built on several battlefields. During the Chancellorsville campaign, Hooker's final line south of the Rappahannock River was a well-entrenched position, firmly held by both infantry and artillery. The strongest works at Gettysburg were probably those constructed by General Henry W. Slocum's Twelfth Corps on Culp's Hill. "Right and left the men felled the trees, and blocked them up into a close log fence," wrote a captain in the Sixtieth New York. "Piles of cordwood which lay near by were quickly appropriated. The sticks, set slanting on end against the outer face of the logs, made excellent battening. All along the rest of the line of the corps a similar defense was constructed."[19] General John W. Geary, commander of the Second Division, Twelfth Corps, reported: "Not only did they [the entrenchments] impede the advance of the overwhelmingly superior numbers of the enemy, but our men were afforded by them a shelter which rendered our casualties surprisingly incompatible with so terrible and prolonged an engagement."[20]

Entrenchments strengthened positions at both Chickamauga and Chattanooga. At Chickamauga the Confederates drove in the Federal center and right. The Federal left, under General George H. Thomas, was covered by strong field entrenchments. The Confederates made their first attacks on September 20, 1863, against Thomas's sector, but without success. William F. G. Shanks, correspondent of the *New York Herald*, wrote: "General Thomas had wisely taken the precaution to make rude works about breast-high along his whole front, using rails and logs for the purpose."[21] One Confederate colonel, whose men charged Thomas's position unsuccessfully, complained: "The enemy was behind his works and we without cover."[22]

---

[18]Grant, "Battle of Shiloh," I, 481.

[19]*OR*, XXV (pt. 1), 1012; John Bigelow, *The Campaign of Chancellorsville* (New Haven, 1910), 416; Jesse H. Jones, "The Breastworks at Culp's Hill," in *Battles and Leaders*, III, 316. On the Twelfth Corps works at Gettysburg, see also *OR*, XXVII (pt. 1), 759, 773, 812, 826, 849, 854.

[20]*OR*, XXVII (pt. 1), 831–32. One of Geary's brigade commanders made a similar comment. Ibid., 856. Geary's Division lost only about 13 percent at Gettysburg. Ibid., 185, 833.

[21]This is quoted in a footnote by the editors in Daniel H. Hill, "Chickamauga—The Great Battle of the West," in *Battles and Leaders*, III, 654n. See also *OR*, XXX (pt. 1), 251–77, and Emerson Opdycke, "Notes on the Chickamauga Campaign," in *Battles and Leaders*, III, 670.

[22]*OR*, XXX (pt. 2), 188. Many Confederate reports mention these works. Ibid., 154, 177, 182, 185, 199, 245, 246. A particular complaint of the Confederates was that the angles in Thomas's works allowed the Federals to enfilade the attackers. Ibid., 162, 171. Thomas's later position on Snodgrass Hill also was improved by works. Ibid. (pt. 1), 436; (pt. 2), 421.

During the Chattanooga campaign, the Confederates built rifle pits at the base of Missionary Ridge and two entrenched lines on the ridge itself.[23]

From the spring of 1864 until the end of the war, extensive and sophisticated field entrenchments were seen in both theaters. Colonel Theodore Lyman, who served on the staff of George G. Meade during the Virginia campaign, wrote to his wife from Spotsylvania Court House: "It is a rule that, when the Rebels halt, the first day gives them a good rifle-pit; the second, a regular infantry parapet with artillery in position; and the third a parapet with an abattis in front and entrenched batteries behind. Sometimes they put this three days' work into the first twenty-four hours. . . . You would be amazed to see how this country is intersected with field-works, extending for miles and miles in different directions and marking the different strategic lines taken up by the two armies, as they warily move about each other." William T. Sherman described the entrenching done during the Atlanta campaign: "Troops, halting for the night or for battle, faced the enemy; moved forward to ground with a good outlook to the front; stacked arms; gathered logs, stumps, fence-rails, anything that would stop a bullet; piled these to their front, and, digging a ditch behind, threw the dirt forward, and made a parapet which covered their persons as perfectly as a granite wall." Oliver O. Howard, Sherman's subordinate in the Atlanta campaign, wrote: "No regiment was long in front of [Joseph E.] Johnston's army without having virtually as good a breast-work as an engineer could plan. There was a ditch before the embankment and a strong log revetment behind it, and a heavy 'top-log' to shelter the heads of the men. I have known a regiment to shelter itself completely against musketry and artillery with axes and shovels, in less than an hour after it reached its position."[24]

The use of field entrenchments increased the advantage of the tactical defensive. Jacob D. Cox claimed after the war: "One rifle in the trench was worth five in front of it." James H. Wilson, who served in both theaters of the war, made the same point, although with more restraint than Cox. "Rifle pits and fieldworks were assaulted many times throughout the war," Wilson said, "but were rarely ever carried." After Theodore Lyman described the Confederate system of entrenching in his letter from Spotsylvania Court

---

[23]Ibid., XXXI (pt. 2), 132, 195, 199, 204; Ulysses S. Grant, "Chattanooga," in *Battles and Leaders*, III, 706–07; Joseph S. Fullerton, "The Army of the Cumberland at Chattanooga," ibid., 725.

[24]Theodore Lyman to Elizabeth Russell Lyman, May 18, 1864, *Meade's Headquarters, 1863–1865* . . . , ed. George R. Agassiz (Boston, 1922), 100; William T. Sherman, "The Grand Strategy of the Last Year of the War," in *Battles and Leaders*, IV, 248; Oliver O. Howard, "The Struggle for Atlanta," ibid., 307. See also Jacob D. Cox, *Military Reminiscences of the Civil War* (2 vols., New York, 1900), II, 215–16.

House, he added: "Our men can, and do, do the same; but remember, our object is offense—to advance."[25]

Civil War commanders hoped that élan would help overcome the advantages of the entrenched tactical defensive. The Rebel yell was intended to promote élan, as were other yells and cheers. A Tennessee colonel whose command advanced with General James Longstreet's Wing at Chickamauga reported after the battle: "I ordered three times three for Old Tennessee and a charge, both of which were responded to with alacrity."[26] Colonel W. F. Tucker of the Fifty-first Mississippi said his men gave "a regular Mississippi yell" as they charged at Chickamauga.[27] Assaulting northern troops gave yells and cheers of their own. During Upton's assault, May 10, 1864, at Spotsylvania Court House, Colonel Emory Upton's men charged "with a wild cheer."[28] After Hancock's assault on the Mule Shoe salient, May 12, 1864, General Winfield S. Hancock reported that his men "broke into a tremendous cheer" as they approached the Confederate works.[29]

The bayonet was well regarded in both the Mexican War and tactical theory, and many Civil War commanders expressed confidence in it. William S. Rosecrans, intending to take the tactical offensive at Murfreesboro, instructed his troops in his attack orders for December 31, 1862, to rush the enemy with the bayonet. "Do this," declared Rosecrans, "and the victory will certainly be yours. Recollect that there are hardly any troops in the world that will stand a bayonet charge, and that those who make it, therefore, are sure to win." General Andrew A. Humphreys concluded at Fredericksburg that only a bayonet charge could carry the Confederate position west of the town. Humphreys led his division of Pennsylvania regiments in one of the many hopeless Union charges against Marye's Heights, convinced that "the only mode of attacking successfully was with the bayonet."[30] A Union lieutenant colonel reported that at Gaines's Mill General Daniel Butterfield had shouted to the Eighty-third Pennsylvania: "Your ammunition is never expended while you have your bayonets, my boys, and use them to the socket."[31]

Confederate commanders often expressed confidence in the bayonet. The final sentence of the Confederate Special Orders No. 8 before Shiloh read: "It is expected that much and effective work will be done with the bayonet."

---

[25]Jacob D. Cox, *Atlanta* (New York, 1882), 129; James H. Wilson, *Under the Old Flag; Recollections of Military Operations in the War for the Union* . . . (2 vols., New York, 1912), I, 181; Lyman to Elizabeth Russell Lyman, May 18, 1864, in Lyman, *Meade's Headquarters*, 100.

[26]*OR*, XXX (pt. 2), 395.

[27]Ibid., 326.

[28]Ibid., XXXVI (pt. 1), 668.

[29]Ibid., 335.

[30]Ibid., XX (pt. 1), 183; XXI, 431.

[31]Ibid., XI (pt. 2), 344.

When the southern advance was delayed at the Hornet's Nest, Albert Sidney Johnston was said to have called to nearby infantry: "Men! they are stubborn; we must use the bayonet." When General John C. Breckinridge's Division made its attack at Murfreesboro, January 2, 1863, its front-line troops were ordered to fire one volley and then use the bayonet. In the southern attack at Peach Tree Creek, July 20, 1864, General A. P. Stewart told his corps that if the Federal line was found to be entrenched "to fix bayonets and carry [the enemy's] works," an order that his subordinates passed on.[32] General Richard Taylor, an aggressive fighter, reported after Pleasant Hill: "Orders were given to all to rely on the bayonet, as we had neither ammunition nor time to waste."[33] Stonewall Jackson was a proponent of the bayonet and advocated its use during his famous stand at First Manassas. At Winchester, during his Shenandoah Valley campaign, Jackson told the colonel of the Thirty-third Virginia that if the Federals brought a battery to the hill in his front, to charge it with the bayonet. When the colonel argued that his regiment was small, Jackson replied, "Take it."[34]

A few Civil War charges included some bayonet fighting. General George McCall's Division fought with the bayonet at Frayser's farm during the Seven Days' battles, and General Cuvier Grover's Brigade made a bayonet charge at Second Manassas. Some of the bloodiest bayonet fighting of the war occurred at Spotsylvania, during Upton's assault and during the fighting at the Mule Shoe salient. Upton reported on his May 10 assault: "The first of our men who tried to surmount the works fell pierced through the head by musket-balls. Others, seeing the fate of their comrades, held their pieces at arms length and fired downward, while others, poising their pieces vertically, hurled them down upon their enemy, pinning them to the ground." Upton included in his report several other examples of fighting with bayonets.[35] Bayonet fighting was done during the Atlanta campaign at Kennesaw Mountain, during the Battle of Atlanta, and at Jonesboro.[36] General Absalom Baird said of Jonesboro: "On no occasion within my knowledge has the use of the bayonet been so general or so well authenticated." Baird's report on Jonesboro included examples of bayonet fencing and fighting.

---

[32]Ibid., X (pt. 1), 395; William Preston Johnston, "Albert Sidney Johnston at Shiloh," in *Battles and Leaders*, I, 564; *OR*, XX (pt. 1), 786, 827; XXXVIII (pt. 3), 871, 876, 882, 894.

[33]*OR*, XXXIV (pt. 1), 567.

[34]Henry Kyd Douglas, *I Rode With Stonewall* (Chapel Hill, 1940), 10; E. Porter Alexander, *Military Memoirs of a Confederate* (reissue, Bloomington, 1962), 35; OR, XII (pt. 1), 755.

[35]*OR*, XI (pt. 2), 392; XII (pt. 2), 439; extract from a letter from General Nelson A. Miles to General Francis C. Barlow, January 6, 1879, quoted in Francis C. Barlow, "Capture of the Salient, May 12, 1864," in *Papers of the Military Historical Society of Massachusetts*, IV, 261; *OR*, XXXVI (pt. 1), 335, 336, 358, 359, 373, 410, 668.

[36]*OR*, XXXVIII (pt. 1), 645, 654, 752, 757, 811; (pt. 3), 156, 227, 253, 565, 582–83, 611–739.

Bayonet fighting also took place at Franklin, at Fort Gregg during the final assault on Petersburg, and at Sayler's Creek.[37]

After the introduction of the rifle, the bayonet was rarely a decisive weapon. In his orders before Murfreesboro, Rosecrans had encouraged his subordinates to use the bayonet. One Federal colonel who fought at Murfreesboro reported after the battle: "I intended to have tried the virtue of the bayonet, according to the instructions of our much-respected general-in-chief. I regret very much to say, after two appeals to the Ninety-ninth Ohio, that regiment failed to come forward."[38] Rifle fire was so destructive that it usually decided an attack before the attackers got close enough to the defenders to use their bayonets. In most successful bayonet charges, the attackers advanced with fixed bayonets, prepared for bayonet fighting, but the defenders gave way before any bayoneting could be done. The Federal bayonet attack at Mill Springs, January 19, 1862, one of the first in the war, took this course: the Confederates retreated before any bayoneting could be done. The colonel of the Ninth Ohio reported, "But few of them [the Confederate defenders] stood, possibly 10 or 12."[39] The official reports of the battle showed that a bayonet charge took place, yet none of the Federal reports claimed that any Southerners were bayoneted.[40] During the Peninsula campaign, Winfield S. Hancock ordered an attack by his brigade at Williamsburg. "A few of the leading spirits of the enemy were bayoneted," wrote Hancock, "the remainder then broke and fled."[41] A Confederate colonel said of an action at Fort Donelson: "This was not, strictly speaking, a 'charge bayonets,' but it would have been one if the enemy had not fled." In many of the most famous bayonet charges of the war, the attacks were decided before any bayonet fighting could be done. The charge of the Fifty-first New York and Fifty-first Pennsylvania across the Lower Bridge at Sharpsburg and the charge of the 125th Ohio at Chickamauga were such cases. The Federal attack on Missionary Ridge was another example. Philip H. Sheridan, a division commander during this assault, said after the war: "At the rifle-pits [at the base of Missionary Ridge] there had been little use for the bayonet, for most of the Confederate troops, disconcerted by the sudden rush, lay close in the ditch and surrendered, though some few fled up the slope to the next line."[42] The official reports of the engagement showed that virtually no

[37]Ibid. (pt. 1), 753; XLV (pt. 1), 256, 260–61, 380, 416; XLVI (pt. 1), 946–47, 998, 1220, 1285.

[38]Ibid., XX (pt. 1), 611.

[39]Ibid., VII, 94.

[40]The official reports on Mill Springs are in *OR*, VII, 80, 85, 94, 96. See also R. M. Kelly, "Holding Kentucky for the Union," in *Battles and Leaders*, I, 389.

[41]*OR*, XI (pt. 1), 540.

[42]Ibid., VII, 342–43; XIX (pt. 1), 444; XXX (pt. 1), 708; Philip H. Sheridan, *Personal Memoirs of P. H. Sheridan* (2 vols., New York, 1888), I, 310.

bayoneting was done either on the slopes or at the crest of Missionary Ridge.[43]

Rifle fire was so powerful that troops were rarely able to use the bayonet. At the beginning of the war, the Confederate cavalryman John S. Mosby observed that the bayonet was of little use at First Manassas. Three days after the battle, Mosby wrote to his wife: "They [the Federals] never once stood to a clash of the bayonet—always broke and ran." Another Confederate cavalryman, Heros von Borcke, examined corpses on the Gaines's Mill battlefield for bayonet casualties, but found none. "These accounts of bayonet fights are current after every general engagement, and are frequently embodied in subsequent 'histories,' so called," von Borcke said shortly after the war, "but as far as my experience goes, recalling all the battles in which I have borne a part, bayonet-fights rarely if ever occur, and exist only in the imagination." Jubal A. Early of the Army of Northern Virginia contended in his *War Memoirs:* "Military commanders sometimes saw the [bayonet] charges, after the fighting was over, but the surgeons never saw the wounds made by the bayonets, except in a few instances of mere individual conflict, or where some wounded men had been bayoneted in the field." In the weeks after the Battle of Shiloh, William T. Sherman denied that any men of his division had been bayoneted in that engagement. On April 22, 1862, Sherman wrote to his brother: "Indeed our brigade surgeon [Dana W.] Hartshorn, has not yet seen a single bayonet wound on a living or dead subject." After the war, Sherman recalled that in close fighting men fought more often with clubbed musket than with the bayonet.[44]

The reports of the medical director of the Army of the Potomac included compilations of the types of wounds treated by the surgeons of that army during the Virginia campaign of 1864 and 1865. These compilations suggest that little bayonet fighting was done in the Virginia campaign, one of the hardest fought campaigns of the war. Many bayonetings were fatal, and many bayonet wounds went untreated or unreported. Even allowing for these cases, the total number of bayonetings during the campaign cannot have been high. The medical director's records show that from May 1, 1864, to July 31, 1864, a period that included the Wilderness, Spotsylvania Court

---

[43]The official reports on Missionary Ridge are in *OR*, XXXI (pt. 2). References to bayoneting such as given on ibid., 528, are very rare.

[44]John S. Mosby to Pauline Mosby, July 24, 1861, *The Memoirs of Colonel John S. Mosby*, ed. Charles Wells Russell (reissue, Bloomington, 1959), 52; Heros von Borcke, *Memoirs of the Confederate War for Independence* (2 vols., Edinburgh, 1866), I, 63–64; Jubal A. Early, *War Memoirs, Autobiographical Sketch and Narrative of the War Between the States* (reissue, Bloomington, 1960), 73; William T. Sherman to John Sherman, April 22, 1862, *The Sherman Letters: Correspondence Between General and Senator Sherman from 1837 to 1891*, ed. Rachel Sherman Thorndike (New York, 1894), 143; William T. Sherman to Ellen Boyle Ewing, April 24, 1862, *Home Letters of General Sherman*, ed. M. A. DeWolfe Howe (New York, 1909), 224–25; William T. Sherman, *Memoirs of General William T. Sherman By Himself* (2 vols., reissue, Bloomington, 1957), II, 394.

House, Cold Harbor, the first assaults on Petersburg, the First Battle of the
Weldon Railroad, the Crater, and other engagements, only thirty-seven
bayonet wounds were treated by surgeons of the Army of the Potomac.[45]
From August to December 1864, a period that included the Second Battle of
the Weldon Railroad, Poplar Spring Church, Boydton Plank Road, and
other engagements, only ten bayonet wounds were treated. From February
to April 1865, a period including Hatcher's Run, Fort Stedman, Five Forks,
the final assault on Petersburg, Sayler's Creek, and other engagements, only
three bayonet wounds were treated.[46]

[45]This follows the statement in *OR*, XXXVI (pt. 1), 265. The individual statements give a
total of thirty-six. Ibid., 225, 237, 241, 251, 261, 262.
[46]Ibid., XLII (pt. 1), 200–02; XLVI (pt. 1), 617–18.

7

Desperate Valor

The basic offensive formation during the Civil War, as in the Mexican War and in tactical theory, was the two-line formation. This formation commonly was used by troops of every army in both theaters throughout the war. When a brigade or division deployed in two lines, the distance between the two lines depended on terrain and other circumstances. Neither Hardee's nor Casey's *Tactics* defined this distance. Hardee's manual had no brigade or division tactics. Casey's *Tactics* specified that for instruction the two lines should be 150 paces distant; for battle conditions the distance would "depend upon circumstances."[1] Lines usually were deployed at close distance. Distances between 150 and 250 yards were most common, but they varied with the battlefield situation and the judgment of a unit's commander.[2] Units also usually deployed at close intervals. (Interval was the space between units forming on the same front.) Casey's *Tactics* provided for an interval of 150 paces between regiments forming on the same brigade line.[3] When a brigade formed in two lines, with more than one regiment in each line, the "battalion of direction" system was often used. One regiment of the first line was designated the "battalion of direction," and all other regiments in the first line were to align on it.[4] Sometimes when a brigade deployed in two lines,

---

[1]Silas Casey, *Infantry Tactics, for the Instruction, Exercise, and Manoeuvers of the Soldier, a Company, Line of Skirmishers, Battalion, Brigade, or Corps D'Armee* (3 vols., New York, 1862), I, 9, 10.

[2]For some examples of both brigades and divisions in the two-line formation and the varying distance between lines, see U.S. War Dept., *The War of the Rebellion: A Compilation of the Official Records of the Union and Confederate Armies* (128 vols., Washington, 1880–1901), Series 1, XVII (pt. 1), 622, 656; XXIV (pt. 1), 606, 609, 643; XXV (pt. 1), 499; XXX (pt. 1), 654, 661; (pt. 2), 321; XXXI (pt. 2), 391–92, 429; XLVII (pt. 1), 1098 (hereinafter cited as *OR*, and unless otherwise indicated all references are to Series 1).

[3]Casey, *Tactics*, I, 9, 10. Official reports rarely mentioned the interval between men or units. Some reports used "interval" to mean "distance" or otherwise confused the usage. See, for example, *OR*, X (pt. 1), 495; XXI, 486.

[4]This system was used with various formations. See, for example, *OR*, XII (pt. 2), 617; XXV (pt. 1), 902, 971, 973; XXVII (pt. 1), 553; (pt. 2), 368, 372, 407, 410–11; XXX (pt. 2), 129, 503, 507; XXXVI (pt. 1), 1068, 1082; XXXVIII (pt. 1), 574; (pt. 2), 246; (pt. 3), 727; XL (pt. 1), 577; XLII (pt. 1), 581.

with more than one regiment on a line, the command of each line was entrusted to a single officer, usually the senior regimental commander of each line.[5]

The two-line formation allowed an attacking unit to throw its firepower along a broad front and have the sustaining power of a second, supporting line. An attack by successive lines in fairly close order was intended to put defenders under continuous pressure. If single lines advanced at too great distances, their attacks became piecemeal and defenders could break up each one separately. In the theory of two-line fighting, the second line could relieve the first line even under battle conditions. The Third Alabama was formed in two lines during Stonewall Jackson's May 2 attack on the Eleventh Corps at Chancellorsville. Captain M. F. Bonham claimed that during this famous attack the Third Alabama was able to actualize the theory of two-line fighting: "The firing of my command was executed in excellent order, the front line firing and loading as they marched on, while the rear came to the front, fired and loaded as the march continued." Effective two-line firing was easier to achieve on the defensive. Colonel Benjamin F. Scribner boasted about his brigade's two-line firing while on the defensive at Chickamauga: "The second line closed up to the first, and at the opportune moment the first line fired; then the second, which caused the enemy to fall back in haste and disorder, leaving the ground strewn with their dead and wounded."[6]

In most cases, the two-line formation could not overcome the firepower of defenders armed with the rifle. Defending rifle fire crippled the front line, which then needed the support of the second. Usually the second line was then also defeated. Attackers moved supporting lines closer and closer together in an effort to overcome the strength of the rifle on the defensive, thus creating one of the greatest tactical problems faced by attackers throughout the Civil War, the intermingling of successive lines with one another. Intermingling destroyed formation and order, crippled the command system, and further increased the advantage of the tactical defensive over the offensive.

On the first day at Shiloh, April 6, 1862, the Confederates attacked in a series of successive lines, a formation that broke down in the confusion of battle and difficult terrain. The Confederates deployed their three corps for the Shiloh attack in successive lines, William J. Hardee's Corps in the front line, Braxton Bragg's Corps deploying 500 yards behind Hardee's, and Leonidas Polk's Corps 800 yards behind Bragg's. John C. Breckinridge's Reserve Division "followed closely the third line."[7] This formation would

---

[5]Ibid., XX (pt. 1), 527; XXX (pt. 1), 595.

[6]Ibid., XXV (pt. 1), 956; XXX (pt. 1), 287.

[7]William Preston Johnston, "Albert Sidney Johnston at Shiloh," in *Battles and Leaders of the Civil War*, ed. Robert U. Johnson and Clarence C. Buel (4 vols., reissue, New York, 1956), I, 557; *OR*, X (pt. 1), 386. P. G. T. Beauregard said after the war that Bragg was not deployed in

have been difficult to maintain in open terrain, and in the broken terrain of the Shiloh battlefield it collapsed altogether. General J. Patton Anderson, commanding a brigade in Bragg's Corps, described the Shiloh terrain as "consisting of alternate hills and boggy ravines overgrown with heavy timber and thick underbrush." Anderson said one thicket was "so dense that it was impossible for a company officer to be seen at platoon distance." The Confederate formation broke down, and the attacking lines became intermingled together. General Patrick R. Cleburne, another southern brigade commander, admitted that by the end of the battle, "My brigade was now completely scattered and disorganized. Many of my officers and men continued fighting in the ranks of other commands or on their own responsibility, but not again in any organization which I could control." J. Patton Anderson, whose brigade began the battle in the second line of Bragg's Corps, reported this experience: "Meeting one of General Bragg's aides . . . I remarked to him that from the position originally assigned me (that of a reserve) I had worked my way into the front line. In a few moments he passed again and said: 'No difference; the general desires you to go wherever the fight is thickest.' " The corps lines became so badly intermingled that informal command agreements replaced the corps command system. A few hours after the attack began, Bragg and Polk met and agreed on a temporary command system, which ignored corps organization.[8]

A singular example of the danger of successive lines attacking at too close distance was the experience of the Second Division, Second Corps, at Sharpsburg. This unit, commanded by General John Sedgwick, was one of the finest divisions in the Army of the Potomac. After a morning of bloody and inconclusive attacks against the left of the Confederate line, Sedgwick's Division advanced to the front and deployed its three brigades into close

lines but in "regiments massed in double columns at half distance," a reserve formation that would have been more flexible. G. T. Beauregard, "The Campaign of Shiloh," in *Battles and Leaders*, I, 584. Beauregard's official report, dated April 11, 1862, states that Bragg was "in the same order as the first" line, that is, "deployed in line of battle." *OR*, X (pt. 1), 386. When writing after the war, Beauregard may have been looking at Special Order No. 8, April 3, 1862, which ordered Bragg to form, "if practicable, with regiments in double columns at half distance, . . . with a view to facility of deployment." Ibid., 393. The same orders said Bragg was to form 1,000 yards behind Hardee. Bragg reported that he deployed 800 yards behind Hardee. Ibid., 393, 464.

[8]*OR*, X (pt. 1), 496, 498, 584, 497, 408, 465–66; Johnston, "Albert Sidney Johnston at Shiloh," I, 562. Albert Sidney Johnston's son, writing after the war to defend his father's reputation, blamed the attack formation on Johnston's second-in-command, Beauregard. "Unfortunately [Beauregard] changed what seems evidently General Johnston's original purpose of an assault by columns of corps into an array in three parallel lines of battle, which produced extreme confusion when the second and third lines advanced to support the first and intermingled with it." Ibid., 552. The most comprehensive biographer of Johnston believes that as army commander he "must bear the ultimate responsibility" for accepting the battle plan. Charles P. Roland, *Albert Sidney Johnston: Soldier of Three Republics* (Austin, 1964), 323.

successive lines. The front-line brigade was commanded by General Willis A. Gorman and was followed by the brigade of General N. J. T. Dana. Dana said he was ordered to remain only seventy-five yards behind Gorman, and when the division came under fire Dana's Brigade was less than seventy-five yards from Gorman.[9] The Philadelphia Brigade, commanded by General Oliver O. Howard, was about "60 to 70 paces" behind Dana's. The division met no opposition until it entered the West Woods. Sedgwick's men were then suddenly struck by fire from three sides, heaviest on the left and in front. "In less time than it takes to tell it," wrote Francis Palfrey, "the ground was strewn with the bodies of the dead and wounded, while the unwounded were moving off rapidly to the north."[10] Sedgwick's lines were in such close order that the division was virtually defenseless. Samuel S. Sumner, a son and staff officer of Edwin V. Sumner, commander of the Second Corps at Sharpsburg, wrote after the war: "In moving forward, the second and third lines of Sedgwick's Division gradually closed on the first line. It was the duty of brigade commanders to preserve proper intervals [distances], but there is always confusion in such movements when under fire, and the natural instinct of the men is to close together." Oliver O. Howard recalled: "Our three lines, each in two ranks, were so near together that a rifle bullet would often cross them all and disable five or six men at a time." Colonel Joshua T. Owen of the Sixty-ninth Pennsylvania thought "the disaster" to the Philadelphia Brigade probably occurred because the brigade was "placed in too great proximity to the other two lines, and thus, while intended to act as a reserve, [was] subjected to as deadly a fire as those it was intended to support." Sedgwick's Division suffered 2,210 casualties at Sharpsburg, most of them in the short time that the division was under fire in the West Woods.[11]

At Murfreesboro the Confederates attempted to attack in successive lines through difficult cedar brake terrain. As had happened at Shiloh, the rough terrain broke up their close-ordered formations. "All parts of our line had to pass in their progress over ground of the roughest character," wrote Braxton Bragg after the battle, "covered with huge stones and studded with the densest growth of cedar, the branches reaching to the ground and forming an almost impassable brake." J. Patton Anderson reported: "It was impossible to preserve a regular and continuous line through such obstacles as the fallen and standing cedars presented."[12]

Bragg determined to attack through this difficult terrain in successive lines

---

[9]*OR*, XIX (pt. 1), 319. The lines were twenty-five to fifty yards distant, at various places. Ibid., 311, 313, 315, 317.

[10]Ibid., 305; Francis Palfrey, *The Antietam and Fredericksburg* (New York, 1897), 87.

[11]Samuel S. Sumner, "The Antietam Campaign," in *Papers of the Military Historical Society of Massachusetts* (14 vols., Boston, 1913), XIV, 11; Oliver O. Howard, *Autobiography of Oliver Otis Howard* (2 vols., New York, 1907), I, 296; *OR*, XIX (pt. 1), 319, 193.

[12]*OR*, XX (pt. 1), 665, 764.

and ordered his attacking corps to form in two lines, 800 to 1,000 yards apart. The divisions in the second line were expected to advance simultaneously with those in front and maintain "a distance of a few hundred yards." Although the Federal right was quickly broken in by Bragg's attack, the rough terrain and increasing Union resistance disordered Bragg's successive-lines formation. As had happened at Shiloh, it was not long before the successive lines were mingled together. "Although my division was originally placed in the second line as a supporting force," said General Benjamin F. Cheatham of Polk's Corps, "it was not long before it was all under fire and hotly engaged with the enemy." General Bushrod Johnson, a brigade commander at Murfreesboro, said that by the end of the day's attack, "The lines were broken and men of different regiments, brigades, and divisions were scattered all over the fields." Bragg himself admitted that by the early afternoon the Confederate lines had "become almost blended."[13]

Bragg complicated his tactical problems at Murfreesboro by incorporating a wheeling movement into his grand tactical plan. His troops were deployed from left to right: Hardee's Corps, Polk's Corps, Breckinridge's Division. Hardee and Polk were expected to execute a wheeling attack, Polk's right pivoting on Breckinridge's left, while attacking in successive lines through difficult terrain. Hardee deployed General J. P. McCown's Division in his front line and General Patrick R. Cleburne's Division about 400 or 500 yards behind McCown's. Hardee's Corps advanced, attempting to pivot as ordered on Polk's left. McCown moved farther and farther to his left, until his division's right flank became exposed and a gap was opened between McCown's right and Polk's left. Cleburne reported afterward: "McCown's line had unaccountably disappeared from my front." Cleburne advanced rapidly from his second-line position and entered the interval between McCown and Polk. Cleburne's advance was much more rapid than McCown's, and Cleburne also outdistanced Polk's two divisions on his right. When Cheatham's Division of Polk's Corps did not move forward with Cleburne's right, Hardee detached General S. A. M. Wood's Brigade to fill the interval between Cleburne and Polk. Bragg's wheeling plan had completely broken down. Cleburne, a fine division commander, admitted that his pursuit of the Federals was "rapid, but not very orderly."[14]

In the January 2, 1863, attack at Murfreesboro, the Confederates again used a close-ordered, successive-lines formation. Bragg ordered General John C. Breckinridge to form his division in two lines to assault the Federal left.[15] The front line consisted of General Roger W. Hanson's Brigade on the left and General Gideon J. Pillow's Brigade on the right. The second line was

---

[13]Ibid., 672, 723, 724, 708, 879, 665.
[14]Ibid., 664, 686, 844, 774, 775, 845.
[15]Ibid., 785.

Colonel Randall L. Gibson's Brigade on the left and General William Preston's Brigade on the right. The two lines, which were probably about 200 yards apart,[16] became intermingled in the course of the charge, hurting Breckinridge's effectiveness. Bragg criticized Breckinridge's deployment: "Our second line was so close to the first as to receive the enemy's fire, and, returning it, took their friends in rear." Colonel Robert P. Trabue, who advanced in the first line, said that the division's retreat was "not in the best order, resulting mainly from the confusion consequent upon the too early advance of the second line into the ground already too much crowded by the first." Preston, whose brigade was in the second line, reported: "Our lines, originally very close in the order of advance, were commingled near the [Stone's] river, and this new [Federal] fire from an overwhelming force from the opposite banks of the stream threw them into disorder."[17]

The Confederates had a similar experience when they used successive lines in the famous attack of Stonewall Jackson's Corps against the Eleventh Corps at Chancellorsville, May 2, 1863. Jackson struck the Federals with three divisions, formed in very close order. General Robert E. Rodes commanded Jackson's front-line division in this attack. General R. E. Colston commanded the next division, which formed about 150 yards to the rear of Rodes. The third division was General A. P. Hill's, which was still deploying when Jackson launched his attack.[18] Once the assault began, the first two divisions soon became intermingled. Rodes reported that by the time his division reached the ridge at Melzi Chancellor's, Colston's men were crossing the Federal works with his own men, and that "from this time until the close of the engagement the two divisions were mingled together in inextricable confusion." Colonel Daniel H. Christie, commanding the Twenty-third North Carolina in Rodes's front line, complained about the close successive-lines formation in his report on Chancellorsville. "It was unfortunate that the supporting line was so close, or not better managed," said Christie. "When

---

[16]Gibson said he was 150 yards behind Hanson. *OR*, XX (pt. 1), 796, 798. Preston said he was 200 yards from Pillow. Ibid., 812. Breckinridge agreed with Preston that the two lines were 200 yards apart. Ibid., 785. Pillow thought that the distance was greater than 200 yards; in two reports, he gave two different distances. Ibid., 808, 810.

[17]*OR*, XX (pt. 1), 668, 827, 813. The Confederate reports agreed that the close successive lines became intermingled. They did not agree on the effect of the intermingling. Breckinridge minimized the effect, reporting that "the two lines had mingled into one, the only practical inconvenience of which was that at several points the ranks were deeper than is allowed by a proper military formation." Ibid., 786. Pillow emphasized the intermingling, complaining that the second line "commingled" with his and blaming much of the failure on the supporting line. Ibid., 810–11.

[18]Rodes said that Colston formed only 100 yards in his rear. *OR*, XXV (pt. 1), 940. Colston said he was 200 yards from Rodes. Ibid., 1004. John Bigelow considered this and other evidence and concluded that the distance was probably about 150 yards. John Bigelow, *The Campaign of Chancellorsville* (New Haven, 1910), 291n.

we first engaged the enemy, this line rushed forward and mingled with the first before there was the least necessity for their assistance. The consequence was, that no officer could handle a distinct command without halting and reforming." Colston reported that as early as fifteen minutes into the attack, his men "were already within a few steps of the first line, and in some places mixed up with them."[19] Colston's engineer officer, Lieutenant Oscar Heinrichs, thought this rapid intermingling of the two divisions took place because of the "eagerness of the men" and because Jackson had "ordered the attack to be vigorous." As at Shiloh, the terrain was so difficult that close successive lines could not move through it without intermingling. Lieutenant Colonel Hamilton A. Brown described the Wilderness terrain through which Jackson's men charged as "a densely thick woods, with undergrowth of scrubby oak, mixed with pine, myrtle, briers, bamboo, and other obstacles to impede the progress of an inhabitant of the wilderness."[20]

By the end of the fighting on May 2, the lines along Jackson's front were completely intermingled. After darkness fell, Henry Kyd Douglas of Jackson's staff joined A. P. Hill at Hill's request and found him "busy getting his division into position to take the place of Rodes and Colston, whose divisions had become intermixed in the confusion of the charge and of the darkness." Colston reported the situation at the end of the evening's fighting: "Owing to the very difficult and tangled nature of the ground over which the troops had advanced, and the mingling of the first and second lines of battle, the formation of the troops had become very much confused, and different regiments, brigades, and divisions were mixed up together." Years after the war, Colston answered the criticism that Jackson's Corps should have accomplished more on the evening of May 2 and referred to the intermingled condition of Jackson's men. "Brigades, regiments, and companies had become so mixed that they could not be handled," explained Colston, "besides which the darkness of evening was so intensified by the shade of the dense woods that nothing could be seen a few yards off. The halt at that time was not a mistake, but a necessity."[21]

At Chickamauga the Confederates again used close successive lines and again experienced the same difficulties. In the first day's fighting, September 10, 1863, General John C. Brown's Brigade was put into battle so closely behind General Henry D. Clayton's Brigade that both brigades came under the same fire. Brown said that he was "so near to Clayton's line that many of

---

[19]*OR*, XXV (pt. 1), 941, 992, 1004. See also ibid., 1032. In his report, Colston said proudly that his men had "passed repeatedly through and beyond the first line" on both May 2 and 3. Ibid., 1008.

[20]Ibid., 1009, 1032.

[21]Henry Kyd Douglas, *I Rode With Stonewall* (Chapel Hill, 1940), 221; *OR*, XXV (pt. 1), 1004–05; R. E. Colston, "Lee's Knowledge of Hooker's Movements," in *Battles and Leaders*, III, 233.

my command were wounded and a few killed before I could return the fire."[22] In the famous assault of Longstreet's Wing on September 20, some intermingling occurred during the Confederate breakthrough and pursuit. In General T. C. Hindman's Division, J. Patton Anderson's Brigade formed a few hundred yards behind the front-line brigade of General Z. C. Deas. During the attack, Anderson's Brigade advanced into Deas's line and became intermingled with some of Deas's units. On another part of the field, Colonel Van H. Manning of the Third Arkansas said his regiment advanced "immediately in rear of another line of troops" on September 20. Manning complained about the successive-line formation: "The distance and speed with which we were required to move before engaging the enemy, together with the annoyance and confusion consequent upon our moving so close in rear of other troops, threw us into battle under serious disadvantages. The fatigue of the men and the deranged condition of the line are some of the prominent evils invariably and unavoidably experienced under the above circumstances."[23]

Battlefield experience taught some subordinate commanders the command and tactical problems created by the use of close successive-line formations. Certain officers tried to anticipate these problems by working out temporary command arrangements before an attack. At Murfreesboro, for example, General Jones M. Withers commanded a front-line division, which was to be followed at 500 to 800 yards by General Benjamin F. Cheatham's Division. Withers had fought at Shiloh, and Cheatham had been at Shiloh and Perryville, so both men had seen successive lines become intermingled and the command system break down. They agreed, before the Confederate advance began, that Cheatham would direct the attack on the left of their front, including Withers's two left brigades, and that Withers would direct the right, including Cheatham's two right brigades.[24]

The alternative to the line formation was the column. Tactical theory before the Civil War was critical of heavy columns but endorsed light columns. Light columns using storm tactics had been successful in the Mexican War and were attempted in the Civil War as early as the Second Battle of Fredericksburg, May 3, 1863. In this action, units of the Sixth Corps assaulted the same front where Federal divisions, attacking in successive lines, had been broken apart on December 13, 1862. General John Newton, commanding the Third Division, Sixth Corps, devised an assault plan that was approved by his corps commander, John Sedgwick. Newton proposed to strike the Confederates with two storming columns, placed at an interval

---

[22]*OR*, XXX (pt. 2), 370.
[23]Ibid., 339, 341, 513.
[24]Ibid., XX (pt. 1), 754. Also see ibid., 710, 724.

great enough that the Confederates would not be able to shift troops to defend both points. The left column consisted of two regiments supported by two others. Newton's two columns were supported by a line formation consisting of one regiment deployed as skirmishers, followed by three other regiments deployed in line. Newton was supported on his left by three similar storming columns from the division of General Albion P. Howe. General Frank Wheaton, a brigade commander in Newton's Division, was ordered to reform all the storming troops after they carried Marye's Heights, putting them into a two-line formation.[25] The columns and supporting line advanced at "double quick time" without firing, were temporarily checked, but eventually carried the Confederate position.[26] The columns succeeded, but Sedgwick suffered severe losses. General Abner Doubleday, in an account written after the war, said that the Sixth Corps lost almost a thousand men in five minutes and quoted Newton as saying that if the Confederates had had another hundred men their line could not have been carried.[27]

At about the same time in the western theater, some Federal brigades made use of both small storming parties and column formations during the May 22 assault on Vicksburg.[28] Some units in each of the three assaulting corps on May 22 used column formations.[29] The Union assaults were repulsed all along the line. No Federal units, regardless of formation, won any significant successes in the May 22 assault.

The column formation was intended to throw maximum force for penetration against a narrow front. Longstreet used this principle in his September 20, 1863, attack at Chickamauga. His brigades and divisions were deployed in lines, arranged on so narrow a front as to achieve the effect of one large column striking the center of the Union line. Longstreet deployed three of his divisions—General T. C. Hindman's, General Bushrod Johnson's, and General A. P. Stewart's—on narrow, two-brigade fronts. In the rear of Bushrod Johnson's Division were formed five brigades (representing two divisions under General John Bell Hood) in a column of brigades with only a distance of one hundred paces between brigades. General William Preston's

---

[25]Abner Doubleday, *Chancellorsville and Gettysburg* (New York, 1882), 57; Huntington W. Jackson, "Sedgwick at Fredericksburg and Salem Heights," in *Battles and Leaders*, III, 227, 228; *OR*, XXV (pt. 1), 559, 599, 617.

[26]*OR*, XXV (pt. 1), 559; Jackson, "Sedgwick," III, 228–29.

[27]Doubleday, *Chancellorsville and Gettysburg*, 58–59. The losses of the Sixth Corps at Second Fredericksburg are difficult to determine because the official reports did not separate the casualties at Second Fredericksburg from those suffered later at Salem Church and Banks's Ford. *OR*, XXV (pt. 1), 188.

[28]*OR*, XXIV (pt. 2), 257, 261, 264, 269, 272–73.

[29]Ibid., 232, 234, 282, 300.

Division, used as a reserve by Longstreet, was also formed on a two-brigade front.[30]

In one of the most famous attacks of the war, Longstreet's Wing struck through the center of Rosecrans's line, driving the Union center and right from the battlefield. Bushrod Johnson credited much of the Confederate success to the depth of Longstreet's formation. "The unusual depth of our columns of attack in this part of the field," reported Johnson, "and the force and power with which it was thrown upon the enemy's line, had now completely broken and routed their center and cast the shattered fragments to the right and left."[31] Federal reports on Chickamauga often remarked about the depth of Longstreet's formation. Colonel John T. Wilder, whose brigade of mounted infantry was in reserve when Longstreet's assault broke through Rosecrans's line, reported: "As the troops on my left moved from their position still farther to the left, a column of rebels, five lines deep, assaulted them, breaking and dispersing the troops at my left, and driving them by weight of numbers in great confusion into the woods in their rear."[32] The Confederate breakthrough was achieved, however, not so much by choice of formation as by good fortune. In the most famous case of its kind during the war, General Thomas J. Wood's Division pulled out of its place in the Federal line just as Longstreet struck, opening a gap into which Longstreet's men advanced.

During the Knoxville campaign the Confederates attempted an unsuccessful column assault against Fort Sanders, November 29, 1863. The Southerners advanced in two columns against the northwest angle of Fort Sanders. The left column was made up of General William T. Wofford's Brigade, and the right column was led by General Benjamin G. Humphrey's Brigade, followed by three regiments of General Goode Bryan's Brigade, all in column of regiments. General Lafayette McLaws, who commanded the division to which these brigades belonged, said he decided on the two-column formation because of the broken terrain and felled timber that lay between the two leading brigades. McLaws also hoped that the friendly rivalry between the Georgians of Wofford's Brigade and the Mississippians of Humphreys's Brigade would promote élan in both columns.[33] Columns had reduced fronts and reduced firepower and therefore often relied on storm tactics. The Con-

---

[30]Ibid., XXX (pt. 2), 288, 303, 363, 456, 457; James Longstreet, *From Manassas to Appomattox: Memoirs of the Civil War in America*, ed. James I. Robertson, Jr. (reissue, Bloomington, 1960), 440; E. Porter Alexander, *Military Memoirs of a Confederate* (reissue, Bloomington, 1962), 459. The front of Bushrod Johnson's Division was two regiments wider than two brigades. *OR*, XXX (pt. 2), 456, 498, 357, 415.

[31]*OR*, XXX (pt. 2), 458.

[32]Ibid., (pt. 1), 448.

[33]Longstreet, *From Manassas to Appomattox*, 503; Orlando M. Poe, "The Defense of Knoxville," in *Battles and Leaders*, III, 741; *OR*, XXXI (pt. 1), 486, 487.

federates were ordered to advance against Fort Sanders with fixed bayonets, moving quietly until they entered the Federal works, when they were to raise a shout. The attack orders declared: "The men should be urged to the assault with a determination to succeed."[34] The columns were slowed by wire entanglements and were stopped by the icy, steep slope of the Fort's parapet. The assault failed.[35]

The best-known Federal column assault of the war was led by Colonel Emory Upton at Spotsylvania Court House, May 10, 1864. Upton, a West Point graduate of 1861, had become disgusted with the conduct of the war and the tactics he had seen his superiors and other officers use.[36] He had seen storm tactics succeed against entrenchments in the small action at Rappahannock Station, November 7, 1863.[37] At Spotsylvania Court House, Upton was given command of twelve regiments with which he was to assault an angle in the well-entrenched Confederate line, near the Scott house. Upton formed the twelve regiments in a column with a three-regiment front, four regiments deep.[38] The three regiments at the head of the column—the 121st New York, the Ninety-sixth Pennsylvania, and the Fifth Maine—all had been at Rappahannock Station; the 121st New York had been Upton's regiment.[39] Of the twelve regiments in Upton's column, all but the Fifth Vermont had been either at Second Fredericksburg or Rappahannock Station. Two regiments, the Sixth Maine and Fifth Wisconsin, had been in both actions.[40]

As in these earlier actions, Upton's column used storm tactics at Spotsylvania Court House. "The pieces of the first line were loaded and capped," said Upton; "those of the other lines were loaded but not capped; bayonets were fixed." The column charged from a pine woods across about 200 yards of open ground to the Confederate entrenchments. "Through a terrible front and flank fire the column advanced, quickly gaining the parapet," Upton reported. After a brief hand-to-hand and bayonet fight, the column carried the first line of works. "Pressing forward and expanding to the right and left, the second line of intrenchments, its line of battle, and the battery fell into our

---

[34]*OR*, XXXI (pt. 1), 461, 486, 487.

[35]Poe, "Defense of Knoxville," III, 743. McLaws emphasized "the slipperiness of the parapet." *OR*, XXXI (pt. 1), 491. The causes of the Confederate failure at Fort Sanders became controversial. Poe, "Defense of Knoxville," III, 744. Longstreet charged McLaws with improper preparations for the assault, but McLaws was eventually exonerated. *OR*, XXXI (pt. 1), 501–06.

[36]George W. Cullum, ed., *Biographical Registrar of the Officers and Graduates of the United States Military Academy, at West Point* (2 vols., New York, 1868), II, 525; Peter S. Michie, *The Life and Letters of Emory Upton* (New York, 1885), 108, 109.

[37]Michie, *Emory Upton*, 83–86; *OR*, XXIX (pt. 1), 575, 576, 586, 588, 589, 592, 593; Martin T. McMahon, "From Gettysburg to the Coming of Grant," in *Battles and Leaders*, IV, 85–87.

[38]*OR*, XXXVI (pt. 1), 660–61, 667.

[39]Ibid., XXIX (pt. 1), 586, 592–95.

[40]Ibid., XXV (pt. 1), 559; XXIX (pt. 1), 586.

hands," Upton said. "The column of assault had accomplished its task." Upton had broken the Confederate line and captured over 1,000 prisoners.[41]

Upton was eventually forced to withdraw when General Gershom Mott's Division failed to come to his support. The Confederate defenders were able to recover and contain Upton's breakthrough on three sides.[42] The attack had not begun until 6 p.m. and at that late an hour the Federals could not arrange for other troops to support Upton. Years after the war, Andrew A. Humphreys, chief of staff of the Army of the Potomac at Spotsylvania, wrote: "Had Mott joined [Upton], the two pressing forward, taking the enemy on the right and left in flank and rear, and receiving further reinforcements from the Sixth Corps as they progressed, the probabilities were that we should have gained possession of Lee's intrenchments."[43]

The success of Upton's column on May 10 led to the adoption of a dense column formation by the entire Second Corps in the May 12 attack on the Mule Shoe salient. For this assault, General Winfield S. Hancock formed the Second Corps about 1,000 yards from the Mule Shoe salient. General Francis C. Barlow formed his division in columns of regiments, each regiment forming a double column on the center. The other three divisions were deployed in lines but with intervals and distances so small that the Second Corps was "almost a solid rectangular mass of nearly 20,000 men." General David B. Birney's Division formed on Barlow's right in two lines that were only a few paces apart. Generals John Gibbon and Gershom Mott formed their divisions in the rear of Barlow's and Birney's divisions, in two close-order lines. Barlow formed even his skirmishers in close order, deploying the Sixty-sixth New York with only one or two paces between each man and directing this skirmish line to stay within 30 yards of the front of the attacking column.[44]

Hancock's attack used storm tactics, advancing at "quick time" for several hundred yards, with Barlow's "heavy column marching over the enemy's pickets without firing a shot." About halfway to the salient, the column broke into "double quick time" and a cheer, and Hancock's men "rolled like an irresistible wave into the enemy's works, tearing away what abatis there was in front of the intrenchments with their hands and carrying the line at all points in a few moments, although it was desperately defended." General John R. Brooke, who commanded one of Barlow's brigades, said that "the

---

[41]Ibid., XXXVI (pt. 1), 667, 668.

[42]Ibid., 490, 668, 673; E. M. Law, "From the Wilderness to Cold Harbor," in *Battles and Leaders*, IV, 129.

[43]*OR*, XXXVI (pt. 1), 667–68; Andrew A. Humphreys, *The Virginia Campaign of '64 and '65* (New York, 1883), 87.

[44]*OR*, XXXVI (pt. 1), 335, 358, 409–10, 421. Gibbon's Division, which consisted of three brigades, was in reserve. Ibid., 335. However, two of these brigades "were almost immediately started in support" and helped carry the Confederate line, and the third brigade "was soon after ordered up." Ibid., 431.

division moved forward steadily in one immense mass" and that his men did not fire until they had mounted the Confederate works. Brooke praised Barlow's column formation, claiming that "nothing but the formation of our attack and the desperate valor of our troops could have carried the point." Hancock's May 12 assault broke the main Confederate line at Spotsylvania, and Hancock claimed the capture of nearly 4,000 prisoners, including two general officers, twenty pieces of artillery, and over thirty colors. Hancock, however, could do no more because his corps was disorganized and, when further pursuit was attempted, it was discovered that the Confederates had constructed "a second formidable line of earth-works" across Hancock's front.[45]

A few less famous column assaults were attempted during the Virginia campaign. On the same day as Upton's assault, the First Brigade, Third Division, Second Corps, also deployed in a column of regiments for an assault on another part of the Confederate lines at Spotsylvania. For the June 1 assault at Cold Harbor, Upton used a formation similar to the one he had used on May 10 at Spotsylvania. Upton formed his brigade on June 1 in four lines. The first three lines were taken up by the Second Connecticut Heavy Artillery, a new and therefore large regiment, deployed in column by battalion. The fourth line consisted of Upton's four other regiments. Choice of formation made little difference in the hopeless offensives at Cold Harbor; there Upton's Brigade fared no better than the other Union brigades. During the June 3 assault at Cold Harbor, two brigades of the Eighteenth Corps formed two close columns by divisions and advanced into the heavy defending rifle and artillery fire. The first column was thrown back onto the head of the second column, and neither brigade was any more successful than any of the other units along the Federal front.[46]

Column assaults also were attempted about the same time in the western theater, on June 27, 1864, at Kennesaw Mountain. For the Kennesaw Mountain attack, Oliver O. Howard, commanding the Fourth Corps, Army of the Cumberland, formed several of his brigades in close columns. The three brigades of General John Newton's Division were each formed in close columns of regimental divisions (half a regiment as a front, the other half immediately behind it). General Charles G. Harker's column formed on Newton's right. General George D. Wagner's column formed on Harker's left at a 100-yard interval. General Nathan Kimball's column was in close support of Wagner, in echelon to the left rear of his column.[47] The front of

---

[45]Ibid., 335, 336, 358, 410.

[46]Ibid., 470, 474, 671, 1012–13.

[47]Ibid., XXXVIII (pt. 1), 199, 295, 304, 319, 326, 329, 335, 355, 361, 364. The journal of the Fourth Corps kept by Lieutenant Colonel Joseph S. Fullerton stated that Harker's Brigade was formed in two columns, each with division front. Ibid., 877. The published official reports did not bear this out. Ibid., 199, 295, 355, 361, 364.

Newton's columns was well covered by skirmishers,[48] and Newton's columns were to be followed by two brigades from General David S. Stanley's Division, both formed in columns of regiments.[49] Howard explained after the war why he chose this column formation. "That formation seemed best for the situation," he said, "first, to keep the men concealed as well as possible beforehand and during the first third of the distance, the ground being favorable for this; second, to make as narrow a front as he [Newton] could, so as to make a sudden rush with numbers over their works." After Newton's Division attacked without success, two brigades of the division of General Jefferson C. Davis, both in columns, also attempted an assault.[50] None of these charges was successful.

Some column assaults were made late in the war during the Petersburg campaign. The unsuccessful Confederate attack against Fort Stedman, March 25, 1865, was made in three columns, preceded by storming parties. In the final assault on Petersburg, April 2, 1865, the brigades of both General Horatio G. Wright's Sixth Corps and General John Parke's Ninth Corps were deployed in column formations. Some brigades deployed in columns of regiments, at close distances.[51] The intention was to have columns with regimental fronts, but regiments varied greatly in numbers in the later campaigns of the war. In many brigades, the lines of a column were determined by numbers and not units, more than one regiment being necessary to give a line a regimental front.[52] Once these columns broke through the Confederate defenses, they were ready to redeploy into lines to exploit their success. These assaults were successful, but the Federal victory on April 2, 1865, must be attributed much less to the choice of formation than to the weak condition of the Army of Northern Virginia in the last week of the eastern war.

Column formations were no more able to overcome the defensive firepower of the rifle than line formations. Infantry advancing in close columns, often relying on the bayonet and storm tactics, offered a vulnerable target to defending rifle and artillery fire. At least one Federal brigade commander at Chickamauga thought Longstreet's deep formation was vulnerable. "The enemy in front was terribly punished as he came up," wrote Colonel John A. Martin. "Our men fired coolly from behind the barricade with terrible effect, the closed ranks and heavy columns of the enemy making their loss very heavy." Nelson A. Miles, who commanded one of Barlow's brigades in the assault on the Mule Shoe salient, said after the war that Barlow's columns

[48]Ibid., 295, 335, 348, 371.

[49]Ibid., 224, 233, 887.

[50]Howard, *Autobiography*, I, 582; *OR*, XXXVIII (pt. 1), 633, 703, 729.

[51]*OR*, XLVI (pt. 1), 317, 322, 332, 902, 954, 963, 968, 1016, 1054, 1057, 1059, 1061, 1067, 1068.

[52]Ibid., 902, 910, 927, 941, 975, 981, 992, 1047.

had presented the Confederate defenders a sizable target. "There were no stray shots or wild shooting at so large a living target," said Miles. Columns could have as much difficulty crossing rough terrain as lines. Barlow admitted after the war that his division, moving in column against the Mule Shoe salient, had been fortunate to find the terrain open. "That we were in that solid formation which was practically irresistible was of course designed," he said, "but that such a formation was practicable was because at the last minute it was found that the nature of the ground permitted it."[53]

The columns used late in the war often had great depth and reduced fronts because of the Civil War organizational system. As regiments lost strength during the war, new regiments were created and added to existing brigades, rather than building up existing regiments. When the three brigades of Newton's Division formed for the Kennesaw Mountain assault in June 1864, with regimental-division front, that front was smaller than it would have been during an earlier campaign. Adding more regiments to an existing brigade also made brigade columns of regiments much deeper.[54] Years after the war, Arthur L. Wagner quoted Luther P. Bradley, who succeeded to the command of one of the brigade columns at Kennesaw Mountain, as saying that the column of regiments in column of divisions was "about the worst possible" choice of formation. Wagner quoted another of the brigade commanders, Nathan Kimball, as saying that "such formations have only the *appearance* of strength, but are really suicidal in their weakness." Jacob D. Cox was critical of the double-column formation used at Kennesaw Mountain, and he criticized the tactical manuals for touting the formation. "Our book of tactics," said Cox, "copying from the French, had taught the regimental column of divisions of two companies, 'doubled on the centre,' was *par excellence* the column of attack."[55]

Columns were often just as unwieldy as lines. Columns, like successive lines, could become intermingled and lose formation. The two Confederate columns sent against Fort Sanders, November 29, 1863, ran together and became intermingled. The Confederate artillerist E. Porter Alexander wrote: "The two columns were soon found to have converged in the darkness too much, and being already deep columns, one of four lines and one of five, they simply coalesced in the darkness into a mass whose officers could no longer separate or distinguish their own men."[56] During Hancock's assault

---

[53]Ibid., XXX (pt. 1), 530; extract from a letter from General Nelson A. Miles to General Francis C. Barlow, January 6, 1879, quoted in Francis C. Barlow, "Capture of the Salient, May 12, 1864," in *Papers of the Military Historical Society of Massachusetts*, IV, 261, 256.

[54]On the influence of the organization system on the formation of Newton's Division at Kennesaw Mountain, see Arthur L. Wagner, *Organization and Tactics* (Kansas City, 1894), 99–100.

[55]Ibid., 100n; Jacob D. Cox, *Atlanta* (New York, 1882), 129.

[56]Alexander, *Military Memoirs*, 488. See also Poe, "Defense of Knoxville," III, 749.

on the Mule Shoe salient, there was much intermingling and confusion among the Federal units, particularly in Barlow's Division, which had formed in close column. Fourteen years after the war, Barlow explained that the intention had been to leave "some small space" as the distance between lines and as the interval between brigades, but that these spaces had disappeared as soon as the division advanced, and that it had become one solid mass. Barlow admitted: "It is easy to say now [1879] that the attacking column, especially if formed in mass, is always thrown into confusion, and that its place should be taken by troops moving up deliberately." Andrew A. Humphreys offered this advice in a footnote to his 1883 book on the Virginia campaign: "It is apparent from this experience of Barlow's division, and from that of Upton's command of the 10th of May, that the first line in columns of attack would have been sufficiently massive to have carried the intrenchments, and that it would have been better to have had the second line in some more open formation, following the first carefully at a distance of several hundred yards."[57]

In an effort to combine the advantages of both line and column formations, commanders sometimes used the two-line combination formation that Mahan had recommended in which the first line was a deployed line and the second line was held in columns. Casey's *Tactics* provided for brigades to use this formation.[58] The first significant use of this formation was made by Federal troops during the Chattanooga campaign in November 1863. When Union troops occupied Orchard Knob on November 23, General Thomas J. Wood's Division used this formation. Two of his brigades advanced with their first lines deployed in line, their second lines massed in close double columns. General Adolph von Steinwehr's Division, which supported the main advance on Orchard Knob, also came to the front in a combination formation of line and closed columns.[59]

The combination formation of lines and columns was used during the main engagement of the battle, the Federal assault against Missionary Ridge, November 25. The left division of this attack was General Absalom Baird's, which advanced in two lines, the first line a deployed line, the second line in double columns.[60] On Baird's right was Wood's Division, which advanced in apparently the same formation.[61] Philip Sheridan's Division formed on

---

[57]*OR*, XXXVI (pt. 1), 373, 410, 491; Humphreys, *Virginia Campaign*, 94; Barlow, "Capture of the Salient," IV, 249, 253–54, 258.

[58]Casey, *Tactics*, I, 10. Hardee's *Tactics* had no brigade or larger unit tactics.

[59]*OR*, XXXI (pt. 2), 254, 263, 280, 289, 292, 359, 362, 272.

[60]Ibid., 508, 512.

[61]Wood did not discuss his formation in his official report. The best evidence is the report of one of Wood's brigade commanders, General Samuel Beatty, who said Wood ordered him to use the combination line and column formation. Ibid., 301.

Wood's right. Sheridan formed his three brigades by deploying Wagner's and Harker's brigades each in two lines, with Colonel Francis T. Sherman's Brigade on their right in a column with a three-regiment front.[62] The right division of the attack was General Richard W. Johnson's, the only division that formed in the standard two-line formation.[63]

The Federal attempt to combine lines and columns at Missionary Ridge was innovative, but it contributed little to the success of the attack. The Federal reports on Missionary Ridge are full of evidence that the Union troops lost their order in the ascent of the ridge and were out of their formations long before they reached the final Confederate line at the summit.[64] "The ground was so broken that it was impossible to keep a regular line of battle," one Union staff officer wrote. "At times their movements were in a shape like the flight of migratory birds—sometimes in line, sometimes in mass, mostly in V-shaped groups, with the points toward the enemy."[65] The combination of lines and columns was later attempted by John Gibbon's Division at Spotsylvania, May 18, 1864, and at Cold Harbor, June 3, 1864, and by Thomas J. Wood's Division at Rocky Face Ridge during the Atlanta campaign, but the formation cannot be credited with any successes.[66]

No tactical formation—line, column, or combination of the two—was ever able to overcome the advantages of the rifle on the tactical defensive. The rifle fire of defenders and difficult terrain quickly broke up many Civil War assaults. One veteran wrote after the war: "It is astonishing how soon, and by what slight causes, regularity of formation and movement are lost in actual battle. Disintegration begins with the first shot. To the book-soldier all order seems destroyed, months of drill apparently going for nothing in a few minutes. Next after the most powerful factor in derangement—the enemy—come natural obstacles and the inequalities of the ground." William T. Sherman said in his *Memoirs* that he rarely saw in the Civil War formations "as

---

[62]Ibid., 189, 195; Philip H. Sheridan, *Personal Memoirs of P. H. Sheridan* (2 vols., New York, 1888), I, 308. One of Harker's regiments was formed in a double-column order but was soon redeployed into line. *OR*, XXXI (pt. 2), 229–30, 233, 236. Sheridan's organization at Chattanooga was complicated by the existence of demibrigades, which were created because the size of regiments had been so depleted by losses. Sheridan, *Personal Memoirs*, I, 297–98.

[63]*OR*, XXXI (pt. 2), 459. On the Federal formations at Chattanooga, see also ibid., 132, 602; Joseph S. Fullerton, "The Army of the Cumberland at Chattanooga," in *Battles and Leaders*, III, 725.

[64]*OR*, XXXI (pt. 2), 202, 207, 208, 219, 282, 286, 309, 513, 521, 535, 538.

[65]Fullerton, "Army of the Cumberland," III, 725. See also extract from a letter of John A. Martin to Joseph S. Fullerton, November 16, 1886, quoted in ibid., 726n.

[66]*OR*, XXXVI (pt. 1), 344–45, 431, 432–33, 436; Charles H. Porter, "The Battle of Cold Harbor," in *Papers of the Military Historical Society of Massachusetts*, IV, 334–35; *OR*, XXXVIII (pt. 1), 445.

described in European text-books." He said that "lines were deployed
according to tactics," but that the generally rough terrain made loose order
more popular.[67]

---

[67]David L. Thompson, "With Burnside at Antietam," in *Battles and Leaders*, II, 660; William
T. Sherman, *Memoirs of General William T. Sherman By Himself* (2 vols., reissue, Bloomington,
1957), II, 394.

8

Grandeur the South Could Not Afford

The use of skirmishers and loose-order formations became more popular as the Civil War went on. Early in the war it was common to detach two companies of a regiment as skirmishers, a practice that evolved from the earlier organizational system that provided for two fixed companies to do all the skirmishing for a regiment or battalion.[1] The detachment of two companies of a regiment as skirmishers was standard practice in both theaters throughout the war.[2] Additional companies often reinforced the first two on the skirmish line, as enemy resistance or other circumstances required.[3] Brigades and divisions also frequently detached additional skirmishers.[4]

The number of skirmishers being deployed escalated noticeably in late 1862. Both the Confederate and Federal official reports on Fredericksburg, December 13, 1862, where Union attacks against each end of the Confederate line were well covered by skirmishers, are filled with references such as

---

[1]Winfield Scott, *Infantry-Tactics; Or, Rules for the Exercise and Manoeuvres of the United States Infantry* (3 vols., New York, 1846), II, 188–89, assumed that one or two companies would do all the skirmishing for a battalion. Silas Casey, *Infantry Tactics, for the Instruction, Exercise, and Manoeuvers of the Soldier, a Company, Line of Skirmishers, Battalion, Brigade, or Corps D'Armee* (3 vols., New York, 1862), I, endorsement on unnumbered page, 6, 8, 11; II, 3–4, originally provided for two fixed companies to do all the skirmishing for a battalion, but this system was suspended by the War Department.

[2]U.S. War Dept., *The War of the Rebellion: A Compilation of the Official Records of the Union and Confederate Armies* (128 vols., Washington, 1880–1901), Series 1, III, 81, 287; XI (pt. 1), 476, 590, 598 (hereinafter cited as *OR;* all references are to Series 1); Abner Doubleday Journal, August 28, 1862 (photostatic copy), Manassas National Battlefield Park; *OR*, XVI (pt. 1), 1085, 1086; XIX (pt. 1), 473; XX (pt. 1), 386, 830; XXI, 280, 595; XXIV (pt. 1), 654, 745; (pt. 2), 242, 244; XXV (pt. 1), 299, 909; XXVII (pt. 1), 309; XXIX (pt. 1), 285; XXX (pt. 1), 298; XXXI (pt. 2), 523; XXXVI (pt. 1), 666, 1068; XLVI (pt. 1), 1004, 1199.

[3]*OR*, XXIV (pt. 2), 23, 24; XLVI (pt. 1), 315, 246–47.

[4]Ibid., XIX (pt. 1), 1007; XXI, 473; XXIV (pt. 2), 132; XXV (pt. 1), 745, 871; XXVII (pt. 1), 543, 547–48; (pt. 2), 630; XXXIV (pt. 1), 605; XXXVIII (pt. 2), 115, 203, 216.

"strong lines of skirmishers," "skirmishers in heavy line," and "clouds of skirmishers."[5]

By the time of the campaigns of 1864 and 1865, extensive use was made of skirmishers in both theaters. Oliver O. Howard noted in his *Autobiography*: "the skirmishers were more and more used as the [Atlanta] campaign progressed. It was always, when taking the offensive, a wise thing to do, to increase the skirmish line enough to give the men confidence, and then push forward till a waiting enemy—one in a defensive position—was sufficiently revealed to enable the commander to determine his next order. On the defensive, a skirmish line well out, and admirably located, would bother an approaching foe as much as a battle line, and at the same time lose but a few lives." In the Petersburg campaign, entire regiments were sometimes deployed as skirmishers.[6] This tactic was used partly because losses had reduced many regiments to small strengths, but it also was done with the intention that loose order would reduce losses. The Second Brigade, Second Division, Second Corps, fought part of the Battle of the Boydton Plank Road, October 27–28, 1864, by advancing in skirmish order and lost only about 12 percent of its members. In the Federal counterattack at Fort Stedman, one small regiment of a hundred men advanced in skirmishing order and captured between twenty-five and fifty Confederate skirmishers, or most of the skirmishers in their front. This Union regiment lost only one man killed, and its major reported, "This small loss is owing chiefly to the regiment having been deployed to cover so long a line." Late in the war, the superior numbers of the Federals allowed them on some occasions to use loose-order tactics to drive the Confederates with minimal Union losses. At the Oconee River crossing during Sherman's march to the sea, a division under William J. Hardee made an entrenched stand on the east bank of the Oconee. After the war, Oliver O. Howard wrote: "Artillery and infantry fire swept our road. [General Peter J.] Osterhaus, excited by the shots, came to me shaking his head and asking how we would get any further. 'Deploy your skirmishers more and more till there is no reply,' I said." Osterhaus followed this advice, and the Southerners gave way.[7]

The increased use of skirmishers and loose order could reduce casualties but could not resolve all the problems of the tactical offensive. Extensive use of loose-order formations was impossible during the Civil War because of the

---

[5]Ibid., XXI, 219, 222, 227, 291, 360, 633, 646. See also Darius N. Couch, "Sumner's 'Right Grand Division,' " in *Battles and Leaders of the Civil War*, ed. Robert U. Johnson and Clarence C. Buel (4 vols., reissue, New York, 1956), III, 111, and J. H. Moore, "With Jackson at Hamilton's Crossing," ibid., III, 139.

[6]Oliver O. Howard, *Autobiography of Oliver Otis Howard* (2 vols., New York, 1907), I, 548; *OR*, XLII (pt. 1), 295, 296, 297, 298, 330, 331, 393, 561, 564, 568, 575, 587; XLVI (pt. 1), 876.

[7]*OR*, XLII (pt. 1), 154, 319, 320; XLVI (pt. 1), 323, 343; Oliver O. Howard, "Sherman's Advance from Atlanta," in *Battles and Leaders*, IV, 665.

problems of communication and control of armies so large. Using the numbers of Grant's and Lee's forces as they began the Wilderness campaign, Alexander S. Webb calculated that Grant's men "properly disposed for battle, would have covered a front of 21 miles, two ranks deep, with one-third of them in reserve," while Lee's men in a similar deployment would have had a front of twelve miles. With such numbers and fronts, loose-order deployment was impossible. Small units could deploy in loose order, but officers found their men more difficult to control when in skirmish order. William T. Sherman said in his *Memoirs*: "When a regiment is deployed as skirmishers, and crosses an open field or woods, under heavy fire, if each man runs forward from tree to tree, or stump to stump, and yet preserves a good general alignment, it gives great confidence to the men themselves, for they always keep their eyes well to the right and left, and watch their comrades; but when some few hold back, stick too close or too long to a comfortable log, it often stops the line and defeats the whole object."[8]

The greatest single innovation made in tactical theory in the 1850s to compensate attackers for the firepower of the rifle was to increase step rates. Hardee's and Casey's *Tactics* provided for a "double quick time" of 165 steps per minute, a rate that was used during the Civil War, beginning with the earliest major battles in both theaters.[9] The "double quick" rate was used in many famous charges of the war, such as the Confederate charge that broke through the Union lines at Gaines's Mill and the charge of Hancock's Second Corps at Spotsylvania, May 12, 1864.[10]

The more rapid step rates did not compensate attackers for the losses that the rifle could inflict on them while they advanced in close order. The "double quick time" and the "run," especially over extended distances, could tire attackers. Officers mentioned this problem in their official reports, sometimes as an excuse for failure, but it was often a serious problem. Major George H. Hildt said the Thirtieth Ohio became "utterly exhausted" when it crossed a plowed field at Sharpsburg at "double quick time." When the Fifth Alabama came into battle on July 1, 1863, at Gettysburg by advancing "frequently at a run" across mixed terrain, many of its soldiers fainted from exhaustion. After the second day of fighting at Gettysburg, an officer of the Fifty-ninth Georgia, in Hood's Division, reported: "We were repulsed the first charge, because the men were completely exhausted when they made it,

---

[8]Alexander S. Webb, "Through the Wilderness," in *Battles and Leaders*, IV, 152; William T. Sherman, *Memoirs of General William T. Sherman By Himself* (2 vols., reissue, Bloomington, 1957), II, 395.

[9]William J. Hardee, *Rifle and Light Infantry Tactics; for the Exercise and Manoeuvres of Troops when acting as Light Infantry or Riflemen* (2 vols., Philadelphia, 1855), I, 26; Casey, *Tactics*, I, 32. For some early examples of the "double quick time" rate, see *OR*, II, 384, 528; III, 83, 292.

[10]E. M. Law, "On the Confederate Right at Gaines's Mill," in *Battles and Leaders*, II, 363; *OR*, XXXVI (pt. 1), 335, 421.

having double-quicked a distance of some 400 yards, under a severe shelling and a scorching sun."[11]

Rapid step rates were so tiring that attackers sometimes advanced in a series of successive rushes. The first significant use of this method of assault was made at Fort Donelson, February 15, 1862, by the two-regiment brigade of Colonel Morgan L. Smith.[12] General Lew Wallace, a division commander at Fort Donelson, oversaw the charge in successive rushes by Smith's Brigade. Wallace said afterward that both of Smith's regiments had had what Wallace called "Zouave training." They were trained to fight in loose order. Wallace said: "Indeed, *purpose* with them answered all the ends of alignment elbow to elbow." Wallace wrote of the Fort Donelson attack: "Now on the ground, creeping when the fire was hottest, running when it slackened, they gained ground with astonishing rapidity, and at the same time maintained a fire that was like a sparkling of the earth. For the most part the bullets aimed at them passed over their heads and took effect in the ranks behind them." In another account, Wallace said: "In the outbursts [of Confederate fire] the assailants fell to their hands and knees, and took to crawling, while in the lulls—occasioned by smoke settling so thickly in front of the defenders that they were bothered in taking aim—yards of space were gained by rushes." General Franz Sigel said that the Federals used similar tactics the following month at Pea Ridge. "When well in action," said Sigel of the second day's fighting, "we advanced slowly from position to position, at the same time contracting our line, the infantry following, rising quickly, and as soon as they had reached a new position lying down again."[13]

By the middle of the Civil War, many soldiers understood the advantages of the tactical defensive. In his official report on the Chancellorsville campaign, General G. K. Warren, chief of topographical engineers of the Army of the Potomac, described Lee's entrenched works along the Rappahannock River in the spring of 1863 and said it was "a conviction in the mind of every private in the ranks" that this line could not be carried. When soldiers of the Twentieth Massachusetts helped defeat Pickett's charge at Gettysburg, they were reminded of their own disastrous experience on the tactical offensive at

---

[11]*OR*, XIX (pt. 1), 470; XXVII (pt. 2), 596, 403.

[12]Arthur L. Wagner, *Organization and Tactics* (Kansas City, 1894), 95–97, discussed this tactical development in a work written a generation after the Civil War. He understood the innovative character of this Federal attack at Fort Donelson, but his recounting of it should be read with the account in Lew Wallace's official report, *OR*, VII, 238–39, and two postwar accounts—Lew Wallace, "The Capture of Fort Donelson," in *Battles and Leaders*, I, 423–24, and Lew Wallace, *Lew Wallace, An Autobiography* (2 vols., New York, 1906), I, 417–18. Wagner (*Organization and Tactics*, 96–97) also mentions the attack of Colonel Jacob G. Lauman's Brigade at Fort Donelson, but his depiction of this brigade's action cannot be entirely reconciled with the regimental reports in *OR*, VII, 227–32.

[13]Wallace, *Lew Wallace*, I, 416; Wallace, "Capture of Fort Donelson," I, 424; Wallace, *Lew Wallace*, I, 417; Franz Sigel, "The Pea Ridge Campaign," in *Battles and Leaders*, I, 329.

Fredericksburg. These Federal infantrymen shouted out "Fredericksburg!" as they fired at Pickett's men.[14]

By the campaigns of 1864, the men in the ranks were expert at evaluating the strength of a defensive line. General Alexander S. Webb reported an action of his brigade on May 10, 1864, at Spotsylvania: "This could hardly be termed a charge. . . . The men had had time to examine the enemy's line. They had found it necessary to hug the ground very closely for some hours, since the firing was severe. They had convinced themselves that the enemy was too strongly positioned to be driven out by assault, and this was evident in the attempt at a charge." At Cold Harbor the Federals lost 12,000 men in hopeless frontal assaults against Lee's entrenched lines. When orders were given for second and third attempts on June 3, a staff officer of the Sixth Corps said that every man at the front knew the offensive could not succeed. "To move that army further, except by regular approaches, was a simple and absolute impossibility," said Martin T. McMahon, "known to be such by every officer and man of the three corps engaged. The order was obeyed by simply renewing the fire from the men as they lay in position."[15]

John Gibbon said that by the time of the Virginia campaign, "it became a recognized fact amongst the men themselves that when the enemy had occupied a position six or eight hours ahead of us, it was useless to attempt to take it. This feeling became so marked that when troops under these circumstances were ordered forward, they went a certain distance and then lay down and opened fire. It became a saying in the army that when the old troops got as far forward as they thought they ought to go 'they sat down and made coffee!' " In a charge on June 18, 1864, at Petersburg, the First Maine Heavy Artillery suffered the greatest recorded loss by a Union regiment in a single attack during the war. When this new and oversized regiment went forward, nearby veteran troops warned the Maine soldiers: "Lie down, you damn fools, you can't take them forts!"[16]

Western soldiers learned the same lessons. Sherman's chief engineer, General Orlando M. Poe, praised Sherman's men for their ability to evaluate defensive positions. "The constant practice of our troops has made them tolerably good judges of what constitutes a good defensive line, and lightened the labors of the engineer staff very materially," Poe reported on the Carolinas campaign. "I was frequently surprised by the admirable location of rifle

---

[14]*OR*, XXV (pt. 1), 195; XXVII (pt. 1), 445.

[15]Ibid., XXXVI (pt. 1), 439; Martin T. McMahon, "Cold Harbor," in *Battles and Leaders*, IV, 218. Colonel Theodore Lyman of Meade's staff thought that this incident at Cold Harbor demonstrated the "staunchness" of the Union troops. Theodore Lyman Journal, June 3, 1864, quoted in *Meade's Headquarters, 1863–1865 . . .* , ed. George R. Agassiz (Boston, 1922), 144.

[16]John Gibbon, *Personal Recollections of the Civil War* (New York, 1928), 229; William F. Fox, *Regimental Losses in the American Civil War, 1861–1865* (Albany, 1889), 16, 17; Bruce Catton, *A Stillness at Appomattox* (Garden City, 1953), 198.

trenches and the ingenious means adopted to put themselves under cover."[17] Colonel Bushrod Jones, who commanded a Confederate brigade at Jonesboro, thought his men could evaluate a strong defensive position all too well. He complained after the battle: "The men seemed possessed of some great horror of charging breast-works, which no power, persuasion, or example could dispel, yet I must say that the officers generally did their duty."[18]

Late in the war, officers sometimes complained that their men were unwilling to attack entrenched lines vigorously and wanted instead to rely on the cover of their own entrenchments. "The best officers and men are liable, by their gallantry, to be first disabled," wrote Theodore Lyman after Cold Harbor, "and, of those that are left, the best become demoralized by the failures, and the loss of good leaders; so that, very soon, the men will no longer charge entrenchments and will only go forward when driven by their officers." General David B. Birney complained of the conduct of some of the Second Corps after the First Battle of the Weldon Railroad, June 22, 1864, at Petersburg: "The impulse seems to have been, both with officers and men, to regain their rifle-pits." On September 4, 1864, John Bell Hood explained his defeat at Jonesboro with this complaint: "It seems the troops had been so long confined to trenches and had been taught to believe that intrenchments cannot be taken, so that they attacked without spirit and retired without proper effort." Hood also said: "I am officially informed that there is a tacit if not expressed determination among the men of this army, extending to officers as high in some instances as colonel, that they will not attack breastworks."[19]

Field commanders made various suggestions about how the advantages of the rifled defensive could be overcome. Nelson A. Miles, a colonel in command of two regiments at Fredericksburg, was convinced by the disastrous Federal attacks there that "nothing but the strictest discipline of both officers and men" would allow a commander to handle his troops in the face of rifle fire. General Carter L. Stevenson of the Army of Tennessee decided at the end of the war that the difficulty in attacking entrenchments was keeping alignment. "My experience with this army," wrote Stevenson on March 30, 1865, "has convinced me that one of the greatest obstacles in the way of our success in assaulting fortified positions of the enemy has been caused by a failure to keep the commands properly aligned, and to move them straight to the front."[20] Major Nathaniel Michler of the Corps of Engineers of the Army of the Potomac concluded at the end of the war that the "new era in field-works" had made temporary entrenchments "almost as strong" as permanent

---

[17]OR, XLVII (pt. 1), 176.
[18]Ibid., XXXVIII (pt. 3), 835.
[19]Lyman, *Meade's Headquarters*, 148n; OR, XL (pt. 1), 326; LII (pt. 2), 730.
[20]OR, XXI, 237; XLVII (pt. 1), 1094.

works and that sieges were now "almost useless." Michler believed the solution to the dilemma was to make direct assaults, which would be costly but might be decisive. "The open assault of works is attended with immense loss of life," admitted Michler, "but at the same time during the slow operations of the siege the sharpshooter so effectually does his work as to produce a large bill of mortality."[21]

Few commanders demonstrated during the war that they understood that the rifle had made the tactical defensive dominant over the offensive. General William B. Hazen, a regular army officer who served in the western theater, showed in his report on the Atlanta campaign that he understood the significance of the rifle and entrenchment. "I must also ask the indulgence of my commanders for calling attention in this report to the subject of 'attacks of the front of an enemy in position,' " wrote Hazen on September 10, 1864, "since the accurate shooting rifle has replaced the random firing musket, since troops now when in position protect their persons by shelters against bullets, and since they can be no longer scared from the line, but see safety in maintaining it." Hazen went on to document his point with statistics from two unsuccessful and costly Confederate attacks in which the losses of Hazen's defending division were very low.[22] In an earlier report on the Chickamauga campaign, Hazen had endorsed the value of entrenchments in reducing losses.[23]

Oliver O. Howard, another regular army officer, concluded after Kennesaw Mountain that frontal assaults against entrenchments were not likely to succeed. In his report on the Atlanta campaign, Howard declared: "My experience is that a line of works thoroughly constructed, with the front well covered with abatis and other entanglements, well manned with infantry, whether with our own or that of the enemy, cannot be carried by direct assault." After the war Howard also wrote: "We realized now [after Kennesaw Mountain], as never before, the futility of direct assaults upon intrenched lines already well prepared and well manned."[24]

Emory Upton, a regular army officer who served with all three arms of the service during the war, was one of the most innovative tacticians of the Civil War. He showed a willingness to experiment with new formations and wrote a new tactical manual after the war. The Federal cavalryman James H. Wilson greatly admired Upton and praised him in his war memoirs, *Under the Old Flag*. Wilson said that few Union commanders "became proficient" at assaulting entrenchments and that Upton "was the only one of them who thoroughly mastered that branch of the military art." Wilson claimed that

[21]Ibid., XL (pt. 1), 291.

[22]Ibid., XXXVIII (pt. 3), 184.

[23]Ibid., XXX (pt. 1), 763.

[24]Ibid., XXXVIII (pt. 1), 199; Oliver O. Howard, "The Struggle for Atlanta," in *Battles and Leaders*, IV, 311.

Upton "never once failed to break through the enemy's works or to make good his hold upon them, where he had been ordered and had sole charge of the arrangements." Wilson thought that Winfield S. Hancock "was next to [Upton] in this complicated work, but no other corps or division commander on either side ever equaled Upton in the uniform success which attended his efforts."[25]

George B. McClellan and George G. Meade have taken criticism, beginning with their contemporaries, for their cautiousness. Both of these soldiers respected the entrenched tactical defensive. During the Peninsula campaign, McClellan spent a month besieging the entrenched Confederate lines at Yorktown because he believed them too strong to be carried by frontal assault. A West Point graduate of 1846 and an engineer officer in Mexico, McClellan wrote afterward that his own personal experience "in this kind of work" was greater than that of any other officer then in the Army of the Potomac. Of the later operations during the Seven Days' battles, McClellan said that he did not feel free to attack Lee until June 25, when McClellan had completed entrenching. Meade contended after Cold Harbor that the heavy losses suffered in the attacks on entrenched positions during the Virginia campaign vindicated his caution at Williamsport and during the Mine Run campaign. On June 5, 1864, Meade wrote to his wife: "I feel a satisfaction in knowing that . . . the results of this campaign are the clearest indications I could wish of my sound judgment, both at Williamsport and Mine Run. In every instance that we have attacked the enemy in an entrenched position, we have failed, except in the case of Hancock's attack at Spotsylvania, which was a surprise discreditable to the enemy. So, likewise, whenever the enemy has attacked us in position, he has been repulsed."[26]

William T. Sherman seems to have learned the high cost of taking the tactical offensive against entrenched positions, although it was probably late in the war before he did so. After the war, Sherman wrote of the Atlanta campaign: "I was willing to meet the enemy in the open country, but not behind well-constructed parapets." Sherman also said he "never intended to assault" the Atlanta defenses and emphasized that he eventually advanced on Jonesboro, which was "*not*" fortified." During the Atlanta campaign, Sherman said that he could not afford the losses that Grant had suffered on the offensive in Virginia. On May 22, 1864, he wrote of Grant's tactics: "Grant's battles in Virginia are fearful but necessary. Immense slaughter is necessary

---

[25]James H. Wilson, *Under the Old Flag; Recollections of Military Operations in the War for the Union* . . . (2 vols., New York, 1912), I, 181.

[26]George W. Cullum, ed., *Biographical Registrar of the Officers and Graduates of the United States Military Academy, at West Point* (2 vols., New York, 1868), II, 140; George B. McClellan, "The Peninsular Campaign," in *Battles and Leaders*, II, 171, 179; George G. Meade to Margaretta Sergeant Meade, June 5, 1864, *The Life and Letters of George Gordon Meade* . . . , ed. George Gordon Meade (2 vols., New York, 1913), II, 201.

to prove that our Northern armies can and will fight." Yet Sherman feared the effect of such costly tactics on his own forces. After Kennesaw Mountain he wrote from Marietta, Georgia: "I think we can whip his [Joseph E. Johnston's] army in fair battle, but behind the hills and trunks our loss of life and limb on the first assault would reduce us too much; in other words, at this distance from home we cannot afford the losses of such terrible assaults as Grant has made." Jacob D. Cox thought that Sherman came to appreciate the high price of the tactical offensive somewhat sooner than Grant, although in both theaters the same lesson was learned. "Grant was slower than Sherman in learning the unprofitableness of attacking field-works," said Cox, "and his campaign was by far the most costly one. . . . There were special reasons which led Grant to adhere so long to the more aggressive tactics, which would need to be weighed in any full treatment of the subject; but I am now only pointing out the fact in both the East and West the lesson was practically the same."[27]

Ulysses S. Grant did not learn to respect the entrenched defensive until very late in the war. In his *Memoirs*, Grant said he regretted ordering the May 22 assault at Vicksburg and the final assault at Cold Harbor. James H. Wilson thought that neither Grant nor Sherman respected the entrenched defensive as much as they should have. "The only chance of victory over such [entrenched] lines, all other things being equal," wrote Wilson, "must be looked for in strategem or in a turning movement. Yet Grant, in the campaign against Richmond and Petersburg, and Sherman in that against Atlanta, in spite of all their previous experience, frequently resorted to the direct assault of temporary entrenchments, and in nearly every instance failed to gain any adequate advantage." Wilson, however, praised Grant for learning after Cold Harbor what many of his soldiers had already known, that his costly offensive tactics would have to be changed.[28]

A few Confederate commanders learned the strength of the tactical defensive and field entrenchments. Joseph E. Johnston was the strongest Confederate exponent of the tactical defensive and was always wary of taking the offensive against entrenchments. After the Battle of McDowell, May 8, 1862, Johnston warned Stonewall Jackson against attacking fortifications.[29] When Johnston attacked McClellan at Fair Oaks/Seven Pines, May 31, 1862,

[27]William T. Sherman, "The Grand Strategy of the Last Year of the War," in *Battles and Leaders*, IV, 253, 254; William T. Sherman to Ellen Boyle Ewing, May 20, 1864, *Home Letters of General Sherman*, ed. M. A. DeWolfe Howe (New York, 1909), 291; William T. Sherman to Ellen Boyle Ewing, June 30, 1864, ibid., 299–300; Jacob D. Cox, *Military Reminiscences of the Civil War* (2 vols., New York, 1900), II, 224.

[28]Ulysses S. Grant, *Personal Memoirs of U. S. Grant* (2 vols., New York, 1885), II, 276–78; Wilson, *Under the Old Flag*, 1, 225, 448–49.

[29]*OR*, XII (pt. 3), 896–97; John D. Imboden, "Stonewall Jackson in the Shenandoah," in *Battles and Leaders*, II, 288.

he ordered that any entrenchments that were encountered were to be turned. Johnston fought most of the Atlanta campaign on the entrenched defensive, and he argued in his memoirs that he had been right in doing so. He wrote, for example, of Rocky Face Ridge: "The Confederate troops suffered little in these engagements, for they fought under the protection of intrenchments." He said the Federals had been repulsed at Kennesaw Mountain "because they had encountered *intrenched* infantry unsurpassed by that of Napoleon's Old Guard, or that which followed Wellington into France, out of Spain." With few exceptions, Robert E. Lee assumed the tactical defensive after the Battle of the Wilderness until the end of the war, and did some of the best fighting of his career. He recognized the value of field entrenchment on the tactical defensive. At Fredericksburg, he added new entrenchments to his line the night after Burnside's attacks. Heros von Borcke heard Lee remark the next morning that these new works strengthened his position as much as reinforcement by 20,000 men.[30] Patrick Cleburne, the most highly regarded Confederate subordinate commander in the west, fought vigorously on the tactical offensive, but he always respected field entrenchments. Cleburne often alerted his superiors when he found field works in his front.[31]

Many Confederate commanders learned the tactical lessons of the war slowly or not at all. After the war, Daniel H. Hill admitted that the Confederates had been too fond of the tactical offensive. "We were very lavish of blood in those days," wrote Hill, "and it was thought to be a great thing to charge a battery of artillery or an earth-work lined with infantry. . . . The attacks on the Beaver Dam intrenchments, on the heights of Malvern Hill, at Gettysburg, etc., were all grand, but of exactly the kind of grandeur which the South could not afford." Braxton Bragg took the tactical offensive in all of his major battles except Chattanooga, and he used close-ordered successive lines and complicated wheeling attacks. Robert E. Lee suffered his most decisive defeats while on the tactical offensive, at Malvern Hill and at Gettysburg. Even when he was successful on the offensive, Lee used up thousands of irreplaceable troops in battles such as Second Manassas and Chancellorsville.[32]

No Confederate commander favored offensive tactics more than John Bell Hood, who fought aggressively as a subordinate commander in battles such as Gaines's Mill, Sharpsburg, and Gettysburg. As an independent commander, Hood constantly sought the tactical offensive until Nashville, when

---

[30]*OR*, XI (pt. 1), 939–40; Joseph E. Johnston, "Manassas to Seven Pines," in *Battles and Leaders*, II, 212; James Longstreet, *From Manassas to Appomattox: Memoirs of the Civil War in America*, ed. James I. Robertson, Jr. (reissue, Bloomington, 1960), 93; Joseph E. Johnston, *Narrative of Military Operations* . . . (reissue, Bloomington, 1959), 307, 343; Heros von Borcke, *Memoirs of the Confederate War for Independence* (2 vols., Edinburgh, 1866), II, 132.

[31]*OR*, XX (pt. 1), 849; XXX (pt. 2), 53.

[32]Daniel H. Hill, "Lee's Attacks North of the Chickahominy," in *Battles and Leaders*, II, 352.

his Army of Tennessee was so fought out that it could only stand on the defensive.[33] In his memoirs, Hood argued for the tactical offensive and contended that Joseph E. Johnston's use of the tactical defensive and entrenchment had ruined the Army of Tennessee. Hood praised the Lee and Jackson "school" for their offensive tactics, which he contrasted with Johnston's defensive ideas. "They [Lee's troops] were always taught to work out the best means to get at the enemy, in order to cripple or destroy him, in lieu of ever seeking the best means to get away from him," declared Hood. "Therefore the Lee and Jackson school is the opposite of the Joe Johnston school, and will always elevate and inspirit, whilst the other will depress and paralyze." Hood insisted that Johnston's continuous defensives and entrenching had made the Army of Tennessee too cautious and had ruined its fighting spirit. "The troops of the Army of Tennessee had for such length of time been subjected to the ruinous policy pursued from Dalton to Atlanta," said Hood, "that they were unfitted for united action in pitched battle. They had, in other words, been so long habituated to security behind breastworks that they had become wedded to the 'timid defensive' policy, and naturally regarded with distrust a commander likely to initiate offensive operations."[34] Hood believed that the use of field entrenchments weakened the morale of troops and made them too cautious.[35] "A soldier cannot fight for a period of one or two months constantly behind breastworks," Hood said, "with the training that he is equal to four or five of the enemy by reason of the security of his position, and then be expected to engage in pitched battle and prove as intrepid and impetuous as his brother who has been taught to rely solely upon his own valor."[36]

Other Confederate leaders agreed with Hood. Stephen D. Lee, who served in both theaters of the war, was also critical of the entrenched defensive. "Troops once sheltered from fire behind works," wrote Lee, "never feel comfortable unless in them. . . . Troops in works, engaged the first time, are always bolder than afterwards—stand erect and deliver their fire with precision as they were used to in the open field; after a few engagements, the thought of constant security is always with them, and their object is to be always covered by works, while under fire. . . . A general who resorts to entrenchments, when there is any chance of success in engaging in the open

---

[33]Even at Nashville, Hood wanted to take the offensive. He said in his memoirs that just before the Confederate line was broken on the second day at Nashville he had finished a plan to leave his position on the Brentwood Heights and attack Thomas's right flank. John Bell Hood, *Advance and Retreat: Personal Experiences in the United States & Confederate States Armies*, ed. Richard N. Current (reissue, Bloomington, 1959), 303.

[34]Ibid., 135, 162.

[35]Ibid., 168–69, 171.

[36]Ibid., 131. See also John Bell Hood to Stepehen D. Lee, January 17, 1874, quoted in ibid., 137.

field, commits a great error." He also said: "To attack entrenchments, give me troops who have never served behind them." Henry Kyd Douglas, who served throughout the war with the Army of Northern Virginia, was very defensive about Robert E. Lee's extensive use of entrenchment during the Virginia campaign. Douglas, who apparently believed entrenchments were evidence of weakness, complained of "the habit of Northern writers to speak of the breastworks and entrenchments constantly constructed in [the Virginia] campaign by Lee's army." Douglas pointed out that "both armies began entrenching in this swinging campaign as soon as they met face to face; and as Grant had a larger army and more diggers and tools, there can be little doubt that the Army of the Potomac made more embankments, trenches, and breastworks than Lee's army."[37]

Regular army officers received little help in solving the tactical problems of the Civil War from either their tactical experience in the Mexican War or from the tactical theory of the 1850s. Nor did volunteer officers learn the tactical lessons of the Civil War any sooner than the regulars. There were many well-known volunteer generals in the Civil War, men such as Nathaniel P. Banks, Francis P. Blair, John C. Breckinridge, Benjamin F. Butler, Howell Cobb, John C. Frémont, John A. Logan, John A. McClernand, Franz Sigel, and Robert Toombs. None of these men made any reputation as tactical innovators. Benjamin Butler and John A. Logan both wrote long books after the war years, and both were critical of the regular army, but neither discussed the tactical lessons of the Civil War. Butler said in his *Autobiography* that his appointment had been criticized by a certain regular army officer. "He said I had no military experience, never having been at West Point," wrote Butler. "He forgot that putting an animal into a stable does not make him a horse; that point being better determined by the length of his ears." Logan's *The Volunteer Soldier of America* warned against the dangers of a professional military elite and praised the volunteer system and the records volunteer soldiers had made in American wars.[38] The Civil War, in Logan's opinion, demonstrated the dangers of "the unwise system of national academies, whereby their graduates were established as the bulwark of the Government," while the volunteer soldier was "crushed in every aspiration and every attempt."[39] Logan believed that too much faith was put in specialized teaching, military or otherwise, and that the most important source of military ability was innate aptitude.[40] There was nothing in either

[37]Stephen D. Lee to John Bell Hood, January 26, 1874, quoted in ibid., 138, 139; Henry Kyd Douglas, *I Rode With Stonewall* (Chapel Hill, 1940), 283.

[38]Benjamin F. Butler, *Autobiography and Personal Reminiscences of Major-General Benjamin F. Butler* (Boston, 1892), 127; John A. Logan, *The Volunteer Soldier of America* (Chicago, 1887), 424, 548–70, 615.

[39]Logan, *Volunteer Soldier*, 425.

[40]Ibid., 115–20.

of these two books, or in the war records of either Butler or Logan, that showed any understanding of the tactical lessons of the Civil War.

James H. Wilson argued that neither the regular nor the volunteer commanders learned the tactical lessons of the war soon enough. Evaluating the conduct of the regulars William T. Sherman and James B. McPherson and the volunteer John A. McClernand during the May 22 assault on Vicksburg, Wilson found all three men wanting. "When it is recalled that neither the brilliant Sherman nor the accomplished McPherson, both distinguished West Point men, had yet mastered the trick of carrying fortified positions by assault," said Wilson, "it need not be thought strange that McClernand, the lawyer and politician, who acquired his first military training in the Black Hawk War, should have failed at this dangerous and complicated business."[41]

When the Civil War began, the problems of the tactical offensive had been greatly increased by the introduction of the rifle. The use of field entrenchments during the war further strengthened the tactical defensive. Traditional ideas about the offensive, élan, the bayonet, and formations became obsolete. Only a few soldiers, such as William B. Hazen, ever identified these problems during the war years. Only a few men, such as Emory Upton, attempted any innovations to adjust to the new tactical situation. Even when the war was over, there was no consensus as to what the tactical lessons of the war had been.

---

[41]Wilson, *Under the Old Flag*, I, 180, 181.

9

Beyond the Noise
No Great Harm Was Done

When the Civil War began, the artillery arm held a high reputation. It had proved its mobility and effectiveness in the Mexican War. In the 1850s, tactical theory regarded artillery as an effective weapon on both the defensive and offensive, and nearly all Civil War commanders respected the artillery arm. Winfield Scott believed that the artillery would be the most important arm in the Civil War. Irvin McDowell warned his troops in his General Orders No. 17, written for the First Manassas campaign, not to make frontal assaults against artillery. "It can hardly be necessary to attack a battery in front," McDowell's orders stated; "in most cases it may be turned." General William N. Pendleton, chief of artillery of the Army of Northern Virginia, referred to the artillery in his report on the Gettysburg campaign as "this great arm of defense."[1]

When used on the defensive, massed artillery was a powerful deployment. This power was first demonstrated at the end of the first day at Shiloh, April 6, 1862. Ulysses S. Grant's last position on that day was greatly strengthened when Colonel J. D. Webster of Grant's staff collected a line of twenty or more guns near Pittsburg Landing. In an article written after the war, P. G. T. Beauregard listed Webster's mass of artillery as one of the major reasons he believed that the Confederates could not carry Grant's last position that evening.[2]

Perhaps the most famous use of artillery on the defensive during the Civil War occurred at Malvern Hill on July 1, 1862. Massed batteries of the Army

---

[1]Cabello, "Rifle and Sabre," *Army and Navy Journal*, VI (January 9, 1869), 326; Philip H. Sheridan, *Personal Memoirs of P. H. Sheridan* (2 vols., New York, 1888), I, 355; U.S. War Dept., *The War of the Rebellion: A Compilation of the Official Records of the Union and Confederate Armies* (128 vols., Washington, 1880–1901), Series 1, II, 305; XXVII (pt. 2), 354 (hereinafter cited as *OR;* all references are to Series 1).

[2]Ulysses S. Grant, "The Battle of Shiloh," in *Battles and Leaders of the Civil War*, ed. Robert U. Johnson and Clarence C. Buel (4 vols., reissue, New York, 1956), I, 474, 475; G. T. Beauregard, "The Campaign of Shiloh," ibid., 590.

of the Potomac, deployed on the commanding ground of Malvern Hill, shot apart the lines of Confederate attackers as they approached across open fields. One Federal soldier who witnessed the Confederate infantry charge against the massed artillery at Malvern Hill wrote: "Their lines melted away. The officers would bring them up again and down they would go head first." The Union artillery defensive at Malvern Hill was widely praised, even by the southern attackers. Stephen D. Lee, a division artillery commander at Malvern Hill, said in an official report written shortly after the battle: "The enemy's artillery was admirably handled in this action, and is admitted to have been the most terrible artillery fire during the war." The Confederate cavalryman Heros von Borcke wrote: "The effect was more disastrous than had been before produced by artillery." In a postwar account, Daniel H. Hill described the advance made late in the battle by nine brigades under General John B. Magruder's orders. "Most of them had an open field half a mile wide to cross," said Hill, "under the fire of field-artillery in front, and the fire of the heavy ordnance of the gun-boats in their rear." He estimated that over half of the Confederate losses at Malvern Hill were caused by field artillery, "an unprecedented thing in warfare."[3]

Events on two battlefields late in 1862 demonstrated the strength of artillery on the defensive. At Fredericksburg, December 13, 1862, the field guns of the Army of Northern Virginia, concentrating their fire on the Federal infantry rather than artillery, made a major contribution to the successful Confederate defense. E. Porter Alexander reported that he ordered his battalion to ignore the Federal guns across the Rappahannock River and to concentrate on the advancing infantry and its supporting batteries close to the town. Colonel Henry C. Cabell, chief of artillery for McLaws's Division, said: "Every battery officer received the instructions that he was to fire with great deliberation, and to fire only upon large bodies of troops."[4] The attacking Union infantry was crippled by the defending artillery fire. "This fire was very destructive and demoralizing in its effects," claimed General James Longstreet, "and frequently made gaps in the enemy's ranks that could be seen at the distance of a mile." When Longstreet and Alexander had reviewed the artillery preparations to cover the field of the Union advance in front of Marye's Hill, Alexander had boasted to Longstreet: "A chicken could not live on that field when we open on it." At Murfreesboro, half a month after Fredericksburg, artillery again proved its effectiveness on the defensive. On the first day of the battle, the Confederates encountered artillery massed on the defensive when they attacked the Round Forest sector. One Federal staff

---

[3]Silas D. Wesson Diary, July 2, 1862 (typescript), United States Army Military History Institute, Carlisle Barracks, Pennsylvania; *OR*, XI (pt. 2), 747; Heros von Borcke, *Memoirs of the Confederate War for Independence* (2 vols., Edinburgh, 1866), I, 71; Daniel H. Hill, "McClellan's Change of Base and Malvern Hill," in *Battles and Leaders*, II, 394.

[4]*OR*, XXI, 576, 586.

officer said of these massed batteries: "They could not fire amiss." The same officer recalled: "The Confederates had no sooner moved into the open field from the cover of the river bank than they were received with a blast from the artillery. Men plucked the cotton from the boles at their feet and stuffed it in their ears. Huge gaps were torn in the Confederate line at every discharge."[5] On January 2, the charge of Breckinridge's Division was repulsed in part by the fire of about fifty-eight field pieces massed by Captain John Mendenhall, chief of artillery for General Thomas L. Crittenden's Left Wing.[6] "In all, fifty-eight pieces of artillery played upon the enemy," wrote one Union staff officer. "Not less than one hundred shots per minute were fired. As the mass of men swarmed down the slope they were mowed down by the score." After the war, Crittenden admitted: "Before this battle I had been inclined to underrate the importance of artillery in our war, but I never knew that arm to render such important service as at this point."[7]

At Chancellorsville in May 1863, massed Union artillery made two important defensive stands, at Hazel Grove and at Fairview. At the Hazel Grove clearing, Captain James F. Huntington and General Alfred Pleasonton massed over twenty guns to help oppose Stonewall Jackson's attack on the evening of May 2.[8] On the Fairview plateau, Captain Clermont L. Best of the Fourth United States Artillery assembled thirty-four guns about 500 yards in the rear of the Federal infantry front. Best's mass of guns fired over the Federal troops in their front and into Jackson's infantry, which was brought

---

[5]Ibid., 570; James Longstreet, "The Battle of Fredericksburg," in *Battles and Leaders*, III, 79; David Urquhart, "Bragg's Advance and Retreat," ibid., 606; G. C. Kniffin, "The Battle of Stone's River," ibid., 628, 629.

[6]*OR*, XX (pt. 1), 456. In his official report, Crittenden said there were fifty-two guns. Ibid., 451. After the war, Crittenden agreed with Mendenhall's figure of fifty-eight guns. Thomas L. Crittenden, "The Union Left at Stone's River," in *Battles and Leaders*, III, 633.

[7]Kniffin, "Battle of Stone's River," III, 630–31; Crittenden, "Union Left at Stone's River," III, 633. It should be said that a counterattack by Federal infantry against Breckinridge's right flank was also an important factor in this action. Grady McWhiney, *Braxton Bragg and Confederate Defeat* (New York, 1969), 367.

[8]Henry J. Hunt said there were twenty-four guns, but General Daniel E. Sickles, Major Clifford Thomson, and Pleasonton all said twenty-two guns. *OR*, XXV (pt. 1), 249, 388, 773, 775; Alfred Pleasonton, "The Successes and Failures of Chancellorsville," in *Battles and Leaders*, III, 179–80, 180n. Huntington said that he assembled eighteen guns on the north side of Hazel Grove without Pleasonton being aware of it. James F. Huntington, "The Artillery at Hazel Grove," ibid., 188. Six of these guns, the six twelve-pounders of Lieutenant Samuel Lewis's Tenth New York Battery, were included by Hunt in his count of twenty-four guns. Ibid., 188n; *OR*, XXV (pt. 1), 249.

L. Van Loan Naisawald argued that Pleasonton exaggerated his role in the Hazel Grove action and its importance. Naisawald said that Huntington, not Pleasonton, was the prime factor in the affair and that Jackson's attack broke down in front of Fairview, not Pleasonton's guns. L. Van Loan Naisawald, *Grape and Canister: The Story of the Field Artillery of the Army of the Potomac, 1861–1865* (New York, 1960), 294–97.

to a halt along the Orange Plank Road. The Federal artillery at Fairview kept up its fire until about 10 p.m. the night of May 2 and was used again during May 3.[9] Captain George E. Randolph, chief of artillery for the Third Corps, claimed that these guns fought well on the defensive on May 3. "Never had artillery a finer opportunity to do good service," said Randolph, "and never was a better use made of favorable circumstances. Twice the columns of the enemy on the [Orange] Plank road were repulsed by the concentration of fire from this line of batteries."[10]

Effective use of artillery on the defensive played an important role in the Union victory at Gettysburg. On the second day of the battle, July 2, 1863, about twenty-five guns held the Plum Run line on the Federal left without any infantry support. On July 3, the Federal artillerymen hoarded their ammunition during the cannonade that preceded Pickett's charge, saving it to use against the Confederate infantry.[11] E. Porter Alexander said after the war that he had never seen the Federals reserve their artillery fire for the Confederate infantry as they did during the Gettysburg cannonade.[12] The Union artillery on Cemetery Ridge contributed to the destruction of Pickett's charge. "The rebel lines advanced slowly but surely," wrote one Federal artillerist; "half the valley had been passed over by them before the guns dared expend a round of the precious ammunition remaining on hand. The enemy steadily approached, and, when within deadly range, canister was thrown with terrible effect into their ranks." Captain Andrew Cowan, commander of the First New York Battery, reported that he fired on Pickett's Division with canister at 200 yards. "My last charge (a double-header) literally swept the enemy from my front," Cowan also said, "being fired at less than 20 yards."[13]

Artillery was sometimes an important defensive weapon in the Virginia campaign of 1864 and 1865. At Spotsylvania Court House on May 10, 1864, Upton's assault was to have been supported by Gershom Mott's Division. The advance of Mott's Division was stopped by Confederate battery fire, and Upton was left unsupported.[14] On May 18, twenty-nine Confederate guns

---

[9]*OR*, XXV (pt. 1), 249, 391, 405, 670, 675, 721. Best, General Henry W. Slocum, and Captain Robert H. Fitzhugh said there were thirty-four guns concentrated at Fairview. Ibid., 670, 675, 721. Sickles said there were only thirty guns. Ibid., 391. Hunt listed the batteries involved and gave a total of thirty-eight guns. Ibid., 249. Batteries were relieved and shifted during May 2 and 3, and the number of guns was probably different at different times.

[10]Ibid., 405. See also Henry J. Hunt, "Artillery," in *Papers of the Military Historical Society of Massachusetts* (14 vols., Boston, 1913), XIII, 123.

[11]Henry J. Hunt, "The Second Day at Gettysburg," in *Battles and Leaders*, III, 310; Henry J. Hunt, "The Third Day at Gettysburg," ibid., 372, 374.

[12]E. Porter Alexander, "The Great Charge and Artillery Fighting at Gettysburg," ibid., 364.

[13]*OR*, XXVII (pt. 1), 480, 690, 428.

[14]Ibid., XXXVI (pt. 1), 490.

under Colonel Thomas H. Carter, firing canister and spherical case, defeated a Federal attack without the aid of any infantry fire.[15] "This attack," said Armistead L. Long, chief of artillery of the Second Corps, "fairly illustrates the immense power of artillery well handled."[16] After Hancock's May 12 assault overran the Mule Shoe salient, several Confederate officers said that the salient had been lost because there had been no Confederate artillery present when the Federals struck. On the mistaken assumption that the Federals were retreating on Fredericksburg, all Confederate artillery pieces in the salient had been removed. When General Edward Johnson reported that the Federals were massing to attack his division, the guns were returned, but only in time for twenty pieces to be captured without ever getting into position or firing a shot. Several Confederate officers, including Richard S. Ewell, Edward Johnson, Armistead L. Long, and E. M. Law, believed that the absence of any defensive artillery fire was a great factor in the Federal success.[17]

Artillery made several contributions on the tactical defensive during the Atlanta campaign. On May 25, 1864, troops of Joseph Hooker's Twentieth Corps attacked a line of log breastworks near New Hope Church, defended by about 5,000 infantrymen and sixteen guns firing canister. The defending artillery fire was so severe that the Federals afterward referred to the position as the "Hell Hole." At Peach Tree Creek on July 20, 1864, Federal artillery fired "terrible discharges" of solid shot, shells, and canister and helped defeat an attempt to turn the flank of George H. Thomas's Army of the Cumberland. On July 28 at Ezra Church, Oliver O. Howard used twenty-six field guns to cover the endangered right flank of John A. Logan's Fifteenth Corps. Howard later credited the infantry with stopping the attack against Logan's flank, but he explained why he thought the artillery support had also been a good idea. "Early in the action," Howard said, "remembering some remarkable experiences on other fields, I thought I would make assurance doubly sure."[18]

Artillery was a powerful defensive weapon throughout the war, but it was less effective on the offensive. Artillery fought aggressively in the Mexican War, sometimes advancing in front of its supporting infantry. Tactical

---

[15]Ibid., 1046, 1087–88.

[16]Ibid., 1087. After the war, E. M. Law said that thirty guns were involved in this action. E. M. Law, "From the Wilderness to Cold Harbor," in *Battles and Leaders*, IV, 134. In their official reports, Long and General William N. Pendleton both said twenty-nine guns. *OR*, XXXVI (pt. 1), 1046, 1087.

[17]*OR*, XXXVI (pt. 1), 1072, 1079–80, 1086; Law, "Wilderness to Cold Harbor," IV, 129–32.

[18]Joseph E. Johnston, "Opposing Sherman's Advance to Atlanta," in *Battles and Leaders*, IV, 269; Oliver O. Howard, "The Struggle for Atlanta," ibid., 306; Oliver O. Howard, *Autobiography of Oliver Otis Howard* (2 vols., New York, 1907), I, 619; II, 23–24; Howard, "The Struggle for Atlanta," IV, 319.

theory before the Civil War regarded artillery as equally an offensive and defensive arm, but Civil War experience proved otherwise.

The aggressive artillery tactics of the Mexican War were attempted at First Manassas, the first important battle of the Civil War. Irvin McDowell, a regular army artillery officer and a veteran of the Mexican War, ordered two of his batteries, commanded by Captains James B. Ricketts and Charles Griffin, to advance in front of the Federal infantry to a position close to the Confederate lines.[19] When approaching Confederate troops were mistaken for battery supports, the Federal artillerymen allowed the Southerners to advance until the attackers fired on them at "pistol range." Griffin said that every one of his cannoneers was shot down and many of his horses killed. Griffin lost three of his six guns in this action and two more later in the Federal retreat. Ricketts was wounded and captured, and all of his guns were lost.[20]

The Confederates attempted to use their artillery on the offensive at Shiloh, the first major battle in the western theater. P. G. T. Beauregard said after the war that he had intended that his corps commanders use their artillery during the first day's attack, in masses of twelve guns at a point. General Daniel Ruggles massed a collection of Confederate batteries that helped reduce the Hornet's Nest position. This assemblage was the first large artillery concentration in North America.[21]

The Confederates attempted an artillery offensive at Malvern Hill against the defending Federal guns, but it ended in failure. James Longstreet said after the war that he had wanted to mass sixty field pieces to fire in support of the Malvern Hill assaults. Difficult terrain forced the Confederates to bring their guns up one or two batteries at a time. "As our guns in front did not engage," Longstreet said, "the result was the enemy concentrated the fire of fifty or sixty guns upon our isolated batteries, and tore them into fragments in a few minutes after they opened, piling horses upon each other and guns upon horses."[22]

At Sharpsburg on September 17, 1862, the Federal infantry assaults were heavily supported by artillery, including many rifled guns on the east bank of the Antietam Creek. Judging from the Confederate accounts of the battle, some of the long-range Federal gunnery was effective. Stonewall Jackson said

---

[19]George W. Cullum, ed., *Biographical Registrar of the Officers and Graduates of the United States Military Academy, at West Point* (2 vols., New York, 1868), I, 559; *OR*, II, 347, 394. Ricketts and Griffin were also regular army artillery officers and veterans of the Mexican War. Cullum, *Biographical Registrar*, I, 581; II, 196.

[20]*OR*, II, 385, 394, 406, 407, 410.

[21]Beauregard, "Campaign of Shiloh," I, 586; *OR*, X (pt. 1), 472–79; Wiley Sword, *Shiloh: Bloody April* (New York, 1974), 291–92.

[22]James Longstreet, " 'The Seven Days,' Including Frayser's Farm," in *Battles and Leaders*, II, 403. See also Hill, "McClellan's Change of Base," II, 393.

that the Union batteries beyond the Antietam opened shortly after dawn on September 17 and enfiladed his line with "a severe and damaging fire."[23] Stephen D. Lee, who commanded an artillery battalion near the Dunker Church, said that his batteries were enfiladed by "about twenty rifle guns" beyond the Antietam. Lafayette McLaws, a division commander at Sharpsburg, found that the Federal artillery was "so far superior" that "after the first experiments" he would not allow his own guns to duel with it. Colonel George T. Anderson, a brigade commander, said of one counterattack that his men made: "We could not pursue them [Federal infantry] as far as I wished, because of the severe fire of artillery directed against us from long-range guns that we could not reach." Daniel H. Hill, whose division held the Sunken Road at the Confederate center, complained: "all the ground in my front was completely commanded by the long-range artillery of the Yankees on the other side of the Antietam, which concentrated their fire upon every gun that opened and soon disabled or silenced it."[24]

In its next major engagement, at Fredericksburg, the artillery of the Army of the Potomac proved ineffective on the offensive. In an attempt to dislodge the sharpshooters of General William Barksdale's Brigade from Fredericksburg, the Federal artillery bombarded the city front. This cannonade damaged buildings but failed to dislodge Barksdale's men. During the hopeless assaults on the Confederate position west of the town, the northern artillery fire was again ineffectual. When the division of Andrew A. Humphreys made its attack against the stone wall position, its artillery support was ineffective. Before Humphreys advanced, Joseph Hooker, who commanded the Center Grand Division at Fredericksburg, "brought up every available battery in the city" to use against the stone wall position. Guns from Battery G, First New York Light Artillery, Battery B, First Rhode Island Artillery, Battery C, First New York Light Artillery, and probably other batteries were engaged.[25] A week after the battle, Hooker admitted that this artillery fire had "no apparent effect upon the Rebels or upon their works." Hooker believed that these guns had been well served but had accomplished little. "They fired as well as batteries could be fired," Hooker said. "But their fire made no impression at all. I do not think one Rebel ran from behind the wall or from the rifle-pits."[26]

The Confederates attempted to use artillery on the offensive at Murfreesboro, but the terrain was unfavorable for this and the artillery accomplished

---

[23]OR, XIX (pt. 1), 956.

[24]Ibid., 845, 858, 910, 1022, 1026.

[25]Longstreet, "Battle of Fredericksburg," III, 75; Lafayette McLaws, "The Confederate Left at Fredericksburg," in Battles and Leaders, III, 86–87; Report of the Joint Committee on the Conduct of the War, 37 Cong., 3 sess. (3 vols., Washington, 1863), I, 668; OR, XXI, 223, 268, 289, 356–57, 435, 436; Darius N. Couch, "Sumner's 'Right Grand Division,' " in Battles and Leaders, III, 115.

[26]Report of the Joint Committee, I, 668, 670.

little. On the first day of the battle, when Confederate infantry failed to carry the Round Forest, Braxton Bragg attempted an artillery concentration against it. Bragg reported that "after two unsuccessful efforts the attempt to carry it [the Round Forest] by infantry was abandoned. Our heaviest batteries of artillery and rifled guns of long range were now concentrated in front of, and their fire opened on, this position."[27] Neither Confederate infantry nor artillery was able to carry the Round Forest.

On January 2, 1863, during the assault of Breckinridge's Division, the Confederates made another unsuccessful effort to use artillery on the offensive. Breckinridge disagreed with the Confederate artillerist Captain Felix H. Robertson about how the artillery should be handled in this assault. Robertson's understanding was that Bragg expected Breckinridge's infantry to make the assault alone and that the Confederate artillery would advance later and occupy the high ground in front after the Federals had been driven from it. Breckinridge wanted the two arms to advance together. Breckinridge intended to advance his division in two lines and wanted Robertson to deploy his pieces between the two lines. "This I declined to do," reported Robertson, "stating as a reason the danger both of confusion and loss from such an arrangement." Breckinridge made the assault with his division artillery immediately in the rear of his infantry, Robertson's guns following Breckinridge's other pieces.[28] Breckinridge's infantry assault failed, and his artillery was thrown into confusion.[29]

The Confederates achieved one of their greatest successes with artillery at Chancellorsville. When the Federals left their defensive position at Hazel Grove, the Confederates quickly massed their own guns there and began firing against both Federal infantry and artillery units. E. Porter Alexander wrote after the war: "Guns had been brought to Hazel Grove from all the battalions on the field—Pegram's, Carter's, Jones's, McIntosh's, and Alexander's. Perhaps 50 guns in all were employed here, but less than 40 at any one time, as guns were occasionally relieved, or sent to the rear to refill."[30] Historian Douglas S. Freeman wrote of this action: "At Hazel Grove, in short, the finest artillerists of the Army of Northern Virginia were having their greatest day." Alfred Pleasonton, the Federal cavalryman, admitted after the war that the southern artillery at Hazel Grove had enfiladed the lines of the Twelfth Corps and also "punished the Third Corps severely."[31]

---

[27]*OR*, XX (pt. 1), 666.

[28]Ibid., 759, 760, 785.

[29]Ibid., 760, 761.

[30]Ibid., XXV (pt. 1), 800, 887, 892, 938, 945, 999–1000; E. Porter Alexander, *Military Memoirs of a Confederate* (reissue, Bloomington, 1962), 347–48. The number of Confederate guns at Hazel Grove was variously reported. Thomas H. Carter said "some twenty-five guns." *OR*, XXV (pt. 1), 1000. Jeb Stuart said he ordered thirty guns to Hazel Grove. Ibid., 887.

[31]Douglas S. Freeman, *Lee's Lieutenants: A Study in Command* (3 vols., New York, 1942–1944), II, 592; Pleasonton, "Successes and Failures," III, 182.

One of the major artillery offensives of the war was the Confederate cannonade that preceded Pickett's charge. The Confederates cannonaded the Union lines with about 142 guns to prepare Pickett's charge, and the Federals replied with 103 pieces.[32] Some Confederate officers argued that the Gettysburg cannonade was a success. Major B. F. Eshleman of the Washington (Louisiana) Artillery claimed that his fire "caused immense slaughter to the enemy." Other southern commanders were more restrained in their claims. Colonel J. Thompson Brown, the acting chief of artillery for the Second Corps, thought that the fire of the guns around him "was well directed, and its fine effect was very noticeable." Brown also said that these guns would have done better if the "proximity" of Confederate infantry and the poor quality of available shells had not forced them to fire only solid shot. Captain Willis J. Dance, a battalion commander, made similar remarks in his official report on Gettysburg.[33]

Many officers criticized the effectiveness of the Gettysburg cannonade. James Longstreet admitted after the war that the cannonade "seemed less effective than we had anticipated." Cadmus M. Wilcox, a brigade commander in General Richard H. Anderson's Division, said: "I do not believe a single battery of the enemy had been disabled so as to stop its fire."[34] Captain Charles A. Phillips, a Union battery commander whose guns were south of the focal point of the cannonade, dismissed the cannonade, remarking that "beyond the noise which was made no great harm was done." Henry J. Hunt, the chief of artillery of the Army of the Potomac, thought the southern artillery fire was too high and "scattered over the whole field."[35]

The Confederates intended to advance artillery in support of Pickett's charge, but the southern artillery was not able to give the infantry much support. E. Porter Alexander said that he intended to advance nine howitzers in front of Pickett's Division but the guns could not be found at the time of the advance.[36] Alexander said that he deployed "fifteen or eighteen" guns behind Pickett's Division, but the Federal artillery ignored them and concentrated on Pickett's men.[37] James Longstreet believed that the Confederate

---

[32]These figures are from the careful study of George R. Stewart, *Pickett's Charge* (Boston, 1959), 114.

[33]*OR*, XXVII (pt. 2), 435, 456, 604. Dance's and many other Confederate guns were not well placed and cannot have accomplished much during the Gettysburg cannonade. Stewart, *Pickett's Charge*, 98.

[34]James Longstreet, "Lee's Right Wing at Gettysburg," in *Battles and Leaders*, III, 343–44; *OR*, XXVII (pt. 2), 620.

[35]*OR*, XXVII (pt. 1), 885; Hunt, "Third Day at Gettysburg," III, 373–74.

[36]Alexander, "Artillery Fighting at Gettysburg," III, 362–63. Longstreet referred to this episode but said seven guns were involved. Longstreet, "Lee's Right Wing," III, 345. George R. Stewart argued that these howitzers could not have contributed much to the charge. Stewart, *Pickett's Charge*, 119–20.

[37]Alexander, "Artillery Fighting at Gettysburg," III, 365.

artillery fire "did not force the Federals to change the direction of their fire and relieve our infantry." B. F. Eshleman said that the artillery was to advance with the infantry, but that low ammunition and losses from the cannonade prevented most of the guns around him from advancing.[38] Robert E. Lee, James Longstreet, and other Confederate officers reported that the southern artillery was low on ammunition after the cannonade.[39]

The Confederates tried to use artillery aggressively at Chickamauga, September 19 and 20, 1863. In a few cases, Confederate field guns were advanced to within less than 100 yards of the Federal infantry lines.[40] Some Confederate gunners succeeded in diverting the flow of Union reinforcements onto the battlefield,[41] and General Simon B. Buckner found an artillery position that enfiladed parts of the entrenched Federal lines around Kelly's field.[42]

The use of artillery on the offensive at Chickamauga was not so successful, however, as the Confederates had hoped. The Confederate plan was that artillery would attack with infantry, batteries following in the rear of the center of brigades.[43] In some cases, the heavily wooded terrain at Chickamauga made it difficult for the artillery to keep up with the infantry. In other cases, the artillery found its field of fire obstructed by the terrain or by the friendly infantry in front.[44]

In the spring campaigns of 1864 in both theaters, there was extensive entrenching. The tactical defensive was strengthened, and the offensive use of artillery was made even more difficult. On some occasions, attempts were made to work field guns near the front lines. During the May 12 assault at Spotsylvania Court House, one section of Battery C, Fifth United States Artillery, under Lieutenant Richard Metcalf was brought up close to the line of Confederate entrenchments. Metcalf's section fired double canister into the Confederate defenders, but nearly all the men and horses of his section were soon casualties. One of Metcalf's men wrote: "We were a considerable distance in front of our infantry, and of course artillery could not live long under such a fire as the enemy were putting through there. Our men went down in short order."[45] A section of Battery B, First Rhode Island Light Artillery, was also said to have been used near the front lines at Spot-

---

[38]Longstreet, "Lee's Right Wing," III, 346; *OR*, XXVII (pt. 2), 435.

[39]*OR*, XXVII (pt. 2), 321, 360, 610, 620.

[40]Ibid., XXX (pt. 2), 154, 176, 197.

[41]Ibid., 177–78, 358–59.

[42]Ibid., 289, 358.

[43]Ibid., 229, 270, 342, 356, 411.

[44]Ibid., 215–16, 256, 270, 286, 360, 370, 382, 411–12, 448.

[45]Ibid., XXXVI (pt. 1), 336, 537, 539, 669; G. Norton Galloway, "Hand-to-Hand Fighting at Spotsylvania," in *Battles and Leaders*, IV, 171–72 and 171n–172n; Sergeant William E. Lines, quoted in a footnote to ibid., 171n.

sylvania.[46] William F. Barry, Sherman's chief of artillery during the Atlanta campaign, reported that Union batteries were sometimes used "upon the actual skirmish line" during that campaign. General John M. Brannan, chief of artillery of the Army of the Cumberland, said his batteries fought "frequently on the skirmish line, within short canister range of strongly intrenched works of the enemy."[47] Extensive entrenching also led to the increased use of coehorn and siege mortars, which threw their shells in a high trajectory and dropped them into the enemy's works. Mortars were used during engagements such as Spotsylvania Court House, Cold Harbor, and Petersburg.[48]

Artillery was rarely an effective offensive weapon in the siege warfare that developed at Petersburg late in the war. The artillery arm was used to prepare assaults against enemy entrenchments and to cover the retreats that often followed. Before the Petersburg Mine assault of July 30, 1864, Henry J. Hunt massed along the front of the Fifth Corps 110 guns and 54 mortars, all of which were to open fire when the mine exploded.[49] After the Mine assault failed, Hunt said he covered the withdrawal "as far as possible" with the artillery.[50] During the final assault on Petersburg, April 2, 1865, some artillery units advanced with the infantry. Artillerymen were also sent forward with the infantry, to be available to work captured guns as they were taken from the Confederates.[51] These tactics were successful, but the Federals owed their success on April 2 much less to the aggressive use of artillery than to the weakened condition of the Confederate defenders.

One reason that artillery was not an effective offensive weapon during the Civil War was that rifling improved infantry fire more than it did artillery fire. Rifling increased the range of cannon, but there were problems with the rifled pieces of the Civil War. Henry J. Hunt was critical of the three-inch ordnance rifle, arguing that it caused ordnance problems that affected accuracy of fire. He believed that the large Parrott rifles had had good opportunities at Sharpsburg and had failed to capitalize on them. Hunt became impatient with the large Parrotts and after Fredericksburg he tried to rid the Army of the Potomac of them. On December 21, 1862, he complained: "the practice in the recent battle [Fredericksburg] with the 20-pounder Parrott was in some

---

[46]*OR*, XXXVI (pt. 1), 336, 509, 533.

[47]Ibid., XXXVIII (pt. 1), 122, 184.

[48]For examples of the use of mortars, see ibid., XXXVI (pt. 1), 527; XL (pt. 1), 280, 433–34, 671–74; Galloway, "Hand-to-Hand Fighting," IV, 173.

[49]*OR*, LX (pt. 1), 280, 288, 483–85, 599–600. On the role of the Eighteenth Corps artillery in supporting the Mine assault, see ibid., 726–27.

[50]Ibid., 281.

[51]For examples of artillery units advancing in the final assault, see ibid., XLVI (pt. 1), 792, 794, 1010, 1011, 1014. For examples of artillerymen accompanying infantry, see ibid., 1010, 1016, 1062, 1068, 1072, 1078, 1081, 1085, 1087, 1088, 1089.

respects very unsatisfactory, from the imperfection of the projectiles, which, notwithstanding the pains which have been taken to procure reliable ones, are nearly as dangerous to our own troops as to the enemy, if the former are in advance of our lines. In addition, the guns themselves are unsafe. At Antietam two of the twenty-two [twenty-pounder Parrotts], and on the 13th instant [at Fredericksburg] another, were disabled by the bursting of the gun near the muzzle."[52] Colonel Charles P. Kingsbury, who was the chief ord-nance officer of the Army of the Potomac during the Peninsula campaign, said that during that campaign the smoothbore batteries "perhaps, proved to be the most efficient part of our artillery." General John D. Imboden, a veteran of the eastern theater, said after the war that he preferred smoothbores to rifles for short-range, open-field fighting, "defensive works not being consi-dered." Jacob D. Cox, a volunteer officer, complained that the regular army artillery officers consistently favored the smoothbore Napoleons over the rifled guns.[53]

The mobility and effectiveness of Civil War field guns were limited by difficult terrain. In the eastern theater, broken ground and Virginia mud often restricted the use of artillery. At Fair Oaks/Seven Pines, for example, the muddy Virginia terrain hindered the guns of both armies. Captain George W. Hazzard, chief of artillery for the First Division, Second Corps, reported: "Ten horses were required to move our guns from one part of the field to another, and our wheel-traces and prolonges snapped like pack-thread." On the Confederate side, General Gustavus W. Smith said that when General W. H. C. Whiting's Division made a rapid advance on the first day of the battle, no artillery accompanied it, "on account of the almost impracticable condition of the ground."[54] The Wilderness region west of Chancellorsville was perhaps the most difficult terrain for artillery during the war because of the dense woods and second growth of the area.[55] The Spotsylvania Court House battlefield, southeast of the Wilderness, was only somewhat more open. Armistead L. Long said of the line of Ewell's Corps at Spotsylvania: "This position, like the one at the Wilderness, was not well adapted to the effective use of artillery, the view being obstructed by forest and old field pine."[56]

The terrain of the western theater was also difficult for artillery. After

---

[52]Hunt, "Artillery," XIII, 115; *OR*, XXI, 189.

[53]*OR*, XI (pt. 1), 156; John D. Imboden, "Incidents of the First Bull Run," in *Battles and Leaders*, I, 233n–234n; Jacob D. Cox, *Military Reminiscences of the Civil War* (2 vols., New York, 1900), I, 182–83.

[54]*OR*, XI (pt. 1), 768; Gustavus W. Smith, "Two Days of Battle at Seven Pines (Fair Oaks)," in *Battles and Leaders*, II, 244.

[55]On the Wilderness terrain and artillery, see *OR*, XXXVI (pt. 1), 430, 1028, 1085; Law, "Wilderness to Cold Harbor," IV, 122.

[56]*OR*, XXXVI (pt. 1), 1086.

Braxton Bragg attacked at Murfreesboro, he admitted that the battlefield terrain had favored the defensive use of artillery. "Our artillery could rarely be used," said Bragg, "while the enemy, holding defensive lines, had selected formidable positions for his batteries and this dense cover for his infantry, from both of which he had to be dislodged by our infantry alone." The Chickamauga battlefield had heavy woods that restricted the use of artillery. One Federal brigade commander referred to the woods around his unit as "a perfect jungle" where "artillery could not be used to advantage." William Preston said that artillery was of little use during the offensive against Snodgrass Hill. "In the attack on the [Snodgrass] hill no artillery could be used by us effectively," Preston reported; "the struggle was alone for the infantry. Few fell who were not struck down by the rifle or the musket." William F. Barry, who served in both theaters, wrote after the Atlanta campaign: "The nature of military operations in a country like ours is peculiar, and often without precedent elsewhere. It is generally unfavorable to the full development and legitimate use of artillery. This is eminently the case in the West, where large tracts of uncleared land and dense forest materially circumscribe its field of usefulness and often force it into positions of hazard and risk."[57]

Some officers regarded field guns as more valuable with inexperienced troops than with veteran troops. In June 1861, Irvin McDowell said that he wanted to add more artillery to his young army because artillery gave confidence to new troops. The artillery arm was thought less important as the war went on. William F. Barry, who served as chief of artillery under both George B. McClellan and William T. Sherman, said that for the Peninsula campaign McClellan had a ratio of more than four guns per 1,000 men, a good ratio for an army composed of new troops. Barry also said that before the Atlanta campaign he recommended, because of "the veteran condition" of Sherman's troops and other factors, that Sherman's artillery be reduced to two guns per 1,000 men, a ratio Sherman endorsed. "Artillery is more valuable with new and inexperienced troops than with veterans," Sherman said after the war. "In the early stages of the war the field-guns often bore the proportion of six to a thousand men; but toward the close of the war one gun, or at most two, to a thousand men, was deemed enough."[58]

By the end of the war, some officers had become skeptical of the value of artillery on the offensive. Jacob D. Cox thought that artillery proved of little value to the Confederate attackers at Peach Tree Creek. "The dense forests made the artillery of little effect in demolishing the works or weakening the

[57]Ibid., XX (pt. 1), 655; XXX (pt. 1), 693; (pt. 2), 417; XXXVIII (pt. 1), 122.

[58]Ibid., II, 721; "Tactics for Field Artillery," 5–6, Proceedings and Report of the Barry Board, in the Papers of the Barry Board, Record Group 94, Adjutant General's Office, Navy and Old Army Branch, National Archives; OR, XXXVIII (pt. 1), 120; William T. Sherman, Memoirs of General William T. Sherman By Himself (2 vols., reissue, Bloomington, 1957), II, 396.

morale of the defenders," Cox said, "and it was essentially an infantry attack upon intrenched infantry and artillery at close range." After the war, Oliver O. Howard questioned the value of artillery cannonades. "I am not sure that this previous artillery practice in battle at long ranges does much good," Howard wrote, "where there are no walls to break down. It may occupy the enemy's artillery and keep it from effective work against our advancing men, but it prevents anything like a surprise."[59]

The artillery arm had won a strong reputation in the Mexican War and was highly regarded at the opening of the Civil War. It was a powerful defensive force on many Civil War battlefields. Attempts were made to use artillery as an offensive arm, but for the most part it was more effective on the defensive. The adoption of rifling benefited the infantry more than the artillery. The difficult terrain of both theaters, and other factors, limited the effectiveness of artillery on the offensive.

[59]Cox, *Military Reminiscences*, II, 277; Howard, *Autobiography*, I, 485.

10

The Cavalry Was Abruptly Checked

When the Civil War began, expectations for what cavalry might accomplish on the tactical offensive were even higher than those for artillery. The mounted arm had performed many difficult duties in the Mexican War. Its units had sometimes fought dismounted, but the saber charges of the war were more memorable and had done much to strengthen confidence in the mounted attack. Tactical theory of the 1850s also stressed the offensive and the saber.

Civil War cavalry leaders of both sides favored using cavalry aggressively. Jeb Stuart, in his official report on his first ride around McClellan's army, quoted his own version of one of Jomini's maxims. Jomini had said that when cavalry attacked cavalry the victor would ordinarily be the commander who had the last squadrons in reserve to throw against his enemy's flank. Stuart said, "he who brings on the field the last cavalry reserve wins the day." In his report on the Seven Days' battles, Stuart stated his disappointment that the campaign had given him no opportunity "for an overwhelming charge." General William E. "Grumble" Jones believed that in cavalry combat "a vigorous assault might put even a small force on a perfect equality with a large one." James H. Wilson wrote in October 1864: "Cavalry is useless for defense; its only power is in a vigorous offensive."[1] Philip H. Sheridan quarreled with George G. Meade during the Virginia campaign because of Sheridan's aggressive ideas about the use of cavalry. From the opening of the campaign, Sheridan wanted the cavalry put on the offensive. The night after the first day's fighting in the Wilderness, he complained in a dispatch to Meade's headquarters: "I cannot do anything with the cavalry except to act on the defensive, on account of [the] immense amount of material and trains

---

[1] Antoine Henri Jomini, *Summary of the Art of War*, trans. O. F. Winship and E. E. McLean (New York, 1854), 312; U.S. War Dept., *The War of the Rebellion: A Compilation of the Official Records of the Union and Confederate Armies* (128 vols., Washington, 1880–1901), Series 1, XI (pt. 1), 1037; (pt. 2), 521; XXVII (pt. 2), 752; XXXVIX (pt. 3), 443 (hereinafter cited as *OR;* all references are to Series 1).

here [Chancellorsville] and on the road to Ely's Ford. . . . Why cannot infantry be sent to guard the trains, and let me take the offensive?" During the movement from the Wilderness to Spotsylvania Court House, Sheridan and Meade had a confrontation that ended with Ulysses S. Grant's decision that Sheridan be allowed to undertake an independent operation.[2]

Tactical theory urged caution about sending cavalry against infantry, but it held that in some circumstances it could be successfully done. In a few exceptional cases, Civil War cavalry attacked and defeated infantry. Colonel Jesse Hildebrand admitted that the Seventy-seventh Ohio of his brigade was attacked successfully by Confederate cavalry after Shiloh. "So sudden and rapid was the charge, shooting our men with carbines and revolvers," Hildebrand reported, "they had no time to reload or fix bayonets, and were forced to fall back under cover of our cavalry. . . . The rebel cavalry literally rode down the infantry." The Union cavalryman William W. Averell said that cavalry attacked infantry successfully during a raid against the Virginia Central and the Richmond and Fredericksburg railroads north of Richmond. During a pursuit operation on May 27, 1862, near Hanover Court House, Federal cavalry belonging to General William H. Emory's Brigade "aggressively attacked infantry," Averell said, "captured whole companies with arms, swept right, left, and rear, and generally filled the ideal of cavalry activities in such a battle."[3]

Federal cavalry fought successfully against Confederate infantry during the Shenandoah Valley campaign of 1864. Sheridan was able to use cavalry to attack infantry in this campaign in part because the infantry that opposed him was often weak and demoralized. Reporting on the skirmishes fought by his cavalry before the battle of Winchester, Sheridan said: "In these skirmishes the cavalry was becoming educated to attack infantry." During the famous Federal counterattack at Cedar Creek, Sheridan's cavalry was deployed on both flanks of his infantry and charged with it. Alfred T. A. Torbert, Sheridan's cavalry commander at Cedar Creek, wrote: "Thus the cavalry advanced on both flanks side by side with the infantry, charging the enemy's lines with an impetuosity which they could not stand."[4]

These cases were exceptional. When cavalry charged infantry the result was more often disastrous for the horsemen. Rifled firepower enabled infantry to break up cavalry charges long before the riders could reach the infantry's lines. One of the best known and most desperate charges of Civil War

---

[2]*OR*, XXXVI (pt. 1), 773; Philip H. Sheridan, *Personal Memoirs of P. H. Sheridan* (2 vols., New York, 1888), I, 354–56, 368–69.

[3]*OR*, X (pt. 1), 263; William W. Averell, "With the Cavalry on the Peninsula," in *Battles and Leaders of the Civil War*, ed. Robert U. Johnson and Clarence C. Buel (4 vols., reissue, New York, 1956), II, 430. The official reports of some of the Union cavalry commanders on Hanover Court House are in *OR*, XI (pt. 1), 685–93.

[4]*OR*, XLIII (pt. 1), 46, 434.

cavalry against infantry was made at Gaines's Mill, June 27, 1862. The Confederate brigade of John Bell Hood broke through the Union lines at Gaines's Mill at the close of the day's fighting. In a hopeless effort to blunt Hood's success, troopers of the Fifth United States Cavalry charged the Confederate infantrymen. Hood's men had just broken through the Federal front and their line, as E. M. Law said, was "ragged and irregular" and only "partly re-formed" when the Union cavalry struck. Even so, the Confederate rifle fire broke apart the cavalry charge within a few minutes. "This episode," Law said, "consumed scarcely more time than it takes to write it."[5] About 250 men of the Fifth Cavalry made this charge and only about 100 riders survived, a loss of about 60 percent. William W. Averell contended: "The charge at Balaklava had not this desperation and was not better ridden."[6]

Another well-known charge of cavalry against infantry was made by the Eighth Pennsylvania Cavalry at Chancellorsville. After Stonewall Jackson had routed the Eleventh Corps on the evening of May 2, 1863, the Eighth Pennsylvania Cavalry rode against Jackson's men in a desperate attempt to slow the Confederate attack. The regiment made a saber charge, riding in column formation,[7] but was broken apart by Confederate rifle fire. John L. Collins, who rode in the charge, later wrote: "We struck it [the Confederate infantry] as a wave strikes a stately ship: the ship is staggered, maybe thrown on her beam ends, but the wave is dashed into spray, and the ship sails on as before." Most of the riders at the head of the column became casualties. Collins said: "Major Keenan, who led his battalion in the charge, the captain in command of the leading squadron, the adjutant, and a few score of their followers went down at this shock together. The detail sent over to recover their bodies after the battle said that the major had thirteen bullets in his body, the adjutant nine, and others fewer."[8] Major Pennock Huey, who commanded the Eighth Pennsylvania Cavalry at Chancellorsville, reported that the regiment lost three officers, thirty men, and about eighty horses in this charge.[9]

---

[5]E. M. Law, "On the Confederate Right at Gaines's Mill," in *Battles and Leaders*, II, 364.

[6]W. H. Hitchcock, "Recollections of a Participant in the Charge," ibid., 346; Averell, "With the Cavalry," II, 430.

[7]Alfred Pleasonton, who commanded a division of cavalry that included the Eighth Pennsylvania Cavalry, claimed that he ordered this charge. *OR*, XXV (pt. 1), 773, 785; Alfred Pleasonton, "The Successes and Failures of Chancellorsville," in *Battles and Leaders*, III, 179. Three men who were then officers in the Eighth Pennsylvania Cavalry—Pennock Huey, J. Edward Carpenter, and Andrew B. Wells—wrote accounts of the charge that disputed Pleasonton's version of it. Pennock Huey, J. Edward Carpenter, and Andrew B. Wells, "The Charge of the Eighth Pennsylvania Cavalry," ibid., 186, 187–88; *OR*, XXV (pt. 1), 785.

[8]John L. Collins, "When Stonewall Jackson Turned Our Right," in *Battles and Leaders*, III, 183.

[9]*OR*, XXV (pt. 1), 784. The regiment's total losses at Chancellorsville, May 1–3, were 102 men and officers. Ibid., 185.

Another famous charge of Federal cavalry against Confederate infantry took place at Gettysburg on July 3, 1863. General Judson Kilpatrick, commanding a cavalry division on the Union left, ordered one of his brigade commanders, General Elon J. Farnsworth, to make a mounted attack against Confederate infantry protected by stone walls. One Federal officer who rode in the charge said that the southern "defensive position" was "one that above all others is the worst for a cavalry charge—that is, behind stone fences so high as to preclude the possibility of gaining the opposite side without dismounting and throwing them down." Farnsworth opposed the charge and protested to Kilpatrick against it, but Kilpatrick insisted that the charge be made. Captain H. C. Parsons of the First Vermont Cavalry said that "each man felt, as he tightened his saber belt, that he was summoned to a ride to death." Farnsworth made the charge in columns of battalions, attacking without any infantry support.[10] Farnsworth's men rode against infantry commanded by E. M. Law, who later wrote: "The course of the cavalry was abruptly checked and saddles were rapidly emptied."[11] About 300 riders made the charge; Farnsworth was killed, and about 100 others became casualties.[12]

Other charges of Civil War cavalry against infantry ended in disaster. The last charge at Cedar Mountain, August 9, 1862, was made by General George D. Bayard's Cavalry Brigade. Four days later, one Confederate infantry brigade commander wrote: "The enemy's cavalry attempted to charge us in two columns, but the fire soon broke them and sent them fleeing across the field in every direction."[13] At Pleasant Hill on April 9, 1864, General Thomas Green ordered General Hamilton P. Bee to make a mounted charge against Federal infantry. Bee advanced two regiments in columns of four and ordered others to follow. He said that his troopers rode into a "disastrous" rifle fire. "Fortunately there were ravines of young pines on our right which furnished somewhat of shelter until the shock could be recovered from," he reported, "but the empty saddles, the men shot and falling in all directions,

---

[10]Ibid., XXVII (pt. 1), 1018–19, 1013, 993; H. C. Parsons, "Farnsworth's Charge and Death," in *Battles and Leaders*, III, 394–96.

[11]E. M. Law, "The Struggle for 'Round Top,'" in *Battles and Leaders*, III, 329.

[12]Parsons gave the number of riders as about 300 and the losses as 65. Parsons, "Farnsworth's Charge," III, 396. This loss figure apparently counted only the First Vermont Cavalry, Parsons's regiment. *OR*, XXVII (pt. 1), 186. Colonel Nathaniel P. Richmond of the First West Virginia Cavalry, who succeeded Farnsworth, reported the brigade losses as 107, and the table accompanying his report gave the total brigade losses for July 3 as 108. Ibid., 1005, 1008. The return on ibid., 186, gave the brigade losses for the entire battle (most of which would have been sustained in this one charge) as 98. The figures in returns such as these were compiled and revised from reported figures and often were lower than the originally reported losses.

[13]L. O'B. Branch Journal, August 13, 1862, quoted in a footnote by the editors to John Pope, "The Second Battle of Bull Run," in *Battles and Leaders*, II, 459n. See also *OR*, XII (pt. 2), 184, 216, 222.

the confusion, produced a scene imperishable on my memory." One regiment lost a third of its men in this charge.[14]

The boldest cavalry action was the saber charge. During the Mexican War, American units had made a few saber charges, such as Kearny's charge after Churubusco and May's at Resaca de la Palma. Attacks such as these increased confidence in the saber. Tactical theory emphasized the saber; Mahan, Halleck, and McClellan had endorsed it. David S. Stanley, chief of cavalry of the Army of the Cumberland, believed that sharp sabers raised the confidence of his troopers. William W. Averell, who led the Third Pennsylvania Cavalry during the siege of Yorktown, recalled after the war, that his regiment's morale improved when it acquired grindstones and sharpened its sabers during the month-long siege.[15]

Some of the most famous saber fighting of the Civil War was done during the Gettysburg campaign. On June 9, 1863, the largest cavalry battle of the war was fought at Brandy Station. General David McM. Gregg, who commanded a division of Union cavalry at Brandy Station, described the opening of the battle by saying that Colonel Percy Wyndham's Brigade charged with drawn sabers and "fell upon" the Confederate cavalry. Judson Kilpatrick's Brigade rode to Wyndham's support, and there was more saber fighting. "Thus for an hour and a half was the contest continued," said Gregg, "not in skirmishing, but in determined charges." Wyndham reported that his brigade made "six distinct regimental charges," and "a number of smaller ones." Later in the same campaign, mounted charges and saber fighting took place during the cavalry battle east of Gettysburg on July 3. General George A. Custer reported that his First Michigan Cavalry "charged in close column upon [General Wade] Hampton's brigade, using the saber only." Captain William E. Miller of the Third Pennsylvania Cavalry wrote after the war that the First Michigan Cavalry formed in column of squadrons and charged into Confederate cavalry that was advancing in the same formation. "As the two columns approached each other the pace of each increased," said Miller, "when suddenly a crash, like the falling of timbers, betokened the crisis. So sudden and violent was the collision that many of the horses were turned end over end and crushed their riders beneath them."[16]

Enough successful saber charges occurred during the war to maintain the reputation of the saber. At Shelbyville, Tennessee, on June 27, 1863, units of Colonel Robert H. G. Minty's Brigade of cavalry rode in column in a saber charge against a Confederate battery and its supports. The charge was led by

---

[14]*OR*, XXXIV (pt. 1), 608. For a Union account of this charge, see ibid., 309.

[15]Stephen Z. Starr, "Cold Steel: The Saber and the Union Cavalry," *Civil War History*, XI (1965), 146; Averell, "With the Cavalry," II, 429.

[16]*OR*, XXVII (pt. 1), 950, 951, 966, 998; William E. Miller, "The Cavalry Battle Near Gettysburg," in *Battles and Leaders*, III, 404.

the Seventh Pennsylvania Cavalry, supported by other units of Minty's command. Lieutenant Colonel William B. Sipes of the Seventh Pennsylvania Cavalry reported that until near the close of the action his men used only their sabers. The Confederates were pursued into Duck River. "Even here," said an officer of the Third Indiana Cavalry, "we used the trusty saber with effect." Minty claimed that the Confederates lost three guns and about 800 men in this charge.[17]

Another decisive saber charge occurred at Winchester on September 19, 1864. Near the close of the battle, Alfred T. A. Torbert sent two cavalry divisions against the left flank of Jubal Early's line. Philip H. Sheridan later said that the ground on the Confederate left "was open, and offered an opportunity such as seldom had been presented during the war for a mounted attack, and Torbert was not slow to take advantage of it." Successive cavalry charges drove in Early's left flank, and the Confederate retreat from Winchester began. One brigade of General Wesley Merritt's Division struck an angle in the southern line. Merritt reported that "the intrepid [General Thomas C.] Devin, with his gallant brigade, burst like a storm of case-shot in their midst, showering saber blows on their heads and shoulders, trampling them under his horses' feet, and routing them in droves in every direction." Devin's men captured over 300 prisoners and three flags.[18]

Saber charges were memorable, but they were not common. "Saber cuts are very rare in the Army of the Cumberland," John Beatty said after the Murfreesboro campaign, "and if young officers were compelled to defer entering into wedlock until they got a wound of this kind, there would be precious few soldiers married." John S. Mosby said that his company of the First Virginia Cavalry was issued sabers at the beginning of the war, "but the only real use I ever heard of their being put to was to hold a piece of meat over a fire for frying. I dragged one through the first year of the war, but when I became a commander, I discarded it."[19]

Some cavalry commanders concluded that the saber had little value, including James H. Wilson, who fought in both theaters of the war. "I think it is demonstrable, both from the experience of the cavalry of the Army of the

---

[17]*OR*, XXIII (pt. 1), 656, 559, 558. Minty's Brigade lost only thirty-six men during the Tullahoma campaign. Ibid., 423. For another account of this charge at Shelbyville, see William B. Sipes, *The Seventh Pennsylvania Veteran Volunteer Cavalry: Its Record, Reminiscences and Roster . . .* (Pottsville, Pa., 1905?), 67–69.

[18]Sheridan, *Personal Memoirs*, II, 26; *OR*, XLIII (pt. 1), 444–45. Merritt also talked about mounted fighting during the Shenandoah Valley campaign of 1864 in an article written after the war. Wesley Merritt, "Sheridan in the Shenandoah Valley," in *Battles and Leaders*, IV, 514, 519–20, 520n.

[19]John Beatty, *The Citizen-Soldier; or, Memoirs of a Volunteer* (Cincinnati, 1879), 213–14; John S. Mosby, *The Memoirs of Colonel John S. Mosby*, ed. Charles Wells Russell (reissue, Bloomington, 1959), 30.

Potomac, as well as that of the Army of the West," said Wilson, "that the sabre is just as much out of date for cavalry in a country like ours as the short sword of the Roman soldier is for infantry. It is in the way and is of no value whatever in a fight, as compared with repeating rifles, carbines, and pistols." Mosby said that "the sabre is of no use against gunpowder" and claimed to be the first Civil War cavalry commander to discard the weapon. He wrote: "My men were as little impressed by a body of cavalry charging them with sabres as though they had been armed with cornstalks." He believed that the saber had been made obsolete when the rifle replaced the musket. After infantry was armed with the rifle, cavalry could no longer rely on shock alone. "In the Napoleonic wars cavalry might sometimes ride down infantry armed with muzzleloaders and flintlocks," Mosby argued, "because the infantry would be broken by the momentum of the charge before more than one effective fire could be delivered. . . . I think that my command reached the highest point [of] efficiency as cavalry because they were well armed with two six-shooters and their charges combined the effect of fire and shock."[20]

During the Civil War, theories about cavalry fighting had to contend with the realities of new weaponry. Some cavalry leaders wanted to take the offensive with saber charges, but they found that their opportunities were rare. At First Manassas, the first major battle of the war, there were only small numbers of cavalry: the Federals had one battalion of regular cavalry and the Confederates had the equivalent of about five regiments. The use of these units at First Manassas typified how cavalry was to be used on battlefields during much of the war. The cavalry leaders there intended to take the offensive, but they used their units primarily in support roles. Colonel Samuel P. Heintzelman said that Major Innis N. Palmer, who commanded the battalion of regular cavalry at First Manassas, "was anxious to engage the enemy," but when Heintzelman saw that there was no opportunity for this he ordered Palmer's cavalry "back out of range of fire." Palmer's Battalion served in detachments and was used to support artillery batteries, perform reconnaissances, and cover the Federal retreat.[21] The Confederate cavalry was only somewhat more active. Jeb Stuart led the First Virginia Cavalry in a charge that rode down the Eleventh New York, the Fire Zouaves regiment.[22] Stuart also used his small cavalry force to cover the flanks of Stonewall Jackson's Brigade, perform reconnaissances, and pursue the Federals after the battle.[23]

---

[20]James H. Wilson, "The Cavalry of the Army of the Potomac," *Papers of the Military Historical Society of Massachusetts* (14 vols., Boston, 1913), XIII, 85; Mosby, *Memoirs of Mosby*, 30, 284–85.

[21]*OR*, II, 315, 470, 403, 393.

[22]Ibid., 347, 483. William C. Davis, *Battle at Bull Run . . .* (Garden City, 1977), 208, shows that it is not clear which side did better in this action, Stuart's cavalrymen or the Zouave infantrymen.

[23]*OR*, II, 481, 483.

In the campaigns that followed First Manassas, cavalry often performed semicombat and noncombat tasks, and it became a standard army joke to ask: "Who ever saw a dead cavalryman?"[24] Mounted units performed tactical reconnaissances, pursued enemy infantry after a victory, and covered friendly infantry after a defeat. Cavalry often was used to cover the flanks of the main lines of infantry on Civil War battlefields in both theaters of the war. Franz Sigel deployed his small cavalry force to cover his flanks at Wilson's Creek. Robert E. Lee used cavalry to guard both of his flanks at Second Manassas, and Braxton Bragg did the same at Chickamauga.[25] At Sharpsburg, George B. McClellan assigned his cavalry to the center of his line rather than the flanks, a deployment for which he was later criticized by such veterans as E. Porter Alexander and Jacob D. Cox.[26]

Cavalry units were sometimes held in the rear of infantry units, where they served as file closers to prevent straggling and desertion. Ulysses S. Grant said that he found that this was the best use for his cavalry at Shiloh. "The nature of this battle was such," Grant wrote, "that cavalry could not be used in front; I therefore formed ours into line, in rear, to stop stragglers, of whom there were many." William W. Averell recalled that at Malvern Hill "my cavalry was deployed as a close line of skirmishers with drawn sabers in rear of our lines, with orders to permit no one to pass to the rear who could not show blood." George B. McClellan reported that one of the tasks of his cavalry at Sharpsburg was "driving up stragglers."[27]

Mounted troops were sometimes used to screen infantry movements and to help achieve tactical surprise. The most famous example of this use of cavalry was the successful screening of Stonewall Jackson's flank march at Chancellorsville by General Fitzhugh Lee's Cavalry Brigade.[28] The mobility and flexibility of cavalry made it the arm most capable of confusing and misleading the enemy. During a rearguard action after Malvern Hill, a squadron of the Third Pennsylvania Cavalry confused pursuing Confederate infantry by sounding artillery bugle calls and deploying like a battery. The cavalry squadron "by a skillful disposition of troopers in sections created a very good semblance of a battery, which moved up under the crest of a hill in front, and

---

[24]After Philip H. Sheridan became Ulysses S. Grant's cavalry commander, he had an interview with President Abraham Lincoln, who ended the interview by quoting this standard army joke. Sheridan, *Personal Memoirs*, I, 347. See also *OR*, XXXVI (pt. 1), 802, and Equites, "Rifle and Sabre," *Army and Navy Journal*, VI (January 30, 1869), 374.

[25]*OR*, III, 86, 87, 89; XII (pt. 2), 556; XXX (pt. 2), 34.

[26]Ibid., XIX (pt. 1), 31; E. Porter Alexander, *Military Memoirs of a Confederate* (reissue, Bloomington, 1962), 270–71; Jacob D. Cox, "The Battle of Antietam," in *Battles and Leaders*, II, 658.

[27]Ulysses S. Grant, "The Battle of Shiloh," in *Battles and Leaders*, I, 474; Averell, "With the Cavalry," II, 431; *OR*, XIX (pt. 1), 31.

[28]*OR*, XXV (pt. 1), 887, 1047.

went through the motions of going into action front." The Confederates were fooled by this ruse and withdrew into a nearby woods.[29] At Second Manassas, Jeb Stuart ordered detachments of cavalry to drag brush along the Manassas and Gainesville road to make it appear to the Federals that the road was being used by columns of infantry. Colonel Thomas L. Rosser, who served under Stuart, said that the brush dragging was done by several companies of cavalry.[30]

When Civil War cavalry units were given combat tasks, they often fought dismounted. James H. Wilson believed that during the Civil War, and "in all modern wars," horses were used "mainly for the transportation of the fighting men."[31] W. S. Burns, a Federal cavalry officer in the western theater, said that he regarded Nathan B. Forrest's men as always being " 'mounted infantry.' " After the war John Bell Hood boasted: "our [Confederate] cavalry were not cavalrymen *proper*, but were mounted riflemen, trained to dismount and hold in check or delay the advance of the enemy." Wesley Merritt wrote of his brigade in the Gettysburg campaign: "The men of the brigade, from long and constant practice, are becoming perfect in the art of foot-fighting and skirmishing."[32] The artillerist Henry J. Hunt considered Brandy Station one of the few "true" cavalry battles of the war because it was chiefly a mounted action. "In nearly all the previous so-called 'cavalry' actions," said Hunt, "the troops had fought as dismounted dragoons." Philip H. Sheridan said of the cavalry engagements of the Virginia campaign: "Indeed, they could hardly have been fought otherwise than on foot, as there was little chance for mounted fighting in eastern Virginia, the dense woods, the armament of both parties, and the practice of barricading making it impracticable to use the sabre with anything like a large force; and so with the exception of Yellow Tavern the dismounted method prevailed in almost every engagement."[33]

---

[29]Ibid., XI (pt. 2), 236; Fitz John Porter, "The Battle of Malvern Hill," in *Battles and Leaders*, II, 423; Averell, "With the Cavalry," II, 432.

[30]This incident appeared in Stuart's report on Second Manassas. *OR*, XII (pt. 2), 736. Rosser testified about it in *Senate Executive Document*, 46 Cong., 1 sess., No. 37 (3 parts), III, 1073–76.

The story of Stuart's deception and its significance became a minor issue in the John Pope–Fitz John Porter controversy. For some differing viewpoints on the incident and its importance, see Pope, "Second Battle of Bull Run," II, 483; James Longstreet, "Our March Against Pope," in *Battles and Leaders*, II, 522; John C. Ropes, *The Army Under Pope* (New York, 1889), 118, 120–21. The historian Ropes concluded: "It seems certainly not unlikely that it [the brush dragging] may have deceived our officers, though its effect was probably much exaggerated by Stuart." Ibid., 121.

[31]James H. Wilson, "The Union Cavalry in the Hood Campaign," in *Battles and Leaders*, IV, 471.

[32]W. S. Burns, "A. J. Smith's Defeat of Forrest at Tupelo (July 14th, 1864)," ibid., 422; John Bell Hood, *Advance and Retreat: Personal Experiences in the United States & Confederate Armies*, ed. Richard N. Current (reissue, Bloomington, 1959), 202; *OR*, XXVII (pt. 1), 944.

[33]Henry J. Hunt, "The First Day at Gettysburg," in *Battles and Leaders*, III, 263; Sheridan, *Personal Memoirs*, I, 424–25.

Cavalry units fought dismounted in the major campaigns of the Civil War, as early as Wilson's Creek, where the Second Arkansas Mounted Rifles dismounted and fought beside Confederate infantry. In the well-known engagement that opened the Battle of Gettysburg, the dismounted cavalrymen of General John Buford's Division opposed General Henry Heth's Infantry Division. During the cavalry battle east of Gettysburg on July 3, mounted charges were made, but units of both sides initially were deployed in dismounted formations. The most decisive use of dismounted cavalry during the war was probably the action of the Federal cavalry at Nashville, December 15 and 16, 1864. James H. Wilson reported that his cavalry corps fought dismounted on December 15, "owing to the roughness of the country."[34] On the second day at Nashville, Wilson's dismounted cavalrymen enveloped Hood's left flank, reached his rear, and cut his line of retreat down the Granny White Pike. Late in the war, cavalry in the eastern theater commonly fought dismounted. Colonel Horace Porter, who was sent by Ulysses S. Grant to observe the engagement at Five Forks, April 1, 1865, later described the fighting done there by the Union cavalrymen, dismounted and armed with repeating rifles. "The dismounted cavalry," said Porter, "had assaulted as soon as they heard the infantry fire open. The natty cavalrymen, with their tight-fitting jackets, and short carbines, swarmed through the pine thickets and dense undergrowth, looking as if they had been especially equipped for crawling through knot-holes."[35]

As the war continued, dismounted cavalry became as adept at defending and attacking entrenchments as infantry. In 1864 dismounted cavalry units defended entrenchments in engagements such as Spotsylvania Court House, Yellow Tavern,[36] Haw's Shop,[37] Cold Harbor, Trevilian Station, and Jonesboro.[38] Dismounted cavalry also successfully attacked entrenchments in engagements such as Five Forks, Nashville, and Selma. After the war, James H. Wilson explained: "Up to that time [Nashville] the cavalry in the West had been reserved for independent operations, and had rarely been seen assaulting fortified positions. Such work had been, by common consent, left

---

[34]*OR*, III, 105, 111, 112; XXVII (pt. 1), 927, 934, 938, 939; Hunt, "First Day at Gettysburg," III, 276, 282; *OR*, XXVII (pt. 1), 956, 957, 998, 1051; (pt. 2), 698; Miller, "Cavalry Battle Near Gettysburg," III, 402, 403; *OR*, XLV (pt. 1), 563. See also ibid., 576.

[35]*OR*, XLV (pt. 1), 40, 564, 591; Henry Stone, "Repelling Hood's Invasion of Tennessee," in *Battles and Leaders*, IV, 463–64; Wilson, "Union Cavalry," IV, 468–69; Horace Porter, *Campaigning with Grant*, ed. Wayne C. Temple (reissue, Bloomington, 1961), 440.

[36]*OR*, XXXVI (pt. 1), 540–41, 879; A Private of the Sixth Virginia Cavalry, "The Death of General J. E. B. Stuart," in *Battles and Leaders*, IV, 194.

[37]*OR*, XXXVI (pt. 1), 854; Theophilus F. Rodenbough, "Sheridan's Richmond Raid," in *Battles and Leaders*, IV, 193.

[38]*OR*, XXXVI (pt. 1), 794; Martin T. McMahon, "Cold Harbor," in *Battles and Leaders*, IV, 214; *OR*, XXXVI (pt. 1), 796, 1095; M. C. Butler, "The Cavalry Fight at Trevilian Station," in *Battles and Leaders*, IV, 238; *OR*, XXXVIII (pt. 2), 860, 870, 871, 872, 881, 883, 885, 888, 891. Other examples can be found in both theaters.

for the infantry; but now, under the influence of organization and discipline, the cavalry, with their Spencer repeating rifles, felt themselves equal to any task." Wilson said he decided on his assault plan at Selma, April 2, 1865, after consulting with Emory Upton, whom he admired for his successes in attacking entrenched positions. Upton served at Selma as a cavalry division commander under Wilson. It was decided that the main burden of attack would be borne by General Eli Long's Division. Long's men were dismounted into a single-rank, loose-order formation, one man per yard. This line of veteran troops, armed with Spencer repeating rifles, advanced and carried the Confederate entrenchments at Selma.[39]

When Civil War cavalry units fought dismounted, a system of horse-holders was used. Every fourth cavalryman remained in the rear of the firing line, holding the reins of his own horse and the horses of three other men on the firing line. Horseholders were responsible for controlling the horses of their dismounted comrades, holding the mounts ready for pursuit or retreat. Horseholders also could be drawn on as a local reserve to reinforce the fighting line, a tactic used, for example, by George A. Custer at Trevilian Station.[40]

The horseholder system was necessary, but it had weaknesses. If any enemy force succeeded in getting between the firing line and the horse-holders, the dismounted men were isolated and vulnerable to capture. Wade Hampton's Cavalry Division lost several hundred men and horses captured at Trevilian Station when the Fifth Michigan Cavalry got between Hampton's dismounted men and their held horses.[41] Horseholders also were vulnerable to artillery fire, which might pass over the firing line and land among the groups of horses in the rear. At Boydton Plank Road, October 27, 1864, during the Petersburg campaign, the horses of Colonel Michael Kerwin's Brigade of Pennsylvania cavalry regiments were driven from one field to another by Confederate artillery fire.[42]

The horseholder system and dismounted cavalry fighting were criticized as a threat to the morale of cavalrymen. Major H. B. McClellan, a member of Jeb Stuart's staff, believed it was dangerous for a horseholder to think that his role was less important than that of a man on the firing line. " 'Number Four' has no right to be exempt from the perils of battle," McClellan said. "He

---

[39]Wilson, "Union Cavalry," IV, 468; James H. Wilson, *Under the Old Flag; Recollections of Military Operations in the War for the Union* . . . (2 vols., New York, 1912), II, 222, 226.

[40]Philip St. George Cooke, *Cavalry Tactics or Regulations for the Instruction, Formations, and Movements of the Cavalry of the Army and Volunteers of the United States* (2 parts, Washington, 1861), I, 163, 164; Theophilus F. Rodenbough, "Sheridan's Trevilian Raid," in *Battles and Leaders*, IV, 234.

[41]*OR*, XXXVI (pt. 1), 785, 796, 823, 1095; Rodenbough, "Sheridan's Trevilian Raid," IV, 233–34. Hampton later regained these captives. *OR*, XXXVI (pt. 1), 785, 1095.

[42]*OR*, XLII (pt. 1), 647.

holds the horses of his comrades only in order that they may more efficiently fight on foot; and he should always be near at hand to give what aid the occasion demands." John Bell Hood, who liked aggressive tactics, was critical of dismounted cavalry fighting, which he compared to infantry fighting behind entrenchments. "In accordance with the same principle," Hood said, "a cavalryman *proper* cannot be trained to fight, one day, mounted, the next, dismounted, and then be expected to charge with the impetuosity of one who has been educated in the belief that it is an easy matter to ride over infantry and artillery, and drive them from the field. He who fights alternately mounted and dismounted, can never become an excellent soldier of either infantry or cavalry proper."[43]

Dismounted cavalry fighting also was criticized because it meant slower operations and slower pursuits. James H. Wilson said that when the Federal cavalry fought on foot at Nashville, "its progress was correspondingly slow, except in [General John H.] Hammond's front." Richard W. Johnson, who commanded a cavalry division under Wilson, said that some of the dismounted cavalry moved slowly on the first day at Nashville. He thought this slowness was partly because the cavalrymen were not used to maneuvering as infantry, partly because they had to cross a creek, and partly because of "their sabers, which the commanding officer of the Fourteenth Illinois Cavalry had, with a singular shortsightedness, permitted his men to bring with them," even after they had dismounted. Wilson wrote of the pursuit after Nashville: "The cavalrymen had, however, become separated from their horses by an unusual distance, and, although the latter were hurried forward as rapidly as possible, and [General John T.] Croxton, who was most available, was ordered to mount and push without delay through Brentwood, to be followed by [General Edward] Hatch and Hammond as soon as they could mount, it had become so dark before they were well under way in pursuit that the men could scarcely see their horses' ears."[44]

Partly in response to the problems of dismounted cavalry fighting, mixed formations of both dismounted and mounted troops were used. Some troops would be dismounted to fight, while others would be held mounted, ready to charge or pursue any success. Federal cavalry units, well armed with repeating rifles, commonly used this system during the last year of the war. Wesley Merritt described an example of combined dismounted and mounted tactics in an account of the skirmish at Cedarville, August 16, 1864: "One regiment of Custer's brigade, dismounted, was moved up to the crest of a hill near the riverbank to meet this force [a Confederate infantry brigade], while the rest of the brigade, mounted, was stationed to the right of the hill. . . . The

---

[43]H. B. McClellan, *I Rode With Jeb Stuart: The Life and Campaigns of Major General J. E. B. Stuart* (reissue, Bloomington, 1958), 208; Hood, *Advance and Retreat*, 132.

[44]Wilson, "Union Cavalry," IV, 468, 469; *OR*, XLV (pt. 1), 599.

enemy advanced boldly, wading the river, and when within short carbine range was met by a murderous volley from the dismounted men, while the remainder of the command charged." On the first day at Nashville, James H. Wilson ordered Edward Hatch to dismount his division, except for one regiment from each brigade to be held as a mounted reserve. The official report of one of Hatch's brigade commanders showed that these orders were followed; the Twelfth Tennessee Cavalry was kept "mounted for a charge, should an opportunity present." During the Petersburg campaign, General J. Irvin Gregg's Division fought a typical dismounted and mounted action near Hatcher's Run on February 5 and 6, 1865. Gregg dismounted two brigades of his division and held a third as a mounted reserve. On February 5, the Thirteenth Pennsylvania Cavalry dismounted and drove a Confederate force in its front. The Second Pennsylvania Cavalry of the same brigade then made a mounted charge, scattering the retreating Confederates. On the next day, the brigade used similar tactics. The Thirteenth and Sixteenth Pennsylvania Cavalry regiments advanced on foot, while the Fourth and Eighth Pennsylvania Cavalry regiments made a mounted charge on their right. Federal cavalry units also used combined tactics at Sayler's Creek during the Appomattox campaign.[45]

The most decisive action of dismounted and mounted cavalry during the war was probably the attack by Federal cavalry against Five Forks, April 1, 1865. The two cavalry divisions commanded by Wesley Merritt, one under Thomas C. Devin and one under George A. Custer, first were deployed dismounted; but after the Confederate lines were broken the two divisions remounted for the pursuit operations. Merritt said that because the terrain was "impracticable for mounted operations," Custer's Division was ordered to dismount, with one of his brigades held as a mounted reserve. "At one time my entire command was dismounted and fighting as infantry in the woods skirting along the enemy's front," Custer reported. "Nothing was accomplished in this manner." Custer later deployed one dismounted brigade across his division front and used his other two brigades in a mounted attack that eventually broke in the Confederate right flank.[46] Devin's Division fought dismounted on Custer's right, holding one regiment mounted and ready to exploit any success. Devin reported: "Captain [Richard S. C.] Lord, First U.S. Cavalry, was ordered to keep his regiment mounted and in readiness to charge should the enemy's line be broken. . . . As the works were carried Captain Lord was ordered to charge with his regiment, and gallantly responded, clearing the breastworks at a bound, and charging far in advance of the division." The combined dismounted and mounted tactics also were

[45]Merritt, "Sheridan in the Shenandoah Valley," IV, 502–03; *OR*, XLV (pt. 1), 576, 589; XLVI (pt. 1), 366, 367–68, 370, 1142, 1145–46, 1158.

[46]*OR*, XLVI (pt. 1), 1100, 1105, 1117, 1118, 1130, 1131.

used at Five Forks by units of General Ranald S. Mackenzie's Cavalry Division of the Army of the James.[47]

Civil War cavalry commanders believed that the cavalry arm should have been used aggressively, but the introduction of the rifle made cavalry attacks against infantry perilous. Infantry armed with the rifle could rapidly empty the saddles of advancing cavalry. Cavalrymen made enough successful saber charges during the war to maintain the saber's reputation, but saber charges were not common. Cavalry often was given semicombat and noncombat assignments, but when it did take a combat role, Civil War cavalry often fought on foot. Dismounted cavalry was used both to defend and attack entrenchments. The Union cavalry, better armed with repeating rifles, was able in the later war period to skillfully combine dismounted and mounted tactics. The Civil War was a period of change in cavalry tactics, and the war left the cavalry arm with an uncertain future.

---

[47]Ibid., 1124, 1128. On Mackenzie's Division, see ibid., 1254–55.

Part Three
Why It Happened

11

We Dashed with Sword and Bayonet on the Foe

Sir Herbert Curzon, K.C.M.G., C.B., D.S.O., the fictional antihero of C. S. Forester's *The General*, distrusted theorists. He considered them to be as "mad as hatters, or even madder. As soon as any man started to talk about the theory of war one could be nearly sure that he would bring forward some idiotic suggestion, to the effect that cavalry had had its day and that dismounted action was all that could be expected of it, or that machine-guns and barbed wire had wrought a fundamental change in tactics, or even— wildest lunacy of all—that these rattletrap aeroplanes were going to be of some military value." One "feather-brained subaltern" who quit Curzon's regiment, the Duke of Suffolk's own Twenty-second Lancers, to serve in the Royal Flying Corps, "actually had the infernal impudence to suggest to the senior major of his regiment, a man with ribbons on his breast, who had seen real fighting, and who had won the battle of Volkslaagte by a cavalry charge, that the time was at hand when aeroplane reconnaissance would usurp the last useful function which could be performed by cavalry." Such treachery infuriated Curzon, but when he accused the young man "of assailing the honour of the regiment with all its glorious traditions, he declared light-heartedly that he would far sooner serve in an arm with only a future than in one with only a past, and that he had no intention whatever of saying anything to the discredit of a regiment which was cut to pieces at Waterloo because they did not know when to stop charging."[1]

Curzon, "hide-bound in his ideas and conventional in his way of thought," was a caricature of the inflexible military leaders who fight the current war just as they fought the last war, usually with disastrous results, but he also illustrated how the "lessons" learned early in a career often determined one's later thoughts and actions. In this sense, he was an example rather than a distortion.

Many of the Civil War's military leaders were as much prisoners of their

---

[1] C. S. Forester, *The General* (London, 1936), 23–24.

past experiences as was Curzon. They had learned the wrong lessons—from
what they had been taught at West Point, from the books they had read, or
from their combat experience. All of the official and unofficial manuals
available in the early 1860s advocated offensive tactics. "Offensive wars . . .
have many advantages; purely defensive ones will always end with submis-
sion," stated a tactical manual published early in the war. "There is one great
maxim . . . *to encounter an advancing enemy by our own advance.*" In 1862 a
Confederate army newspaper advised troops: "charge impetuously. No
Federal regiment can withstand a bold and fearless bayonet charge. . . . The
greatest minds in the South are coming to the conclusion, that our liberties
are to be won by the bayonet. Those regiments or companies that most
distinguish themselves in bayonet charges will march on the true road to
honor and preferment."[2]

Men who had been told to rely upon the bayonet and assault tactics and
who had witnessed the success of such charges were understandably slow to
appreciate the advantage the new rifles gave defenders. It is significant that
some of the first leaders to recognize the full extent of the rifle's killing power
when fired from entrenchments were Federals who had seen no action during
the Mexican War—either such West Point graduates as Generals William T.
Sherman, William B. Hazen, and Oliver O. Howard, or such citizen soldiers
as General Jacob D. Cox and Colonel Theodore Lyman. "Put a man in a
hole," noted Lyman, "and he will beat off three times his number, even if he
is not a very good soldier." A few entrenched men armed with rifles could
hold a position against great odds. General Cox declared: "One rifle in the
trench was worth five in front of it." Perhaps he exaggerated a bit, but
unquestionably the rifle and the spade had made defense much stronger than
offense.[3]

Yet most Confederate leaders, and some Federals such as Grant, seemed
unwilling to give up the old tactics. "There was a tremendous assault along
the line . . . [at Cold Harbor on June 3, 1864, but it] failed with a loss . . . of
8000 men on our side," admitted a Union officer. "In the evening the Rebs.
assaulted our lines, but were repulsed." Two assaults by General Richard
Taylor, who had been with his father, Old Zach, in Mexico, cost the Confederacy 500 casualties in 1862 and taught Taylor nothing. "What the hell are
you dodging for?" Taylor had screamed as his men wavered in one assault.
"If there is any more of it, you will be halted under fire for an hour." Taylor
led his brigade to within fifty yards of the enemy "in perfect order, not firing
a shot." He proudly reported that the men closed "the many gaps made by

[2]Emil Schalk, *Summary of the Art of War: Written Expressly for and Dedicated to the U.S. Volunteer
Army* (Philadelphia, 1862), 2, 118; Corinth (Mississippi) *Missouri Army Argus*, May 12, 1862.

[3]Theodore Lyman, *Meade's Headquarters, 1863–1865* . . . , ed. George R. Agassiz (Boston,
1922), 224; Jacob D. Cox, *Atlanta* (New York, 1882), 129. See Chapter 8.

[the enemy's] fierce fire" and preserved "an alignment that would have been creditable on parade." The following year at Milliken's Bend one of Taylor's brigades, "in obedience to orders, attacked with the bayonet" and lost 100 men. Such aggressive actions were popular with Southerners. "We want Stonewall Jackson fighting . . . that . . . hurls masses against . . . the enemy's army," a Confederate officer announced in November 1862. "The policy of intrenching . . . will ruin our cause if adopted here. The truth is it never paid anywhere."[4]

Confederates were still attacking in the last months of the war, but in every instance they paid a ruinous price. "This war has demonstrated that earthworks can be rendered nearly impregnable . . . against direct assault," noted Captain Henry O. Dwight of the Twentieth Ohio Infantry. "An attack on fortified lines must cost a fearful price, and should be well weighed whether the cost exceed not the gain. This, then, is what an assault means—a slaughter-pen, a charnel-house, and an army of weeping mothers and sisters at home." Writing in 1864 during the Atlanta campaign, Dwight observed that if the Federal army had "been as experienced at Shiloh as it is now Beauregard would have come up and broken his army to pieces on our fortifications, instead of finding our whole army lying exposed to his attacks on the open field. At Fort Donelson, too, where we had to attack fortifications, we ourselves had no sign of a work upon which we could fall back after each day's repulse; nor did the enemy seem to realize the value of his own works, for instead of quietly waiting the attack, he threw away his army by fighting outside his works. It is now a principle with us to fight with movable breast-works, to save every man by giving him cover, from which he may resist the tremendous attacks in mass of the enemy." In March 1865 a North Carolinian informed his aunt that the men in Lee's army were "depleted and discouraged," but they were still proud and "when called on to fight, even tho they may not charge the enemy with the same old spirit," they nevertheless would "drive [the Federals] from the field" because "Grant's Army . . . is possessed of a wholesome dread of our men."[5]

When the Civil War began not even the writers of military texts, the

---

[4]Marsena Rudolph Patrick, *Inside Lincoln's Army: The Diary of Marsena Rudolph Patrick*, ed. David S. Sparks (New York, 1964), 380; Richard Taylor, *Destruction and Reconstruction . . .* , ed. Charles P. Roland (reissue, Waltham, 1968), 68–69; John H. Worsham, *One of Jackson's Foot Cavalry* (New York, 1912), 87; U.S. War Dept., *The War of the Rebellion: A Compilation of the Official Records of the Union and Confederate Armies* (128 vols., Washington, 1880–1901), Series 1, XXIV (pt. 2), 459 (hereinafter cited as *OR*, and unless otherwise indicated all references are to Series 1); E. John Ellis to his father, November 29, 1862, E. John, Thomas C. W. Ellis and Family Papers, Louisiana State University, Baton Rouge.

[5]Henry O. Dwight, "How We Fight at Atlanta," *Harper's New Monthly Magazine*, XXIX (1864), 663–66; Jos. C. Webb to his aunt, March 5, 1865, Lenoir Family Papers, Southern Historical Collection, University of North Carolina, Chapel Hill.

so-called brains of the army, had understood that the rifle would create a need for new tactics. Professor Dennis Hart Mahan, who had taught the art of war at the United States Military Academy for nearly twenty years, wrote in 1855: "What effect the enormously heavy ordnance, now coming into general use, and the greater and more effective range of small arms are going to produce on the Art [of war] as it is now practiced remains to be seen. At Sebastopol [in the Crimea] things seem to be going on pretty much in the old way—trenches are dug, batteries are thrown up and attack by 'skill and industry' seem still the order of the day. The Minie rifle takes men off at 600 or 1000 yards, instead of the old distances of from 2 to 300; but strong holds will be reduced not much the sooner by this means, particularly as it is a game at which both parties play without odds." Mahan's view that the rifle would make little impact upon tactics was reiterated in a military manual published in 1861, the same year its author, Henry W. Halleck, became a Union major general. "Some of the light troops used as sharp-shooters carry the rifle," announced Halleck, "but this weapon is useless for the great body of infantry."[6]

No one could have been more mistaken; it was the rifle that won the war for the North—the rifle along with the refusal of Southerners to admit until they had bled themselves nearly to death that the rifle's killing power could check even the most courageous charges. Had Civil War armies still been armed with smoothbores, the Confederates well might have retained their independence. They favored assault tactics and they charged with much recklessness. Such aggressiveness, which would have been an advantage in prerifle warfare, was self-destructive in the 1860s.

Professor Mahan is often credited with being the primary molder of military theory in antebellum America. Between 1832 and the Civil War every graduate of the United States Military Academy had to pass Mahan's course on civil and military engineering, which included instruction in the art of war. The most influential of his six books—*An Elementary Treatise on Advanced-Guard, Out-Post, and Detachment Service of Troops, and the Manner of Posting and Handling Them in Presence of an Enemy* (1847)—was a summary of his lectures.[7]

Never without his umbrella, Mahan was too cautious to teach an unqualified offensive dogma. "Great prudence must be shown in advancing," he warned, "as the troops engaged are liable at any moment to an attack on their

[6]Dennis Hart Mahan to Joseph G. Swift, February 17, 1855 (copy), Alfred T. Mahan Papers, Library of Congress; Henry W. Halleck, *Elements of Military Art and Science* (New York, 1862), 260.

[7]U.S. War Dept., *The Centennial of the United States Military Academy at West Point, New York, 1802–1902* (2 vols., Washington, 1904), II, 310; Russell F. Weigley, *Towards an American Army: Military Thought from Washington to Marshall* (New York, 1962), 38–53.

flank."[8] He also recognized and taught some of the timeless principles of warfare. He opposed the waste of either men or material. "*To do the greatest damage to our enemy with the least exposure to ourselves*," he stressed, "is the military axiom lost sight of by ignorance of the true ends of victory."[9] Some positions were "more favorable to the defensive than the offensive," and he advised that "barricades should not be attacked in front, except for very grave reasons, as, if skillfully defended, they can only be carried at great cost of life." Security was so important that no less than a third of an army should be assigned to outpost duty. "Our purpose, in all cases," lectured Mahan, "should be to keep the enemy in a state of uncertainty as to our actual force and movement." He considered the collecting and arranging of military information one of the most vital duties an officer could perform.[10]

Yet Mahan's students seemed to listen most attentively when he preached two themes: the necessity of a professional army and the superiority of offensive over defensive warfare. Amateurs had no place in a sound army, said Mahan: "An active, intelligent officer, with an imagination fertile in the expedients of his profession, will seldom be at a loss as to his best course when the occasion offers; to one without these qualities, opportunities present themselves in vain."[11] Only offensive-minded professionals with a broad knowledge of warfare could win future conflicts. Mahan taught his students that boldness in an officer was as essential as military skill. Fortifications might help exhaust an enemy, but they were useless if they encouraged passive defense. Forts should be springboards for assaults. "Carrying the war into the heart of the enemy's country," he insisted, "is the surest plan of making him share its burdens and foiling his plans."[12] Disciplined forces led by professionals should be aggressive. "If the main-body falters in its attack," Mahan counseled, "the reserve should advance at once through the intervals, and make a vigorous charge with the bayonet." He favored "successive cavalry charges" to check infantry and artillery, and he advocated that artillery take an active role in assaults. In addition, Mahan was certain that a "charge by column, when the enemy is within fifty paces, will prove effective, if resolutely made." He believed that Napoleon had proved the advantage of offensive warfare. "To him," Mahan announced, "we owe those grand features of the art, by which an enemy is broken and utterly dispersed by one and the same blow."[13]

Mahan's students trimmed and oversimplified their master's lessons. Enamored with professionalism and offensives, they ignored many of his warn-

---

[8]Dennis Hart Mahan, *An Elementary Treatise on Advanced-Guard* . . . (New York, 1861), 43.
[9]Ibid. (New York, 1864), 30–31.
[10]Ibid. (New Orleans, 1861), 37, 112, 50, 74, 46, 49.
[11]Ibid., 143.
[12]Ibid. (New York, 1864), 198–99, 202.
[13]Ibid. (New Orleans, 1861), 13, 45, 11; ibid. (New York, 1864), 30.

ings and qualifications and much of his discussion of timeless principles. Their commitment to professionalism and the tactical offensive soon became orthodoxy in the regular army, although both concepts were foreign to the American tradition of citizen soldiers and defensive warfare. Curiously, this quiet revolution in military thought went almost unnoticed outside the army. Only a few citizens complained that Mahan's "aristocratic and anti-republican" doctrines "utterly and forever excluded [amateur soldiers] from holding any office of honor, trust, or emolument in the [United States] military service."[14]

Without real protest from any quarter, the antebellum army's young professional officers elevated the offensive to an inviolate canon of American military policy. They found, or believed that they found, support for the offensive dogma in the works of Napoleon and Jomini, besides Mahan the antebellum West Pointer's most revered authorities on the theory of warfare. Several of Mahan's students wrote books before the Civil War that emphasized the advantage of offensive over defensive operations.[15]

But it would be a mistake to assume that Mahan molded the minds of all the young men who were in his classes. Far more important in shaping the ideas of young officers on the art of war was what they learned or thought they learned during the Mexican War. Ulysses S. Grant is an excellent example. There is no evidence to indicate that Mahan, Jomini, or Napoleon had much influence on Grant's military thinking. Grant claimed that he had never read any of Jomini's works, and there is no reason to doubt this. Jomini's works were all written in French, a language in which, Grant admitted, "my standing was very low." Not until 1859, long after Grant had left West Point, was Jomini's *Summary of the Art of War* used as a textbook in tactics at the military academy, and then only in translation. There may have been books by Jomini in the West Point library when Grant was a cadet, but there is no indication that he looked at any. Most of the books Grant read at the academy were, he guiltily confessed, novels.[16]

Grant knew something of Napoleon's campaigns, but references to the Corsican are brief in Grant's writings and suggest no more than what Grant

[14]John A. Logan, *The Volunteer Soldier of America* (Chicago, 1887), 225–26. Henry W. Halleck, who favored a professional army, quoted Napoleon as saying, "It was neither the volunteers nor the [recruits] who saved the Republic; it was the 180,000 old troops of the monarchy." Halleck's Military Note Book, begun January 1, 1843, Henry W. Halleck Papers, Library of Congress.

[15]Weigley, *Towards an American Army*, 64–67, 72–73, 75, 85, 95, 140, 194–95, 224, 55–78; Nathaniel C. Hughes, Jr., *General William J. Hardee: Old Reliable* (Baton Rouge, 1965), 41–50.

[16]T. Harry Williams, "The Military Leadership of North and South," in *Why the North Won the Civil War*, ed. David Herbert Donald (Baton Rouge, 1960), 43; Ulysses S. Grant, *Personal Memoirs . . .* (2 vols., New York, 1885), I, 39; Samuel E. Tillman, "The Academic History of the Military Academy, 1802–1902," *Centennial of the Academy*, I, 278–79; Edward S. Holden and W. L. Ostrander, "A Tentative List of Text-books Used in the United States Military Academy at West Point from 1802 to 1902," ibid., 458, 464.

might have remembered from his studies at West Point. For example, in 1845 Grant teasingly told his fiancée that her brother would have time "to prove himself a second Napoleon as you always said he would." Later, in describing the American flanking movement at Cerro Gordo, Grant suggested that the "undertaking [was] almost equal to Bonapartes Crossing the Alps." And finally, in his *Memoirs*, Grant wrote: "I never admired the character of the first Napoleon; but I recognize his great genius."[17]

It is true that Grant was exposed to Mahan's views in class, but there is no real evidence that he either fully understood them or was affected by them. Unlike his friend William T. Sherman—who announced in 1862: "Should any officer high or low . . . be ignorant of his tactics, regulations, or . . . of the principles of the Art of War (Mahan and Jomini), it would be a lasting disgrace"—Grant never mentioned his old professor in letters or reminiscences. Mahan recalled years later that Cadet Grant had quiet manners and a boyish face and that he was not an outstanding student.[18]

There are several reasons why Grant learned little about the art of war at West Point. None of his instructors, including Mahan, excited him. His earliest hero was not a professor, but General Winfield Scott. "During my first year's encampment," recalled Grant, "General Scott visited West Point, and reviewed the cadets. With his commanding figure, his colossal size and showy uniform, I thought him the finest specimen of manhood my eyes had ever beheld, and the most to be envied. I could never resemble him in appearance, but I believe I did have a presentiment for a moment that some day I should occupy his place on review."[19]

Another reason why Grant, as well as other cadets, learned little about the art of war at West Point was because too little time was devoted to the subject. Mahan mixed lessons on strategy and tactics into his engineering course for fourth-year students. "But few lectures [on the art of war] were given by Professor Mahan," recalled a former cadet, "and these were restricted almost entirely to short descriptions of campaigns and battles, with criticisms upon the tactical positions involved." An officer told a commission that was investigating instruction at the academy in 1860: "I do not think enough importance is attached to the study or standing in the several branches of tactics. These are not taught sufficiently."[20]

---

[17]Grant, *Memoirs*, I, 252–53; Grant to Julia Dent, July 6, 1845, *The Papers of Ulysses S. Grant*, ed. John Y. Simon (6 vols. to date, Carbondale, 1967–   ), I, 46–47; Grant to John W. Love, May 3, 1847, ibid., 136; Grant, *Memoirs*, II, 547.

[18]*OR*, XVII (pt. 2), 119; Dennis Hart Mahan, "The Cadet Life of Grant and Sherman," *Army and Navy Journal*, IV (March 31, 1866), 507.

[19]Grant, *Memoirs*, I, 41.

[20]U.S. War Dept., *Report of the [1860] Commission to Examine into the Organization, System of Discipline, and Course of Instruction of the United States Military Academy at West Point* (Washington, 1881), 74, 156, 76, 164, 133.

It was easy enough for young cadets, studying in an environment where academic standards were not especially high and most learning was done by rote, to misinterpret, oversimplify, or simply forget much of what Mahan taught. Grant and most other cadets apparently learned just enough to satisfy their examiners, but once they had passed the course—like so many students before and after them—they quickly forgot what they had been taught. That was not difficult. Mahan's views were neither unequivocal nor always precisely stated.[21]

Nor was much done at West Point or at army posts to stimulate men to further study. Regulations sometimes discouraged cadets from using the library, and some did not check out a single volume during their four years at the academy. "One of the important objects of education is to give habits of judicious reading," noted General Joseph E. Johnston. "The present academic course [at West Point] is not calculated to do so." An instructor at the academy testified: "I have never known . . . of a single instance of an officer studying theoretically his profession (when away from West Point) after graduating." Another officer pointed out that the army offered "no incentive to exertion and study beyond the personal satisfaction each officer must feel who has consciousness of having done his duty. The careless and ignorant officer is promoted, in his turn, with as much certainty as the accomplished and conscientious one."[22]

Neither his letters nor his reminiscences suggest that Grant spent any time studying his profession after he left West Point. Perhaps that is why he could write: "Soldiering is a very pleasant occupation generally." Years later he recalled that except for one instance, "I . . . never looked at a copy of tactics from the time of my graduation." That exception occurred when he received his first Civil War command. "I got a copy of [Hardee's] tactics and studied one lesson," Grant admitted. "I perceived at once, however, that Hardee's tactics—a mere translation from the French with Hardee's name attached— was nothing more than common sense. . . . I found no trouble in giving commands that would take my regiment where I wanted it to go. . . . I do not believe that the officers of the regiment ever discovered that I had never studied the tactics that I used."[23]

Grant clearly favored experience over theory, but questions about whose theories influenced whom and to what extent have caused certain disagreements among scholars. In 1956 David Herbert Donald argued that the devo-

[21]Dennis Hart Mahan, *A Complete Treatise on Field Fortification* (New York, 1862); Mahan, *Advanced-Guard*; Mahan to "Dear Sir," April 5, 1834, David B. Harris Papers, Duke University.

[22]War Dept., *Report of the [1860] Commission*, 82, 100, 170, 77, 114, 79. Library policy apparently discouraged book borrowing at West Point. Several people complained in 1860 that cadets were allowed to "take out but a single volume, and that from Saturday noon till Monday morning."

[23]Grant, *Memoirs*, I, 252–53.

tion of Jefferson Davis and his generals to the outmoded military ideas of Jomini contributed significantly to Confederate defeat. Northerners innovated and won; Southerners remained inflexible and lost. Donald claimed that Davis—a "military martinet, stiff and unbending," who "was constitutionally incapable of experimenting"—"retained to the end . . . faith in Jomini's maxims." T. Harry Williams thought Jomini's influence was strong and detrimental to Confederate generals, especially to Robert E. Lee, but Williams made no claim that Jomini's ideas shaped Davis's policy. Frank E. Vandiver admitted that Jomini's maxims probably influenced Davis, who "had studied principles of war at West Point," but Vandiver insists that the Confederate president developed his own "bold and original war policy, which he called the 'offensive-defensive.' " The most recent writers emphasize "Confederate strategy's strong conformity to the teachings of Jomini and Napoleon, and the prominent role of [General P. G. T.] Beauregard in securing this conformity." Thomas L. Connelly and Archer Jones argue that Davis favored a defensive or a counteroffensive strategy preached by Beauregard. Indeed, Connelly and Jones conclude that the "story of Confederate strategy can be perceived as a belated triumph for the western concentration bloc and for Beauregard's ideas."[24]

All of these writers agree that to some extent Jomini shaped Confederate military thinking, but they disagree on just how strongly Davis and his generals were influenced and in what way. Donald argues that Davis consciously followed Jomini's maxims; Vandiver claims that Davis, though schooled in Jominian principles, adopted an "original war policy"; and Connelly and Jones insist that Beauregard's ideas, which came from Jomini and Napoleon, ultimately dominated Davis and Confederate warfare.[25]

The conclusions of these distinguished scholars seem to be supported more by logic than by evidence. Their syllogism: Mahan taught Jomini's ideas at West Point, which Davis and most high-ranking Confederate generals attended; Jomini's works were available in antebellum America, either in French or in translation; consequently, it appears reasonable that West Point graduates, who had studied French and had taken courses in military science, were thoroughly familiar with the writings and maxims of Jomini.

But were they? Almost none of the letters by Confederate generals that we have examined mentions Jomini. In 1860 General Joseph E. Johnston recommended that Jomini's *Art of War* be dropped as a textbook at West Point

---

[24]David Herbert Donald, *Lincoln Reconsidered: Essays on the Civil War Era* (New York, 1956), 82–102; Williams, "Military Leadership North and South," 23–47; T. Harry Williams, *Americans at War: The Development of the American Military System* (New York, 1962), 55–73; Frank E. Vandiver, *Their Tattered Flags* (New York, 1970), 88, 94; Thomas L. Connelly and Archer Jones, *The Politics of Command: Factions and Ideas in Confederate Strategy* (Baton Rouge, 1973), 172–77.

[25]Donald, *Lincoln Reconsidered*, 91; Vandiver, *Tattered Flags*, 88, 94; Connelly and Jones, *Politics of Command*, 172–73.

because he considered Decker's *Tactics* and "three little works by Frederick the Great" more "instructive." It is sometimes overlooked that none of Jomini's books was used as a text while Jefferson Davis, Albert Sidney Johnston, Robert E. Lee, or Joseph E. Johnston was at West Point. At that time an English translation of Guy de Vernon's *Treatise on the Science of War and Fortification* was the text for the course on engineering and the art of war. It was taught not by Dennis Hart Mahan but by David B. Douglass, an 1813 graduate of the academy.[26] Connelly and Jones admit that neither Davis nor Lee "enunciated their [military] principles clearly nor showed to whom, if anyone, they were indebted."[27]

If Davis got his Jomini indirectly from Beauregard, as Connelly and Jones claim, the Confederate president must have done so unconsciously, for he and Beauregard hated each other.[28] "My plan of campaign at Drewry's Bluff [in 1864] would have given us a glorious triumph . . . and probably peace and independence," boasted Beauregard, "but that obstinate and obstructive man who was at the head of our affairs ruined everything! He was no more fit to comprehend a bold and important military operation than a Benedek!"[29]

More important to the argument presented by Connelly and Jones is whether Beauregard was a Jominian. Such a question may seem absurd. He must have been; this "Napoleon in Gray," as his biographer called him, this dapper Creole who reminded people of "Paris and Napoleon and Austerlitz and French legions."[30] Jomini's overwhelming influence upon such a man's military ideas would appear as certain as Beauregard's supposed admiration for all things Gallic. But concrete evidence is scarce. We have been unable to

---

[26]War Dept., *Report of the [1860] Commission*, 170; Tillman, "Academic History," I, 276–77; Jefferson Davis, *The Papers of Jefferson Davis*, ed. Haskell M. Monroe, Jr., and James T. McIntosh (2 vols. to date, Baton Rouge, 1971–   ), I, 95.

[27]Connelly and Jones, *Politics of Command*, 174.

[28]On Davis's hatred of Beauregard, see Mary B. Chesnut, *A Diary from Dixie*, ed. Isabella D. Martin and Myrta Lockett Avary (New York, 1905), 248–49; Jefferson Davis, *Jefferson Davis: Private Letters, 1823–1889*, ed. Hudson Strode (New York, 1966), 156, 378, 396–97; Jefferson Davis to James Lyon, August 13, 1876 (copy), Jefferson Davis Papers, Library of Congress; Jefferson Davis to Lucius B. Northrop, April 9, 1879, Jefferson Davis Papers, Duke University; Thomas Bragg Diary, January 8, April 7, 1862, Southern Historical Collection, University of North Carolina, Chapel Hill.

[29]P. G. T. Beauregard to Thomas Jordan, November 4, 1866 (copy), Pierre Gustave Toutant Beauregard Papers, Library of Congress. The reference is to Ludwig von Benedek, the Austrian general who was disastrously defeated at Sadowa in 1866. Later Beauregard wrote: "Do you recollect what I used to say sometimes at Charleston, to-wit: 'That if Alexander, Caesar, Frederick the Great and Napoleon had been surrounded by such men as Mr. Davis had selected to be members of his cabinet and of the Government Bureaux and command some of his armies the names of those Great Emperors would hardly have been heard of in history except through their errors & defeats.' " Beauregard to Jordan, March 6, 1867 (copy), Beauregard Papers, Library of Congress.

[30]T. Harry Williams, *P. G. T. Beauregard: Napoleon in Gray* (Baton Rouge, 1955), 1–2.

find any place where Beauregard acknowledged Jomini's influence upon him. On the contrary, what has appeared are tantalizing bits and pieces of evidence that are in no way conclusive but together raise some doubts about Beauregard's admiration for Jomini. For example, it was not Jomini that Beauregard recommended to his brother-in-law, Charles Villeré, in 1862. "I did not take up my pen to give you a lecture on the 'Art of War,' " Beauregard wrote; "if you wish to learn something on that important subject, study 'The Theory of War' by Lt. Col. P. L. MacDougall—1 vol. London, & look particularly at from page 51 to 169. It is the best 'Field Book' I have yet read on that subject."[31]

Again in 1862, in a letter to General Braxton Bragg, Beauregard recalled not the lessons taught by Jomini or his interpreter at West Point, Dennis Hart Mahan, but rather those of the natural and experimental philosophy professor, William H. C. Bartlett. "In *tactics* as in *statics*," wrote Beauregard, "the force is equal to the mass multiplied by the square of the velocity, as Professor Bartlett used to teach us at West Point. We must profit by his lessons to put to rout those abolition hordes."[32]

In 1867 Beauregard admitted to a friend that he did not own Jomini's works, but even more startling perhaps is his criticism of French tactics. "You are aware that the French &, generally, Latin races, generally attack in *columns* of Regts., Brigades or Divs.," Beauregard announced, "whereas the Anglo-Saxon races, Americans &c, always attack in *line* of battle. I prefer definitely the latter which gives a much greater development of fire—which after all decides the fight."[33] That Beauregard always signed his letters G. T. or Gus, and never Pierre, may tell us more than we have suspected about his cultural identification.

The Mexican War had a profound influence upon Beauregard, as it did on many of the men who would make military decisions in the Civil War. One of eight young officers on General Scott's staff who became Union or Confederate generals, Beauregard—along with Robert E. Lee, George B. McClellan, and others—received high praise from Scott for bravery and skill during the campaign against Mexico City, and his military thinking was shaped by close association with the commanding general and the way he fought. Years later, in explanation of why he considered himself better qualified to command an army in 1861 than Joseph E. Johnston, Beauregard wrote: "Having been attached . . . to the staff of the Commander-in-chief, General Scott, in the Mexican War, General Beauregard had taken a leading

---

[31]Beauregard to Charles Villeré, September 16, 1862 (copy), Beauregard Papers, Library of Congress.

[32]Beauregard to Bragg, November 16, 1862 (copy), ibid.

[33]Beauregard to Thomas Jordan, January 6, 1867 (copy), ibid.; Beauregard to Jubal A. Early, September 1, 1876, Jubal A. Early Papers, Library of Congress.

part in the reconnaissances and conferences that had led and determined the marches and battles of that campaign; and as to what was really essential in these respects to the command of an army he had a practical military experience beyond any opportunities of General Johnston."[34]

Beauregard, Lee, Jackson, Grant, Bragg, Davis, and a host of other Civil War leaders found their military heroes and models during the Mexican War. "Our Genl. [Scott] is our great reliance," Lee wrote from Mexico. "He is a great man on great occasions. Never turned from his object. Confident in his powers & resources, his judgment is as sound as his heart is bold & daring." Lee's admiration for his old commander never waned. Less than a month before he surrendered at Appomattox, Lee wrote his wife: "I have put in the bag Genl. Scott's autobiography, which I thought you might like to read. The Genl. of course stands out very prominently & does not hide his light under a bushel, but he appears the bold sagacious truthful man as he is."[35]

Lee was not the only Southerner to extol Scott's boldness. William Montgomery Gardner, who would become a Confederate general, praised Scott's "brilliant operations" in 1847. "The idea of 10,000 men marching upon a capital containing upwards of 200,000 inhabitants, defended by more than 30,000 troops, having more than 100 pieces of cannon, fortified both by nature and act is enough to astound the world," Gardner informed his brother. "As for myself I will be proud to my dying day to have participated in the successes of the Army of Mexico." In the opinion of Stonewall Jackson, Scott's campaign against Mexico City excelled "any military operations known in the history of our country."[36]

General Zachary Taylor, much admired by those who served in his army, was as much a hero as Scott to many young officers. Future Union General Robert Anderson wrote from Mexico: "There is not a better soldier or braver man than Genl. Z. Taylor, . . . but those who fight under him must incur with their Genl., who is nearly always in the front of the battle . . . , the full dangers of an open direct attack." Future Confederate General Samuel G.

---

[34]Winfield Scott, *Memoirs of Lieut.-General Scott, LL.D. Written by Himself* (2 vols., New York, 1864), II, 450, 508, 533–34; G. T. Beauregard, *A Commentary on the Campaign and Battle of Manassas of July, 1861, Together with a Summary of the Art of War* (New York, 1891), 15–16, 44. The eight officers on Scott's staff who became generals were Robert E. Lee, P. G. T. Beauregard, Gustavus W. Smith, and Benjamin Huger (Confederate); and George B. McClellan, Isaac Ingalls Stevens. Zealous B. Tower, and John Gray Foster (Federal).

[35]Robert E. Lee to John MacKay, October 2, 1847, Robert E. Lee and Custis Lee Papers, United States Army Military History Institute, Carlisle Barracks, Pennsylvania; Robert E. Lee, *The Wartime Papers of R. E. Lee*, ed. Clifford Dowdey and Louis H. Manarin (Boston, 1961), 918–19.

[36]William M. Gardner to his sister, November 22, 1847, and to his brother, October 24, 1847, William Montgomery Gardner Papers, Southern Historical Collection, University of North Carolina, Chapel Hill; Jackson quoted in Lenoir Chambers, *Stonewall Jackson* (2 vols., New York, 1959), I, 90.

French called Taylor "the brave old soldier" who "would fight the enemy, wherever he found them, to the end." Taylor's paymaster recalled that he was roused from bed by the general on the morning of the Battle of Monterey, told to "come with me and I will give you a chance to be shot," and remained with Taylor for "eight hours under fire." Stonewall Jackson, who served under both Taylor and Scott in Mexico, informed his sister in 1847: "you may imagine that I esteem General Scott more than General Taylor. But such is not the case. I esteem General Scott more only as a military man." Taylor, said Jackson, was "as brave as a lion."[37]

The campaigns of Taylor and Scott were the highlights of Ulysses S. Grant's pre–Civil War military education. From them Grant learned strategies and tactics he would use in the Civil War. For example, his Vicksburg campaign was similar to Scott's bold march to Mexico City. Grant's account in his *Memoirs* of Scott's campaign could have been, with only a few changes, a fair description of his own brilliant moves that culminated in the capture of Vicksburg.[38]

Grant saw Taylor's and Scott's forces attack and drive the Mexicans both from open fields and fortified positions. He reported with some amazement after the Battle of Resaca de la Palma: "Grape shot and musket balls were let fly from both sides making dreadful havoc. Our men [con]tinued to advance . . . in sp[ite] of [the enemy's] shots, to the very mouths of the cannon an[d] killed and took prisoner the Mexicans." After the Americans had successfully stormed Monterey, Grant wrote: "taking together the strength of the place and the means the Mexicans had of defending it it is almost incredible that the American army now are in possession here."[39]

After a time Grant accepted as standard tactics the attacks that at first he had considered incredible. Why not? They always succeeded. The American forces were invincible. Not only had they won every battle, but when they attacked they inflicted heavier casualties than they suffered. By the spring of 1847 Grant could write of the American attack at Cerro Gordo, which he witnessed: "As our men finally swept over and into the [Mexican] works, my heart was sad at the fate that held me from sharing in that brave and brilliant assault."[40]

Grant never forgot those assault tactics that had been so successful in Mexico. He used them repeatedly in the Civil War, often to his own detri-

---

[37]Robert Anderson, *An Artillery Officer in the Mexican War, 1846–47: Letters of Robert Anderson, Captain, 3rd Artillery, U.S.A.* (New York, 1911), 151; Samuel G. French, *Two Wars: An Autobiography* (Nashville, 1901), 67; Ephraim Kirby Smith, *To Mexico with Scott; Letters of Captain E. Kirby Smith to His Wife,* ed. Emma Jerome Blackwood (Cambridge, Mass., 1917), 72; Thomas J. Jackson to his sister, May 1, 1847, Thomas J. Jackson Papers, Library of Congress.

[38]Grant, *Memoirs,* I, 166.

[39]Grant to Julia Dent, May 11, October 3, 1846, in Grant, *Papers of Grant,* I, 85–86, 112.

[40]Grant to unknown addressee, April 24, 1847, ibid., 134.

ment. They failed to work as well for him as they had for Scott and Taylor, of course, because rifles could halt assaults the smoothbore muskets could not stop, but Grant never fully accepted the fact that the rifle had revolutionized tactics. After losing more than 7,000 men in a frontal attack at Cold Harbor in June 1864, Grant wrote: "I regret this assault more than any one I have ever ordered. I regarded it as a stern necessity, and believed that it would bring compensating results; but, as it proved, no advantages have been gained sufficient to justify the heavy losses suffered."[41]

Some lessons are difficult to unlearn, especially those taught to young people by respected instructors. Taylor and Scott were more than Grant's commanders—they were his heroes. It is understandable that their method of warfare had a lasting influence upon him. "I never thought at the time to doubt the infallibility of these two generals," Grant confessed.[42]

Though he admired and learned from both Taylor and Scott, Grant left no doubt which man influenced him the most. "Both were pleasant to serve under—Taylor was pleasant to serve with," wrote Grant, who announced after the Mexican War's opening battles: "history will count the victory just achieved [by General Taylor] one of the greatest on record." And Grant later informed his fiancée that he had so much confidence in Taylor's military skill that "I do not feel my Dear Julia the slightest apprehention [sic] as to our success in ev[e]ry large battle that we may have with the enemy no matter how superior they may be to us in numbers."[43]

What Grant later recalled in his *Memoirs* about Taylor is especially significant because it reveals not only what Grant admired in his old general but also how many of Taylor's characteristics and military practices he adopted. Taylor "was opposed to anything like plundering by the troops," Grant noted. So was Grant. "Taylor was not an officer to trouble the administration much with his demands, but was inclined to do the best he could with the means given him." So was Grant. "Taylor never made any great show or parade, either of uniform or retinue." Neither did Grant. Taylor "moved about the field in which he was operating to see through his own eyes the situation." So did Grant. "Taylor was not a conversationalist." Neither was Grant. On paper Taylor "could put his meaning so plainly that there could be no mistaking it. He knew how to express what he wanted to say in the fewest well-chosen words." So did Grant. And finally, Grant said of Taylor what so many writers have said of Grant: "No soldier could face either danger or responsibility more calmly than he. These are qualities," Grant noted, "more rarely found than genius or physical courage."[44]

---

[41]Horace Porter, *Campaigning with Grant*, ed. Wayne C. Temple (reissue, Bloomington, 1961), 179.

[42]Grant, *Memoirs*, I, 167.

[43]Grant to Julia Dent, May 11, June 5, 1846, in Grant, *Papers of Grant*, I, 87, 90.

[44]Grant, *Memoirs*, I, 85, 99–100, 138, 139.

The similarities between Taylor and Grant are too great to be categorized as coincidence. At the outset of the Mexican War Grant doubtless admired Taylor partly because Grant, even as a young soldier, was already much like the old general. But it also seems clear that Taylor, to a greater extent than has been realized, became Grant's military model. No other man so profoundly influenced Grant's pre–Civil War military education. "The art of war is simple enough," Grant once remarked. "Find out where your enemy is. Get at him as soon as you can. Strike at him as hard as you can, and keep moving on."[45] Zachary Taylor himself could not have given a better definition of how to fight.

No Civil War general—not even Lee—was more aggressive than Grant. He assumed the offensive in nearly every campaign or battle he directed. One exception was when he was surprised by a Confederate attack at Shiloh, but there he opened the second day of fighting with a sustained counterattack that eventually drove the Confederates from the field. His offensives against generally mediocre Confederate generals (John B. Floyd, Gideon Pillow, John C. Pemberton, and Braxton Bragg) in the western theater of operations early in the war were, despite a few disappointments, remarkably successful. He opened an invasion route into the Deep South by taking Forts Henry and Donelson, survived a bloody action at Shiloh, captured Vicksburg after a daring campaign, and finally relieved Chattanooga and drove the Confederates from Tennessee. All of this success cost him only 23,551 casualties, and 10,162 of these occurred at Shiloh. The exact number of casualties he inflicted on the Confederates in these various operations is uncertain, but at Vicksburg alone 29,396 southern soldiers surrendered to him.[46]

It is impossible to determine whether Grant would have done as well early in the war against more formidable opponents, but one thing is certain: he remained as aggressive as ever when he moved on to Virginia later in the war, even though his offensive tactics there, practiced against Robert E. Lee, cost the Federals horrendous losses. Grant's casualties in only twelve months of combat in Virginia exceeded by some 47,000 men his losses over twenty-two months in the West. In a few days in the Wilderness and at Spotsylvania during his opening offensive in the East, Grant lost 26,302 men, or 2,751 more than he lost during his entire tenure in the West.[47] (See table 6.)

The Civil War might have ended sooner if all Union generals had been as aggressive as Grant, but the outcome well could have been an independent Confederacy. Aggressiveness helped the Federals win at Vicksburg and at Missionary Ridge, but it brought them bloody failures at Fredericksburg and

---

[45]Grant quoted in Williams, "Military Leadership North and South," 51.

[46]Thomas L. Livermore, *Numbers & Losses in the Civil War in America: 1861–65* (reissue, Bloomington, 1957), 140–41, 100.

[47]Ibid., 140–41. See table 5.

Table 6

SIGNIFICANT CAMPAIGNS AND BATTLES
DIRECTED BY ULYSSES S. GRANT

Action Before 1864:	Grant's Force	Grant's Losses
Fort Donelson	27,000	2,608
Shiloh	62,682	10,162
Champion's Hill	29,373	2,254
Vicksburg	45,556	3,052
Chattanooga	56,359	5,475
	220,970	23,551

Action in 1864–65:		
Wilderness through Cold Harbor	c. 122,000	c. 50,000
The Mine	20,708	2,865
Deep Bottom Run	27,974	2,180
Weldon Railroad	20,289	1,303
New Market Heights	19,639	2,682
Boydton Plank Road	42,823	1,194
Dabney's Mills	34,517	1,330
Appomattox campaign	112,992	9,066
	c. 400,942	c. 70,620
TOTALS:	c. 621,912	c. 94,171

Cold Harbor. "What luck some people have," Joseph E. Johnston wrote after news reached him of Lee's victory at Fredericksburg. "Nobody will ever come to attack me in such a place."[48]

Fortunately for the Federals, not all of their military leaders were as committed as Grant to frontal assaults and showdown battles. Several commanders, such as George G. Meade and George H. Thomas, made their reputations as defensive fighters. General William S. Rosecrans, whom Beauregard admitted was "astute, wily, active, & intelligent," informed General Henry W. Halleck in July 1862 that "a thousand cavalry will do more damage to the rebels by seizing and destroying their means of subsistence than a brigade of infantry."[49] Unlike his friend Grant, William T. Sherman (who was stationed in California during the Mexican War and missed serving with either Taylor or Scott) rarely attacked; he favored moves that forced the enemy to attack him. A Union officer who knew Grant and Sherman recalled: "General Grant and General Sherman . . . were as unlike as day and night. Grant had no nerves, while Sherman was made up of nerves. Grant never gave himself any concern in regard to an enemy he could not see, while a concealed foe was more dreadful to Sherman than one in full view. Grant's strategy consisted in getting as near an enemy as possible, and then 'moving on his works without delay.' Sherman was more of a strategist, and believed in surprising his enemy by a masterly move. . . . Grant reached Richmond by more fighting than strategy. Sherman reached Atlanta by more strategy than fighting." Fairly early in the war the Union commander-in-chief recognized just how much manpower and material were consumed in offensive operations. In May 1862 Abraham Lincoln stressed the advantage enjoyed by defenders in a letter to General McClellan: "if we can not beat him [the enemy] when he bears the wastage of coming to us, we never can when we bear the wastage of going to him. This proposition is a simple truth, and is too important to be lost sight of for a moment. In coming to us, he tenders us an advantage which we should not waive."[50]

The Confederates were unwilling to acknowledge Lincoln's "simple truth" about the "wastage" of their offensive tactics. One reason for this point of view was their Mexican War experiences. Of the eighty-five men who obtained the rank of major general or higher in the Confederate service, 71 percent were graduates of the United States Military Academy and 61 percent actually participated in the conflict with Mexico. Even more significant,

---

[48]Joseph E. Johnston to Louis T. Wigfall, December 15, 1862, Louis T. Wigfall and Family Papers, University of Texas, Austin.

[49]P. G. T. Beauregard to Braxton Bragg, November 16, 1862 (copy), Beauregard Papers, Library of Congress; *OR*, XVII (pt. 2), 108.

[50]Richard W. Johnson, *A Soldier's Reminiscences in Peace and War* (Philadelphia, 1886), 307; Abraham Lincoln to George B. McClellan, October 13, 1862, *The Collected Works of Abraham Lincoln*, ed. Roy P. Basler (9 vols., New Brunswick, 1953–1955), V, 461.

all of the men who commanded a Confederate army in one or more of the major campaigns or battles of the Civil War—Albert Sidney Johnston, P. G. T. Beauregard, Joseph E. Johnston, Robert E. Lee, Braxton Bragg, John C. Pemberton, John Bell Hood, and Jubal A. Early—or who commanded a corps in four or more major battles—James Longstreet, Thomas J. "Stonewall" Jackson, William J. Hardee, Leonidas Polk, A. P. Hill, and Richard S. Ewell—were West Point graduates, and all but three (Hood, Polk, and Early) of these fourteen men had served in the Mexican War.[51] These and scores of other Southerners who led troops in the 1860s were fossilized by what they saw and did while under the command of Taylor and Scott.

Grant was not the only young officer who learned the wrong lessons in Mexico. Braxton Bragg, whose battery was credited with saving the day at Buena Vista, was completely enamored with Taylor as well as with Old Zach's reckless attacks and stubborn defenses. What Bragg missed in his enthusiasm was the real lesson of Buena Vista, which was the great advantage that defenders with sufficient mobile firepower enjoyed over attackers. This failure to understand what had happened and how it could be applied to later battles is both significant and curious. It is curious because a close examination of the Buena Vista battlefield convinced Bragg that artillery had accounted for "nine-tenths of the [enemy's] killed and wounded."[52]

Just how committed these Mexican War veterans were to assault tactics is evidenced by their words and actions in the Civil War. James Longstreet, who had won two brevets for gallantry in Mexico, wrote before his costly and unsuccessful attack upon Federal fortifications at Knoxville, Tennessee, in late 1863: "I am entirely convinced that our only safety is in making the assault upon the enemy's position." Confederate General William H. T. Walker, who also had won two brevets in Mexico, complained in 1861 that "this sitting down and waiting to be whipped . . . is to me the most disgusting. If it be my fate to lose my life in the cause . . . in Heavens name let me die like a soldier with sword in hand boldly leading my men on a fair and open field." Stonewall Jackson, another winner of two Mexican War brevet promotions for gallant conduct, favored and practiced offensive tactics until he was mortally wounded at Chancellorsville. General Alexander R. Lawton claimed that Jackson "did not value human life. . . . He could order men to

[51]These figures are based upon information found in Ezra J. Warner, *Generals in Gray: Lives of the Confederate Commanders* (Baton Rouge, 1959), and Francis B. Heitman, *Historical Register and Dictionary of the United States Army* (2 vols., Washington, 1903). Hood was too young to be in the Mexican War. Polk, who had resigned from the United States Army in 1827, did not volunteer for service in Mexico. Early did volunteer; he became a major in a Virginia regiment, but he saw no action in the Mexican War.

[52]Grady McWhiney, *Braxton Bragg and Confederate Defeat* (New York, 1969), 77–90; Braxton Bragg to James Duncan, April 4, 1847, James Duncan Papers, United States Military Academy.

their death as a matter of course. Napoleons French conscription could not have kept him supplied with men, he used up his command so rapidly." In less than six months in 1862 Jackson's tactics cost the South over 20,000 casualties—the equivalent of one entire army corps—or almost twice the number of men under Jackson's command when the campaign began. Jackson was so committed to conventional offensive tactics that he once actually requested that some of his troops be equipped with pikes instead of muskets. Pikes, he explained, should be "6 or more inches longer than the musket with the bayonet on, so that when we teach our troops to rely upon the bayonet they may feel that they have the superiority of arm resulting from its length." Lee apparently saw nothing wrong with such a request; he approved it and ordered Josiah Gorgas, chief of ordnance, to send pikes to Jackson. Gorgas sent muskets instead.[53]

Five of the six men who at one time or another commanded the Confederacy's two largest armies were devoted to aggressive warfare. Albert Sidney Johnston, P. G. T. Beauregard, Braxton Bragg, John Bell Hood, and Robert E. Lee all preferred to be on the offensive. Of the major field commanders, only Joseph E. Johnston really enjoyed defense, but he protested in 1864 against the charge that he only wanted to fight on the defensive and retreat. "I learn that it is given out that it has been proposed to me to take the offensive with a large army, & that I refused," Johnston wrote a friend. "Don't believe any such story. I have been anxious to take the offensive." Though a cautious man, Johnston had attacked strongly at Fair Oaks in 1862 and a month before that battle had written to Lee: "We must . . . take the offensive, collect all the troops we have in the East and cross the Potomac with them, while Beauregard, with all we have in the West, invades Ohio. Our troops have always wished for the offensive, and so does the country."[54]

Perhaps one reason Joe Johnston was cautious was that he had been wounded several times in action against Indians and Mexicans before the 1860s and was again hit twice at Fair Oaks—first by a bullet in the shoulder

---

[53]James Longstreet to Lafayette McLaws, November 28, 1863, Lafayette McLaws Papers, Duke University; William H. T. Walker to his wife, July 12, 1861, William Henry Talbot Walker Papers, Duke University; Mary B. Chesnut, *A Diary from Dixie*, ed. Ben Ames Williams (reissue, Boston, 1961), 330; *OR*, XII (pt. 3), 842. The campaigns and Jackson's losses were 2,095 in the Shenandoah Valley; 6,700 during the Seven Days; 1,365 at Cedar Mountain; 4,629 at Second Manassas; and 6,095 in the Maryland campaign. Robert U. Johnson and Clarence C. Buel, eds., *Battles and Leaders of the Civil War* (4 vols., reissue, New York, 1956), II, 300–01, 315–16, 496, 500, 601–02.

[54]Joseph E. Johnston to Louis T. Wigfall, April 30, 1864, Wigfall Papers; *OR*, XI (pt. 3), 477. A contemporary noted: "As to the policy of war advised by the general officers of the Confederate army, Bragg . . . in the fall of 1861 wrote to the Secretary of War urging concentration and the offensive. Albert Sidney Johnston, Lee, Beauregard, and Forrest urged the same policy." John Witherspoon Du Bose, "Gen. Joseph Eggleston Johnston, C.S.A.," *Confederate Veteran*, XXII (1914), 176–77.

and a few moments later by a shell fragment, which unhorsed him. For nearly six months during the critical summer and fall of 1862 he was incapacitated, and even after he returned to duty he often was, in his own words, "too feeble to command an army." In April 1863, when President Davis ordered Johnston to take command of the South's second most important army, he was "seriously sick." Johnston explained: "I . . . am not now able to serve in the field." Later, when he was ordered to assume command of forces in Mississippi, he replied: "I shall go immediately, although unfit for field-service."[55]

Albert Sidney Johnston died early in the war, but the one big battle that he directed was an attack. "What we have got to do must be done quickly," he announced. "The longer we leave them to fight the more difficult will they be to defeat." In the 1840s Johnston had favored the invasion of Mexico and a bold offensive against Mexico City, and in 1862 he launched a furious strike against the Federals at Shiloh, where he was killed in action. "Gentlemen," he told some of his generals who feared that the enemy would not be surprised and the Confederate assault would fail, "we shall attack at daylight tomorrow." As the generals returned to their units, Johnston told a staff officer: "I would fight them if they were a million."[56]

Beauregard, who helped Albert Sidney Johnston plan the bloody attack at Shiloh, favored a Confederate invasion of Maryland in 1861, and he announced in 1862: "I desire to . . . retake the offensive as soon as our forces . . . have been sufficiently reorganized." Relieved of command before he could make another attack, Beauregard repeatedly advocated offensives. He favored throwing "masses against fractions" of the enemy, "of crushing one of his fractional masses by a concentrated attack on either one of them." In November 1862 he wrote Braxton Bragg: "I am glad to hear . . . that you are again about to take the offensive. I would concentrate my forces well in hand—let him [the enemy] show his game, & then precipitate with lightning speed my whole mass (as we did at Shiloh) on one of his fractions." In 1863 Beauregard told Joe Johnston that "the surest way to relieve the State of Mississippi and the Valley of the Mississippi from the presence of the

---

[55]Robert M. Hughes, *General Johnston* (New York, 1893), 21, 25, 32, 144; Heitman, *Historical Register*, II, 26; Joseph E. Johnston, *Narrative of Military Operations*, ed. Frank E. Vandiver (reissue, Bloomington, 1959), 164, 168, 173; *OR*, XXIII (pt. 2), 745. John Jones noted that it was Johnston's "misfortune to be wounded in almost every battle he fights." John B. Jones, *A Rebel War Clerk's Diary*, ed. Earl S. Miers (reissue, New York, 1958), 82.

[56]*Confederate Veteran*, III (1895), 83; Charles P. Roland, *Albert Sidney Johnston: Soldier of Three Republics* (Austin, 1964), 105, 110–11, 115, 128, 312–13, 323–25; William Preston Diary, April 5, 1862, War Department Collection of Confederate Records, National Archives; William Preston Johnston, "Albert Sidney Johnston at Shiloh," in *Battles and Leaders*, I, 555. Johnston reportedly told an Arkansas regiment just before it charged at Shiloh: "Men of Arkansas! they say you boast of your prowess with the bowie-knife. Today you wield a nobler weapon—the bayonet. Employ it well." Roland, *Johnston*, 327.

Enemy's Army is suddenly and boldly to take the offensive." And in 1864 Beauregard hoped to obtain reinforcements from Lee's army and "to take the offensive and attack [General Benjamin F.] Butler vigorously" at Drewry's Bluff. Though he failed to get the men he requested, Beauregard reported on May 20: "We have driven the enemy line about a mile along the whole extent of his front and have succeeded after a severe struggle."[57]

Bragg, who objected to trenches because he believed they destroyed an army's aggressiveness, attacked in three of the four major battles that he directed. In 1862 he revealed to another general just how he would attack the enemy: "I shall promptly assail him in the open field with my whole available force, if he does not exceed me more than four to one." In a draft of his report on Shiloh, Bragg suggested that the most "valuable lesson" to be learned from that bloody action was "never on a battle field to lose a moment's time, but . . . to press on with every available man giving a panic stricken and retreating foe no time to rally."[58]

The man who took command of the Army of Tennessee after Joe Johnston's removal, John Bell Hood, was the general most committed to assault tactics. Johnston's defense of Atlanta in May and June 1864 cost the Federals 3,000 more men than the Confederates lost. Hood lost 12,500 more men than Sherman in assaults on the Federals around Atlanta from late July to early September 1864. After his failure to damage the Federals at Jonesboro, where he directed two corps "to attack . . . with the utmost celerity and energy," Hood blamed Johnston for the failure. "It seems," Hood informed the government, "the troops had been so long confined [by Johnston] to trenches and had been taught to believe that intrenchments cannot be taken, so that they attacked without spirit and retired without proper effort." After President Davis saw this letter he scribbled on it: "it is sad to hear such feeling as is described in any portion of our troops who are required to act offensively."[59]

---

[57]Jones, *Rebel War Clerk's Diary*, ed. Miers, 40; *OR*, XVII (pt. 2), 599; XXVIII (pt. 2), 399–400; P. G. T. Beauregard to Thomas Jordan, July 12, 1862 (copy), Beauregard Papers, Library of Congress; Beauregard to Braxton Bragg, November 16, 1862 (copy), ibid.; Beauregard to J. E. Johnston, May 15, 1863 (copy), Wigfall Papers; Beauregard to Braxton Bragg, May 14, 16, 20, 1864, Pierre Gustave Toutant Beauregard Papers, Duke University.

[58]Braxton Bragg to Mansfield Lovell, January 8, 1862, Mansfield Lovell Papers, Henry E. Huntington Library, San Marino, California; Bragg's Report of Shiloh, April 30, 1862 (rough copy), William P. Palmer Collection of Braxton Bragg Papers, Western Reserve Historical Society, Cleveland. In April 1863 President Davis's military aide wrote: "General Bragg says heavy intrenchments demoralize our troops." *OR*, XXIII (pt. 2), 761. And a member of Bragg's staff noted about the same time: "The Engineers are busy in strengthening the field works around Tullahoma. Gen. Bragg has never shown much confidence in them—Murfreesboro for example." George William Brent Diary, April 13, 1863, Palmer Collection.

[59]Livermore, *Numbers & Losses*, 119–21, 122–26; John Bell Hood to Braxton Bragg, September 4, 1864, Davis Papers, Duke University.

Long after the war Hood continued to argue against the use of field works and entrenchments. He claimed that "General Lee never made use of entrenchments, except for the purpose of holding a part of his line with a small force, whilst he assailed the enemy with the main body of his Army. . . . He well knew that the constant use of breastworks would teach his soldiers to look and depend upon such protection as an indispensable source of strength; would imperil that spirit of devil-me-care independence and self-reliance which was one of their secret sources of power, and would, finally, impair the morale of his Army." Hood insisted that a "soldier cannot fight for a period of one or two months constantly behind breastworks . . . and then be expected to engage in pitched battle and prove as intrepid and impetuous as his brother who has been taught to rely solely upon his own valor. The latter, when ordered to charge and drive the enemy, will—or endeavor to—run over any obstacle he may encounter in his front; the former, on account of his undue appreciation of breastworks . . . , will be constantly on the look-out for such defences. His imagination will grow vivid under bullets and bombshells, and a brush-heap will so magnify itself in dimension as to induce him to believe that he is stopped by a wall ten feet high and a mile in length. The consequence of his troubled imagination is that, if too proud to run, he will lie down, incur almost equal disgrace, and prove himself nigh worthless in a pitched battle."[60]

Lee, too, liked to attack. He often suggested offensives to the president and urged other generals to be aggressive. In May 1862, a month after what Lee called the Confederate "victory of Shiloh," he advised Beauregard to invade Tennessee. When Lee assumed command of Confederate forces in Virginia in June 1862 he promptly abandoned defensive warfare and launched two offensives—one by Jackson in the Shenandoah Valley and Lee's own Seven Days' campaign against McClellan. The president's wife recalled that "General Lee was not given to indecision, and they have mistaken his character who supposed caution was his vice. He was prone to attack." In June 1863 Lee informed the secretary of war: "As far as I can judge there is nothing to be gained by this army remaining quietly on the defensive."[61]

Though Lee was at his best on defense, he adopted defensive tactics only after attrition had deprived him of the power to attack. His brilliant defensive campaign against Grant in 1864 made the Union pay in manpower as it had never paid before, but the Confederates resorted to defensive warfare too

---

[60]John Bell Hood, *Advance and Retreat: Personal Experiences in the United States & Confederate States Armies*, ed. Richard N. Current (reissue, Bloomington, 1959), 131.

[61]*OR*, X (pt. 2), 546; Varina H. Davis, *Jefferson Davis . . . A Memoir* (2 vols., New York, 1890), II, 318–19; R. E. Lee to James A. Seddon, June 8, 1863, in Lee, *Wartime Papers*, 505.

late; Lee started the campaign with too few men, and he could not replace his losses as could Grant.[62]

Even after the Wilderness campaign Lee still wanted to take the offensive. He continued to hope that he could maneuver Grant out into the open and attack him. In May 1864 Lee wrote Davis: "[Grant's] position is strongly entrenched, and we cannot attack it with any prospect of success without great loss of men which I wish to avoid if possible. . . . [M]y object has been to engage him when [his army is] in motion and . . . I shall continue to strike him whenever opportunity presents itself." After the war the defenders of Lee were quick to point out that their hero had been as aggressive as ever in the last years of the conflict. "It is a very popular error to speak of General Lee as acting on the defensive in the campaign of 1864, and his 'retreating' before General Grant," contended one writer. "The truth is that from the day Grant crossed the Rapidan until . . . he sat down to the siege of Petersburg . . . Lee never made a move except to meet and fight the enemy, and that . . . he craved nothing so much as 'an open field and a fair fight.' " Another observer wrote that nothing was "more false" than the view that "Lee was strong only in defence, and was averse to taking the offensive." His "genius was aggressive," and he detested defensive warfare, for no leader "knew better than he that axiom of the military art which finds the logical end of defence in surrender." Just two weeks before he surrendered, Lee lost 3,500 men in an unsuccessful assault on the Federal fortifications at Petersburg. "I was induced to assume the offensive," Lee explained to President Davis, "from the belief that the point assailed could be carried without much loss." As it happened, Lee's attack cost the Confederates three times as many men as the defenders lost.[63]

The man most responsible for the Confederacy's military policies, Jefferson Davis, also had formed his ideas on the art of war in Mexico. There Zachary Taylor, the only army commander under whom Davis ever served, became his military idol. Taylor was the "great captain of the age," Davis avowed; "the world held not a soldier better qualified." A great commander, Davis informed Beauregard in 1861, was a man of moral strength, dauntless courage, and the "power that moves and controls the mass. This is not an ideal," insisted the Confederate president, "but a sketch of Taylor." Davis

---

[62]One study estimates that Grant lost about 50,000 men between the Wilderness and Cold Harbor, or about the number with which Lee started the campaign. Clifford Dowdey, *Lee's Last Campaign* (Boston, 1960), 299.

[63]R. E. Lee to Jefferson Davis, May 18, 1864, *Lee's Dispatches . . . to Jefferson Davis . . .* , ed. Douglas S. Freeman and Grady McWhiney (New York, 1957), 183–84; Anon., "General Lee's Offensive Policy in the Campaign of 1864," *Southern Historical Society Papers*, IX (1881), 137; Captain John Hampden Chamberlayne, "Address on the Character of General R. E. Lee," ibid., III (1877), 34–35; Lee to Davis, March 26, 1865, in Lee, *Lee's Dispatches*, 341–42.

romanticized his only commander into something he was not—a soldier skilled in "military science." But it was Taylor's "manly courage" that Davis most appreciated. Of the first Mexican War battles, Davis wrote that Taylor "paused for no regular approaches, but . . . dashed with sword and bayonet on the foe."[64]

Davis believed that this was the way war should be fought. At Monterey he impatiently led his regiment against a Mexican redoubt. "Now is the time," he reportedly shouted as his troops slowed their advance. "Great God, if I had fifty men with knives I could take the fort." The men, with Davis in front, rushed forward and drove the Mexicans from their strong position. Davis's "power" and "courage" inspired a young soldier to write: "I verily believe that if he should tell his men to jump into a cannon's mouth they would think it all right, and would all say, 'Colonel Jeff . . . knows best, so hurrah, boys, let's go ahead.' He is always in front of his men, and ready to be the first to expose himself. . . . I never wish to be commanded by a truer soldier than Colonel Davis."[65]

The concepts of leadership that he had formed before the Civil War guided his appointments as president of the Confederacy. Davis especially admired courage, modesty, boldness, and experience, and he discovered these characteristics in such men as Albert Sidney Johnston and Robert E. Lee. Davis also found, at least to his own satisfaction, these same admired qualities in less likely individuals. Many of the men he appointed to high military rank had no better qualifications than that Davis had known and liked them at West Point, in the Old Army, or in Mexico.[66]

If the president appointed and retained men who seemed to him to possess those personal traits that he considered essential in military leaders, he also denounced and sometimes removed those who did not. From the war's outset Davis tended to personalize disagreements and to reduce the standards by which he evaluated military competence to a moral question—whether or not he deemed an individual to have character.

The two most famous examples are the cases of Joseph E. Johnston and Beauregard. As early as 1861 Davis decided that these two men lacked

[64]Jefferson Davis, *Jefferson Davis, Constitutionalist: His Letters, Papers and Speeches*, ed. Dunbar Rowland (10 vols., Jackson, 1923), I, 80, 47–49; *OR*, V, 903–04; Davis to his brother, January 26, 1847, Jefferson Davis Papers, Chicago Historical Society.

[65]Justin H. Smith, *The War With Mexico* (2 vols., New York, 1919), I, 252; Joseph Davis Howell to his mother, October 13, 1846, in Davis, *Jefferson Davis: Private Letters*, 44.

[66]Jefferson Davis, *The Rise and Fall of the Confederate Government* (2 vols., reissue, New York, 1958), I, 307–08; II, 144, 310; Davis to John Letcher, September 12, 1861, Davis Papers, Duke University; Grady McWhiney, *Southerners and Other Americans* (New York, 1973), 87–97; the favorable testimony of Lucius B. Northrop at Davis's court-martial is in Davis, *Papers of Davis*, I, 371–72; John B. Jones, *A Rebel War Clerk's Diary at the Confederate States Capital*, ed. Howard Swiggett (2 vols., New York, 1935), II, 188.

soldierly qualities. Part of the problem appears to have been their refusal to acknowledge that Davis knew as much about the art of war as they did. Soon the president concluded that they were too contentious, too jealous of their prerogatives and reputations, and ultimately he decided that they were petty and dishonest men devoid of character and consequently untrustworthy. After Davis and Johnston had a dispute over rank early in the war they never trusted each other. In 1863 an observer noted: "the President detests Joe Johnston . . . and General Joe returns the compliment with compound interest." As the Confederacy collapsed in April 1865, Davis complained to his wife: "J. E. Johnston and Beauregard were hopeless. . . . Their only idea was to retreat." And after the war Davis frequently denounced Johnston for his bad character, "selfishness," "convenient" memory, "malignity and suppression of the truth." While in prison, Davis told his doctor that Vicksburg fell because Johnston "failed to obey the positive orders to attack General Grant" and that if Johnston "had vigorously attacked Sherman at Atlanta when directed, the fortunes of the war would have been changed, and Sherman hurled back to Nashville, over a sterile and wasted country—his retreat little less disastrous than Napoleon's from Moscow. He did not do so, and was relieved—General Hood, a true and spirited soldier, taking his place—but the opportunity was then gone; and to this delay, more than any other cause, the Southern people will attribute their overthrow, whenever history comes to be truly written."[67]

Davis revealed his contempt for Beauregard as well as his conviction that the man was not resolute when he wrote in October 1862: "Beauregard was tried as Commander of the Army of the West and left it without leave, when the troops were demoralized and the country he was sent to protect was threatened with conquest." When a delegation of Tennesseans asked him to restore Beauregard to command, Davis replied that he would refuse if the whole world requested it.[68]

Davis not only judged men by the standards that he had adopted before 1861, he also brought with him to the presidency a limited perspective based on his personal experiences and prejudices that would shape Confederate military affairs and tactics. His belief that war could be both just and glorious

[67]Chesnut, *Diary from Dixie*, ed. Martin and Avary, 248–49; Davis, *Jefferson Davis: Private Letters*, 156, 378, 396–97; Davis to James Lyon, August 13, 1876 (copy), Davis Papers, Library of Congress; Davis to Lucius B. Northrop, April 9, 1879, Davis Papers, Duke University; James P. Jones, ed., " 'Your Left Arm': James H. Wilson's Letters to Adam Badeau," *Civil War History*, XII (1966), 243–44; John J. Craven, *Prison Life of Jefferson Davis* . . . (reissue, Biloxi, 1979), 128–29.

[68]Thomas Bragg Diary, January 8, April 7, 1862, Southern Historical Collection, Chapel Hill; Davis to Edmund Kirby Smith, October 29, 1862, Edmund Kirby Smith Papers, Southern Historical Collection; Edward A. Pollard, "The Confederate Congress," *The Galaxy*, VI (1868–1869), 749.

helped give him the confidence he needed to initiate hostilities in 1861.[69] He considered Southerners a martial people who would fight magnificently, or as he told a woman in June 1861: "we will do all that can be done by pluck and muscle, endurance, and dogged courage, dash, and red-hot patriotism."[70] His own fondness for combat caused him to favor bold—indeed, sometimes reckless—generals. He had some understanding of the strategic value of railroads, but his bias against the navy caused him to neglect that vital service.[71]

His concept that wars should be fought only between organized armies prevented him from encouraging extensive espionage, sabotage, or guerilla warfare. His strong views on race kept him from supporting the use of slaves in the Confederate army until it was too late for them to help the South. The standards by which Davis evaluated men roused much criticism. Though he disliked political generals, he appointed enough of them to irritate professional soldiers but not enough to satisfy the politicians. By early 1862 Howell Cobb complained that the president preferred "drunken West Point men . . . to worthy and accomplished men from private life." And in 1863 the head of the Bureau of War claimed that even "Mr. Davis's friends say that he is . . . the worst judge of men in the world, apt to take up with a man of feeble intellect or character, and when he has once done so, holds on with unreasoning tenacity." The Confederate president held to his military views with equal tenacity. A few years before his death Davis wrote his old friend Lucius B. Northrop, the Confederacy's much criticized commissary general: "The fact is you showed extraordinary capacity, but, like myself, were wanting in the quality to conciliate men who had private ends to serve, or who were vain enough to believe that they could teach us about things on which we had labored exhaustingly, and of which they were profoundly ignorant."[72]

Of all the military influences upon Davis before 1861, those from the Mexican War unquestionably were the most profound. The Confederacy's defeat may not have been insured, as Bernard DeVoto flippantly remarked, by what Jefferson Davis learned "in exactly five days of action" in Mexico, but those months with Taylor's army provided Davis with a reservoir of military experiences from which he continually drew lessons and judgments.

---

[69]Grady McWhiney, "Jefferson Davis and the Art of War," *Civil War History*, XXI (1975), 101–12.

[70]Chesnut, *Diary from Dixie*, ed. Martin and Avary, 71.

[71]William N. Still, Jr., *Iron Afloat: The Story of the Confederate Armorclads* (Nashville, 1971), 5–6.

[72]Cobb quoted in Horace Montgomery, *Howell Cobb's Confederate Career* (Tuscaloosa, 1959), 39; Robert G. H. Kean, *Inside the Confederate Government: The Diary of Robert Garlick Hill Kean*, ed. Edward Younger (New York, 1957), 72; Davis to Lucius B. Northrop, March 3, 1885 (copy), Jefferson Davis Papers, Mississippi Department of Archives and History, Jackson.

After the Civil War, in a dispute over some military matter, Davis insisted that he knew a point he had made was correct. How did he know? His "experience as commander of volunteers" in Mexico convinced him that he was right.[73]

---

[73]Bernard DeVoto, *The Year of Decision, 1846* (Boston, 1943), 203, 284; Davis to Jubal A. Early, April 7, 1878, Davis Papers, Duke University.

12

The Rebels Are Barbarians

It is significant that most of the Confederacy's military leaders practiced in the 1860s the offensive tactics that they had seen work so well in Mexico in the 1840s, but the tactical preferences of a few men—even those in high command—could scarcely have prevailed if a majority of the southern people had opposed offensive warfare. The simple fact is that Southerners were aggressive.

They were culturally conditioned "for offensive war," explained a Richmond newspaper in August 1862: "The familiarity of our people with arms and horses gives them advantages for aggression, which are thrown away by delay. Ten thousand Southerners, before the Yankees learnt to load a gun, might have marched to Boston without resistance." Such confidence in their ability to drive the enemy was typical of Confederates, especially in the first years of the war. The cultural isolation of their society fostered a contempt for outsiders, particularly Yankees, and a romantic vision of southern self-prowess. Many a Southerner, contended a native of the South, "at all times feels able and prepared—cocked and primed, in his own vernacular—to flog the entire North." The common view in the antebellum South was that Northerners would not fight. "Such shameful cowards these Yankees are," proclaimed a Southerner. "I am sorry to hear of the times being so hard in old Blount [County, Alabama] but I think they will be better in 12 months & I have a good reason for thinking so," a young Confederate soldier wrote in October 1861. "Because we are going to kill the last Yankey before that time if there is any fight in them still. I believe that J. D. Walker's Brigade can whip 25,000 Yankees. I think that I can whip 25 myself."[1]

---

[1]*Daily Richmond Whig*, August 26, 1862; Daniel R. Hundley, *Social Relations in Our Southern States*, ed. William J. Cooper, Jr. (reissue, Baton Rouge, 1979), 224; John Washington Inzer, " 'The Yankees are the Meanest People on Earth,' " comp. Clarke Stallworth, in *Birmingham News*, November 4, 1980, B-1; T. B. Deaver to Thomas Hendricks, October 8, 1861, *Cherished Letters of Thomas Wayman Hendricks*, comp. Josie Armstrong McLaughlin (Birmingham, 1947), 86.

Combat was more highly esteemed in the Old South than in the Old North. "To such an extent does the military fever rage," observed one Southerner, "a stranger would conclude at least every other male citizen to be either 'Captain or Colonel, or Knight at arms.' Nor would he greatly err, . . . for . . . he would find more than every other man a military chieftain of some sort or other." Southerners were quick to anger and to fight. "I heard today of another instance of the barbarous manner which the Floridians have in settling difficulties," wrote a visitor. "Two men had a slight difficulty about some hogs. They became enraged & meeting each other both fired at the same time. The one was killed & the other dangerously wounded." Such encounters were customary. "Human life is a cheap commodity [in the South], and the blow of anger but too commonly precedes or is simultaneous with the word," explained a foreigner. "The barbarous baseness and cruelty of public opinion, dooms young men, when challenged, to fight," noted a traveler. "They must fight, kill or be killed, and that for some petty offence beneath the notice of the law. Established names only . . . may refuse to fight, but this is rarely done; to refuse is a stain and high dishonour." The southern habit of regarding a fighter—soldier or dueler—as a hero horrified many Northerners. "Cruel horrid custom thus to butcher & destroy men for the false code of honor," pronounced a Yankee preacher. Unlike Southerners, Northerners "were not so military in their habits," observed a contemporary, "because, though equally brave . . . , they were more industrious, more frugal, and less mercurial in their temperament. Religion was with them a powerful spring of action, and discouraged all wars except those of self-defence. The social and moral virtues, the sciences and arts, were cherished and respected; and there were many roads to office and to eminence, which were safer and more certain, and not less honourable, than the bloody path of warlike achievement."[2]

Their attitude toward combat was only one of the many ways in which Southerners and Northerners differed. Antebellum observers pointed out that Southerners practiced, as an Englishwoman put it, "a mode of life which differs entirely from that prevailing in the Northern States."[3] A wide range of eyewitnesses characterized Southerners as more hospitable, generous, frank, wasteful, lazy, lawless, and reckless than Northerners, who were in turn more reserved, thrifty, shrewd, disciplined, enterprising, acquisitive, careful, and practical than Southerners. The Old South was a leisure-

[2]Hundley, *Social Relations*, 127–28; Henry B. Whipple, *Bishop Whipple's Southern Diary, 1843–1844*, ed. Lester B. Shippee (London, 1937), 29–30; Charles Mackay, *Life and Liberty in America, . . . in 1857–8* (New York, 1859), 173; William Faux, *Memorable Days in America . . .* (London, 1823), 187; Frederick Hall, *Letters from the East and from the West* (Washington, 1840), 287–88. The South's chivalric cult is emphasized in Rollin G. Osterweis, *Romanticism and Nationalism in the Old South* (New Haven, 1949).

[3]Catherine C. Hopley, *Life in the South . . .* (2 vols., reissue, New York, 1974), I, 73–74.

oriented society where people favored the spoken word over the written and enjoyed their sensual pleasures—singing, dancing, eating, drinking, gambling, riding, hunting, fishing, and fighting. Family ties reportedly were stronger in the South than in the North; Southerners, whose values were more agrarian, wasted more time and consumed more tobacco and liquor. Yankees, on the other hand, were cleaner, neater, more orderly and progressive, worked harder, and kept the Sabbath better than Southerners.[4]

Yankee culture was in large part transplanted English culture; southern culture was Celtic—Scottish, Scotch-Irish, Welsh, Cornish, and Irish.[5] The Confederate diarist who wrote in 1863 that "the war is one between the Puritan & Cavalier" was close to the mark, and so was the English traveler who observed that "the slave-holding states appeared to stand in about the same relation to the free, as Ireland does to England; every thing appears slovenly, ill-arranged, incomplete [in the South]; windows do not shut, doors do not fasten; there is a superabundance of hands to do every thing, and little is thoroughly done."[6]

---

[4]See, for example, Thomas Ashe, *Travels in America* . . . (3 vols., London, 1808), I, 123; Carl David Arfwedson, *The United States and Canada, in 1832, 1833, and 1834* (2 vols., London, 1834), I, 364; II, 181; [Carlo Barinetti], *A Voyage to Mexico and Havana; including some General Observations on the United States* (New York, 1841), 29–30; James Silk Buckingham, *The Slave States of America* (2 vols., London, 1842), I, 286–87; Moritz Busch, *Travels Between the Hudson & the Mississippi, 1851–1852*, trans. and ed. Norman H. Binger (Lexington, 1971), 150–53; George William Frederick Howard, Earl of Carlisle, *Travels in America* (New York, 1851), 76–77; Michel Chevalier, *Society, Manners and Politics in the United States*, trans. Thomas Gamaliel Bradford (Boston, 1839), 149–50; Louis Auguste Felix, Baron de Beaujour, *Sketch of the United States* . . . , trans. William Walton (London, 1814), 133–34; Ebenezer Davies, *American Scenes—and Christian Slavery: A Recent Tour of Four Thousand Miles in the United States* (London, 1849), 104, 208; Faux, *Memorable Days*, 35–36; William Kingsford, *Impressions of the West and South During a Six Weeks' Holiday* (Toronto, 1858), 53; Charles Joseph Latrobe, *The Rambler in North America* . . . (2 vols., London, 1835), I, 60–61, II, 5; Alexander Mackay, *The Western World; or Travels in the United States in 1846–47* . . . (3 vols., London, 1849), I, 204; II, 134, 143; David W. Mitchell, *Ten Years in the United States; Being an Englishman's View of Men and Things in the North and South* (London, 1862), 192; Charles G. Parsons, *Inside View of Slavery; or, A Tour Among the Planters* (Cleveland, 1855), 164; Alexis de Tocqueville, *The Republic of the United States of America, and Its Political Institutions*, trans. Henry Reeves (New York, 1858), 427, 560; Whipple, *Southern Diary*, 26, 43–44.

[5]Forrest McDonald and Grady McWhiney, "The Antebellum Southern Herdsman: A Reinterpretation," *Journal of Southern History*, XLI (1975), 147–66; Grady McWhiney, "The Revolution in Nineteenth-Century Alabama Agriculture," *Alabama Review*, XXXI (1978), 3–32; Forrest McDonald, "The Ethnic Factor in Alabama History: A Neglected Dimension," ibid., 256–65; Grady McWhiney, "Saving the Best from the Past," ibid., XXXII (1979), 243–72; Forrest McDonald and Ellen Shapiro McDonald, "The Ethnic Origins of the American People, 1790," *William and Mary Quarterly*, XXXVII (1980), 179–99; Forrest McDonald and Grady McWhiney, "The South from Self-Sufficiency to Peonage: An Interpretation," *American Historical Review*, LXXXV (1980), 1095–1118.

[6]T. Otis Baker Diary, October 8, 1863, T. Otis Baker and Family Papers, Mississippi Department of Archives and History, Jackson; Carlisle, *Travels in America*, 54–55.

After the Civil War an orator contrasted the Teutonic and Anglo-Saxon North with the Celtic South. There had been in the past a time when "the need of the hour was an emphasis of the Teutonic . . . , an exaltation of idea, of organization, of concentration. . . . But every victory, as everybody knows, has its reacting danger. Business enterprise is good; commercial integrity is good; a genius for management, for execution, these are good; but all of them put together are not enough. And these, which are the smaller part of Teutonism, are just what are being exalted to-day far above their place. Now has come a time for reassertion, for . . . an emphasis upon Celticism. Organization, tending to pass over into tyranny," had produced "the triumphant commercialism of the North." Only Southerners, with their Celtic ways, could counterbalance the evils of this business culture, insisted the orator: "The intimate friendship with nature, the tender feeling for all the aspects of earth and sky; the almost passionate attachment to particular places; that irrational devotion to lost causes which we call Quixotism; that infinite sympathy with failure; that tolerance of dreamers and visionaries; that regard for grace and fancy—in a word, the impractical imagination, has been beaten down beneath the hammers of trade. But in the South," he said, "the conditions of the last thirty years appear to have been just those which tend to develop this sort of imagination. In the South, if anywhere, remains a flowering of Celticism, or romance, or poetry."[7]

The way that Southerners fought was one of the strongest indicators that their cultural heritage was Celtic. They attacked with such boldness that French General A. Collard dubbed them "admirable [fighters]—the first in the world. I have no hesitation in paying this deserved praise," he wrote in 1864, "and the whole world thinks as I do." President Davis cited the "pluck . . . , courage, [and] dash" that characterized the Confederate soldier, and General Hood spoke of "the spirit of devil-me-care independence" that drove the Rebel infantryman to "run over any obstacle he may encounter in his front." Or as one veteran Confederate put it: "a spirited charge,—the forte of southern soldiers,—often decides the fate of an action."[8]

Celtic warfare may best be described as a continuum. Not only have people of Celtic culture exhibited an abiding love of combat; they have

---

[7]Herman Justi, ed., *Official History of the Tennessee Centennial Exposition* (Nashville, 1898), 474. This reference was supplied by Professor Don H. Doyle of Vanderbilt University.

[8]A. Collard to James Trudeau, February 12, 1864 (trans. H. B. Lee), Jefferson Davis Papers, Duke University; Mary B. Chesnut, *A Diary from Dixie*, ed. Isabella D. Martin and Myrta Lockett Avary (New York, 1905), 71; John Bell Hood, *Advance and Retreat: Personal Experiences in the United States & Confederate States Armies*, ed. Richard N. Current (reissue, Bloomington, 1959), 131; Henry E. Handerson to his father, September 11, 1861, in *Yankee in Gray: The Civil War Memoirs of Henry E. Handerson, with a Selection of His Wartime Letters*, ed. Clyde Lottridge Cummer (Cleveland, 1962), 91.

fought much the same way for more than two thousand years. Consider, for example, the similarities of three climactic battles in Celtic history: Telamon, Culloden, and Gettysburg. In each of these battles Celtic forces used the same tactics with the same results. Boldly they attacked a strongly positioned enemy, who knew what to expect and was prepared to meet the charges. The enemy always had better weapons; in each encounter, superior military technology and defensive tactics overcame Celtic dash and courage. The Celts risked everything on the outcome of their charges and every time they lost not just a battle but a war.

Coincidence? Possibly, but more likely an example of cultural continuity—the persistence of accustomed ways despite traumatic interaction with other groups. That, at least, is what Celtic warfare from 225 B.C. to A.D. 1863 suggests.

In 225 B.C. the fate of Rome was at stake. For some time the Romans had been at war with "barbarians," people called Celts who had pushed across the Alps into Italy's Po Valley. When the Romans made the mistake of ignoring their own laws and meddling in Celtic affairs, the Celts, who were temperamentally unable to abide such an affront, took up their arms. At Telamon, north of Rome, the Celtic army led by Aneroëstes found its advance blocked by well-placed Roman forces. Their strong position on a hill gave the Romans a decided tactical advantage, especially because the Celts did exactly what they were expected to do—attack. They rarely did anything else. In earlier encounters their favorite tactic was a wild, reckless assault accompanied by what the Romans considered "weird, discordant" music and "horrible and diverse yelling" that curdled an opponent's blood.

As the Romans waited, the Celts prepared to attack. The "imposing appearance of the Celtic host in arms and the wild tumult" was a frightening spectacle, recalled a Roman; "since the whole [Celtic] army took up a war-chant, a din arose so immense and terrifying that . . . the very hills around seemed to be raising their voices in echo."[9]

The Celts rushed forward with their customary vigor, but their charges failed to break the Roman lines. It was obvious that the Romans were better equipped than the Celts and that the Celtic charges, which the Romans were prepared to meet, no longer paralyzed them as they had before. The Celts really had no chance. The shields used by the Romans covered the entire body; those used by the Celts were much shorter. The Celts "stormed against the enemy" as usual, but they were easy targets for the Romans, who used their tall shields like a wall and thrust out with their swords at the exposed Celts. Not only were the naked or lightly clad Celts painfully vulnerable, they could neither thrust back with their blunt swords nor cut

⁹Gerhard Herm, *The Celts: The People Who Came out of the Darkness* (New York, 1977), 14–26; Barry Cunliffe, *The Celtic World* (New York, 1979), 58.

through the Roman shields. The pointed Roman sword could be used to thrust as well as to cut; the rounded swords used by the Celts could only cut. Moreover, as Polybius noted, the Celtic sword was so poorly constructed that a single blow against a Roman shield would bend it badly enough that the wielder would have to stop fighting, "wedge it against the ground, and straighten it with his foot." While doing this, the Celts were slaughtered.

At Telamon the Celtic charges not only failed but also gave the Romans a total victory. Some 40,000 Celts were killed and another 10,000 were captured.[10]

Celtic power waned after Telamon. The Celts remained as combative and as courageous as ever, and even learned from the Romans certain mechanical military skills, but they never became as rigidly disciplined military technicians as were the Romans. To have done so would have been foreign to the Celtic nature. The Celts were excellent fighting men, but they were far too proud, impetuous, and independent to become first-rate soldiers. Culturally conditioned to prefer bold rather than cautious actions, they lacked self-discipline, patience, and tenacity. They still believed in and practiced the Celtic charge; like wishful thinking, it was one of their folkways.[11]

They again proved their aggressiveness some seventy years after their defeat at Telamon, during Caesar's Gallic Wars. The Celts of Gaul, according to Caesar, believed that "it was better to die in battle than to fail to recover their ancient glory in war and the liberty which they had inherited from their ancestors." He also noted that the Celts were "reckless," given to "sudden impulsive decisions," and possessed a "rash impetuosity." All of these traits worked to the advantage of the Romans. Caesar reported with pleasure that the Celts "had learned from their fathers and their ancestors to fight with courage rather than with guile or recourse to stratagems."[12]

Nevertheless, before they were subdued, these simple warriors inflicted several defeats on the Romans. Of a Celtic charge led by Ambiorix in 54 B.C. that annihilated a Roman cohort, Caesar wrote: "The natives at once raised their customary cry . . . , and, yelling and screaming, charged down upon our army and broke through the ranks." That same year in Britain the Romans had their lines broken by another Celtic charge. And though Caesar tried to explain away his defeat by the Celts at Gergovia in 52 B.C., a series of charges led by Vercingetorix drove the Romans from the field.[13]

Eventually, of course, Caesar won. His skill, cunning, and the might of the Roman military machine were too much for the Celts to overcome. "In

---

[10]T. G. E. Powell, *The Celts* (New York, 1958), 107–08; Herm, *Celts*, 26.

[11]Anne Ross, *Everyday Life of the Pagan Celts* (London, 1970), 54–77; Cunliffe, *Celtic World*, 56–57.

[12]Julius Caesar, *War Commentaries of Caesar*, trans. Rex Warner (New York, 1960), 137–38, 60, 17.

[13]Ibid., 104–05, 153–64.

the grip of their *furor* the Celts forgot all the rules of prudence," wrote Gerhard Herm; "[they] took on whatever stood in their path and thus threw away in one day the fruits they had so painfully garnered. . . . Caesar, quick as ever to react, seized the chance he was offered, allowed the attackers to charge as far as the legionaries' wall of shields and then, manoeuvring with parade-ground precision, took them in a deadly pincer movement. From then on it was the same old story. Celtic swords were broken on Roman lances, Celtic rage on Roman discipline." After his victory, Caesar wrote critically of the Celts. He concluded that while they were "quick and eager to start a war; they lack[ed] the strength of character and resolution necessary for enduring disasters."[14]

There were disasters aplenty for the Celts. Driven westward by their enemies, the Celts retreated to the British Isles, where for centuries they and their descendants—the Welsh, Cornish, Irish, and Scots—fought on against the Romans, Saxons, Normans, and finally the English.[15]

In the long struggle to survive, the Celtic peoples fought fiercely if not always successfully. In A.D. 83 Roman forces barely survived a wild attack by Scots at Loch Ore. In 183 and again in 207 the Scots broke through the northern Roman wall in Britain. They also invaded England in 306, 345, 360, and 398. During the reign of English King Henry II (1154–1189) parts of Ireland fell under English control, the Scottish king was captured and forced to render homage to Henry, and much of Wales was compelled to acknowledge nominal subjection to him; but the Celts were as yet unconquered. For two centuries after the Norman invasions, until Llewellyn's defeat in 1282 by English King Edward I, the Welsh fought vehemently to retain their traditions and independence. Even then not all Welshmen accepted English rule; another Welsh revolt occurred in 1294 and discontent lingered.[16]

Rebellion became a way of life in Ireland. English King Richard II (1377–1399) managed to pacify the Irish for a time; the Tudors also made a determined effort to conquer Ireland, but every attempt for the next 450 years failed. Oliver Cromwell's systematic endeavor to exterminate the Irish, in which more than half the people of Ireland died, was followed by rebellion after bloody rebellion—led by Owen Roe O'Neill in 1649, by Patrick Sarfield in 1689, by Wolfe Tone in 1798, by Robert Emmet in 1803, by Young

[14]Herm, *Celts*, 193; Caesar, *War Commentaries*, 66.

[15]Lloyd Laing, *Celtic Britain* (New York, 1979), 104–13, 129–43.

[16]Ibid., 149; Michael Hechter, *Internal Colonialism: The Celtic Fringe in British National Development, 1536–1966* (Berkeley, 1975), 47–78; J. P. MacLean, *An Historical Account of the Settlement of Scotch Highlanders in America* . . . (reissue, Baltimore, 1978), 32–33; Goldwin Smith, *A History of England* (4th ed., New York, 1974), 63–64, 122–28.

Ireland in 1848, by the Fenians in 1867, by the Easter rebels in 1916, and by the Provisional IRA in recent years.[17]

Armed resistance to English domination continued in Scotland for several centuries. In 1314 at Bannockburn, where twenty-one clans participated, the Scots attacked and killed 30,000 Englishmen. In 1513 King James IV of Scotland led an assault on the English at Flodden. The shock effect of this charge almost carried the Scots to victory, but the English archers and pikemen rallied and slaughtered the Scots. Among those killed were James and fifteen clan chiefs. "At Flodden," wrote an Englishman, "our bows and bills slew all the flower of their honour." At Pinkie in 1547, after their initial attack succeeded, the Highlanders stopped to plunder and lost the battle. At Killiecrankie Pass in 1689 the "wild charge" of John Graham's Highlanders routed Hugh Mackay's government troops. At Prestonpans in 1745 a single charge by his clansmen won the battle for "Bonnie Prince Charlie," but the next year the Highlanders were decisively defeated when their charges failed to break the English ranks.[18]

This happened on April 16, 1746, at Drumossie Moor, near Culloden, where Prince Charles and about 5,000 Jacobites faced the Duke of Cumberland and 9,000 Englishmen. Short of supplies as usual, the "tired and starving" Highlanders attacked bravely, inspired by the hair-raising sounds of their fierce yells and their bagpipes. The Englishmen had been trained by Cumberland to resist the Highland charges. Supported by eighteen pieces of artillery, the English infantry awaited the assaults in three ranks—the first kneeling, the second stooping, and the third standing. As one authority explained, the English guns and musket fire "caused great distress to the Highlanders," whose desperate efforts were repulsed. The battle cost them more than 2,000 killed or wounded; the English lost only 50 killed and 200 wounded.[19]

The defeat at Culloden was important in Celtic history: a powerful effort followed to Anglicize all Scots, and this in turn drove many of them to America. A Scot noted that the clans made their last stand at Culloden, "and it is for their bravery and loyalty in a 'lost cause' that they are chiefly

---

[17]Alwyn Rees and Brinley Rees, *Celtic Heritage: Ancient Tradition in Ireland and Wales* (London, 1961), 118–19, 174–75; Nicholas Mansergh, *The Irish Question, 1840–1921* (Toronto, 1966), 20–21; Hechter, *Internal Colonialism*, 103–08. On the Irish hero warrior, see M. L. Sjoestedt, *Gods and Heroes of the Celts*, trans. Myles Dillon (London, 1949). For classical Celtic and Irish battle parallels, see E. Hull, "Observations of Classical Writers on the Habits of the Celtic Nations, as Illustrated from Irish Records," *Celtic Review*, III (1907), 62–76, 138–54.

[18]Wallace Notestein, *The Scots in History* (reissue, Westport, 1970), 37–40; MacLean, *Scotch Highlanders*, 33–36; Smith, *History of England*, 127, 211, 435; Henri Hubert, *The Greatness and Decline of the Celts* (London, 1934), 165–84.

[19]Peter Hume Brown, *History of Scotland* . . . (3 vols., Cambridge, 1909–1912), III, 321–24; William Ferguson, *Scotland, 1689 to the Present* (New York, 1968), 152–53.

remembered today." After Culloden the English sought to destroy the clans. Jacobites were hunted down, their houses burned, and their cattle stolen. The English adopted laws that declared a number of clan leaders traitors, disarmed the Highlanders, proscribed their dress, confiscated the estates of all attained persons, and abolished the traditional relationships between clansmen and their chiefs. More destructive yet to the Celtic way of life in Scotland were the changes in tenancy, animal husbandry, and work patterns. Traditional ways and social customs were outlawed to be replaced by the ways of a "money economy." Consequently, great numbers of Scots moved to America, where they were able to practice their old ways. After the Jacobite Rebellion, migration from the Highlands to America reached what Dr. Samuel Johnson called an "epidemical fury." More than 20,000 people left the Highlands for North America between 1763 and 1775, when an official ban was placed on emigration to America.[20]

Both before and after the Jacobite Rebellion great numbers of people from the Celtic, non-English, areas of the British Isles—from Cornwall, Wales, Ireland, Scotland, and those "Celtic fringe" counties of England in the extreme north and along the Welsh border—settled in America. By 1790, when the first United States Census was taken, over three-quarters of the people living in New England were of English origins and the middle states had a mixed population, but from Pennsylvania south and west the population became increasingly Celtic. In the South, especially in the Carolinas and in the backcountry, Celts constituted an overwhelming majority. The same pattern existed at the time of the American Civil War—the majority of the white people in the South in the 1860s were of Celtic origins and most of those who were not had become culturally Celticized; the majority in the North were of English origins and many who were not had become culturally Anglicized.[21]

This cultural dichotomy in America was not only the major cause of the Civil War but it explains why the war was fought the way it was. Because the American Civil War was basically a continuation of the centuries-old conflict between Celts and Englishmen, it is understandable that Southerners would fight as their Celtic ancestors had and that Yankees would follow the ways of their English forebears, even to the extent of recruiting foreigners and blacks to do some of their fighting for them.[22]

---

[20]Brown, *History of Scotland*, III, 325–47; R. W. Munro, *Highland Clans and Tartans* (London, 1977), 56–66.

[21]McDonald and McDonald, "Ethnic Origins, 1790," 179–99; McDonald and McWhiney, "Self-Sufficiency to Peonage," 1107–11; Forrest McDonald and Grady McWhiney, "The Celts Did It: Migration and Southern Culture," in *When the South Was West: The Old Southwest, 1780–1840*, ed. Cleveland Donald, Jr. (Jackson, 1982).

[22]Half a million of the Federal soldiers were foreign born and an additional 180,000 were blacks. E. B. Long and Barbara Long, *The Civil War Day by Day: An Almanac, 1861–1865* (Garden City, 1971), 705, 707. A foreign observer noted: "The Southerners . . . estimate

From the war's outset the Confederates fought in the traditionally Celtic way: they attacked. The best-known example of their recklessness was Gettysburg, where the Confederates lost nearly 23,000 men in three days of attacks. Losses were so severe at Gettysburg because the Confederates did just what the Federals wanted and expected them to do—attack strongly defended positions. "The plan of [Confederate General Robert E. Lee's] . . . attack seems to have been very simple," noted a foreign observer. Indeed it was; General Lee, reportedly a descendent of the Scottish military hero Robert Bruce, matched the raw courage of his men against the deadly fire of rifled muskets and artillery. The results can best be described in the words of participants in the slaughter. A Union soldier recalled that on the first day a line of Rebels "nearly a mile in length" attacked. "First we could see the tips of their color-staffs coming up over the little ridge, then the points of their bayonets, and then the Johnnies themselves, coming on with a steady tramp, tramp, and with loud yells." When they neared the Union position they were met by a "tornado of canister" that swept their line "so clean . . . that the Rebels sagged away. . . . From our second round on a gray squirrel could not have crossed the road alive."[23]

Of his brigade's bayonet assault on the Union line at Gettysburg, a Confederate wrote: "[we] pressed on to within about twenty or thirty paces of the [enemy's] works—a small but gallant band of heroes daring to attempt what could not be done by flesh and blood. The end soon came. We were beaten back to the line from which we had advanced with terrible loss, and in much confusion."[24]

Charge after charge failed. "My men . . . advanced about half way to the enemy's position," wrote the commander of an Alabama regiment, "but the fire was so destructive that my line wavered like a man trying to walk against a strong wind, and then slowly, doggedly, gave back. . . . My dead and wounded were then nearly as great in number as those still on duty. They literally covered the ground. The blood stood in puddles in some places . . . ; the ground was soaked with the blood of as brave men as ever fell on the red field of battle."[25]

---

highest the Northwestern Federal troops. . . . The Irish Federals are also respected for their fighting qualities; whilst the genuine Yankee and Germans (Dutch) are not much esteemed." Arthur J. L. Fremantle, *The Fremantle Diary* . . . , ed. Walter Lord (Boston, 1954), 133.

[23]Fremantle, *Diary*, 210; William Winston Fontaine, "The Descent of General Robert Edward Lee from King Robert the Bruce, of Scotland," *Southern Historical Society Papers*, IX (1881), 194–95; Douglas S. Freeman, *R. E. Lee: A Biography* (4 vols., New York, 1934–1935), I, 160; Augustus Buell, *"The Cannoneer": Recollections of Service in the Army of the Potomac* (Washington, 1890), 63–64.

[24]Randolph H. McKim, *A Soldier's Recollections: Leaves from the Diary of a Young Confederate* . . . (New York, 1910), 195–206.

[25]William C. Oates, *The War Between the Union and the Confederacy and Its Lost Opportunities, with a History of the 15th Alabama Regiment* . . . (New York, 1905), 210–12, 218–21.

The final Confederate attack at Gettysburg was made late in the afternoon on July 3 when General George E. Pickett, a romantic figure whose hair hung "almost to his shoulders in curly waves," led his division across an open valley to assault the Union forces on Cemetery Ridge. "None on that crest now need be told that *the enemy is advancing*," recalled a Federal who was there; "the dull gray masses deploy, man touching man, rank pressing rank, and line supporting line. The red flags wave [it was no accident that the Confederates adopted as their battle flag the Celtic St. Andrew's cross], their horsemen gallop up and down; the arms of eighteen thousand men, barrel and bayonet, gleam in the sun, a sloping forest of flashing steel. Right on they move, . . . magnificent, grim, irresistible." As they came within range of rifle and cannon, the Federals opened fire. "The enemy advanced magnificently, unshaken by the shot and shell which tore through his ranks," reported the Union chief of artillery. "When our canister fire and musketry were opened upon them, it occasioned disorder, but still they advanced gallantly until they reached the stone wall behind which our troops lay. Here ensued a desperate conflict, the enemy succeeding in passing the wall and entering our lines, causing great destruction of life, especially among the batteries. Infantry troops were, however, advanced from our right; the rear line of the enemy broke, and the others, who had fought with a gallantry that excited the admiration of our troops, found themselves cut off."[26]

Those Confederates who were still alive and could move retreated. All three of Pickett's brigade commanders had charged with their men. Two were killed; the other was wounded and captured.[27] Pickett's charge, like the other Confederate charges at Gettysburg, had failed, and with them the Confederacy.

Southerners lost the Civil War because they were too Celtic and their opponents were too English. The distinguished historian of the war's common soldiers, Bell I. Wiley, concluded that in many ways Johnny Reb and Billy Yank were quite different. Rebels fought "with more dash, *élan* and enthusiasm"; they were more emotional, more religious, more humorous and poetical, says Wiley. They also had a more "acute sense of the ludicrous, the dramatic or the fanciful." Yanks, on the other hand, were more practical, more materialistic, more literate, and they displayed "more of tenacity, stubbornness en masse and machinelike efficiency."[28] These, and other distinc-

[26]Richard B. Harwell, ed., *Two Views of Gettysburg: By Sir Arthur J. L. Fremantle and Frank A. Haskell* (Chicago, 1964), 189; U.S. War Dept., *War of the Rebellion: The Official Records of the Union and Confederate Armies* (128 vols., Washington, 1880–1901), Series 1, XXVII (pt. 1), 239 (hereinafter cited as *OR*, and unless otherwise noted all references are to Series 1).

[27]Edwin B. Coddington, *The Gettysburg Campaign: A Study in Command* (New York, 1968), 518, 525.

[28]Bell I. Wiley, *The Life of Billy Yank: The Common Soldier of the Union* (Indianapolis, 1951), 358–61.

tions that Wiley failed to mention, are significant. They suggest that the Civil War was a conflict between two distinct peoples and they also indicate the persistence over time of cultural patterns that seriously influenced, if they did not absolutely determine, the war's outcome.

All of the differences that Wiley recognized are cultural characteristics that separated not merely Rebels and Yankees but Celts and their historic enemies from antiquity to the American Civil War. Romans and Englishmen, like Yankees, were more practical, more materialistic, more literate, more tenacious, and more machinelike than the Celts they fought, just as the Confederates and their Celtic forebears were more emotional, foolhardy, romantic, and undisciplined than their opponents.

Some of these characteristics, particularly those that shaped Celtic warfare and tactics, deserve closer analysis. First, it is important to recognize that their enemies always considered themselves morally superior and more civilized than the Celts. Such views doubtless influenced how both sides fought. The Romans, for example, considered themselves the defenders of "civilization." They believed their Celtic neighbors to be primitive and disgusting savages. The historian Polybius called them lazy and their "existence very simple." Similar charges were made against the Welsh and the Irish, whom the English often regarded as impossible to civilize and fit only for extermination. At the beginning of the seventeenth century the king of Scotland still considered many of his subjects barbarians. "As for the Hielands," wrote King James V, "I shortly comprehend them all in two sorts of people: the one, that dwelleth in our main land that are barbarous, and yet mixed with some show of civilitie: the other that dwelleth in the Isles and are all utterlie barbarous, without any sort of show of civilitie." The king advised his son and heir to move against these clans, to reduce them to subservience, and to civilize or exterminate them, but "to think no other of them than of wolves and wild boars." After the conquest of Canada, English General James Wolfe concluded: "The Highlanders are very useful, serviceable soldiers. . . . They are hardy, intrepid, accustomed to a rough country, and no great mischief if they fall. How can you better employ a secret enemy than by making his end conducive to the common good?"[29]

Yankees viewed Southerners with fully as much contempt as Englishmen viewed Celts. Before the Civil War a Northerner, with typical Anglo-Saxon arrogance, advised Yankees to "mingle freely" with Southerners, "and . . . strive to bring up their habits, by a successful example, to the New England standard." When that proved impossible, stronger measures were recommended. "I believe," announced a saintly Northerner, "that the great conception of a Christian society, which was in the minds of the Pilgrims of the Mayflower, . . . is to displace and blot out the foul [South] . . . , with all its

---

[29]Herm, *Celts*, 7; Hechter, *Internal Colonialism*, 73–78; Munro, *Highland Clans*, 36, 62.

heaven-offending enormities; that . . . our vast and heterogeneous . . . population is either to be subdued and won to its principles and its blessings or to give place to the seed of the righteous." A Massachusetts soldier favored a policy of genocide toward Southerners. "I would exterminate them root and branch," he wrote just after the war. "They have often said they preferred it before subjugation, and, with the help of God, I would give it them. I am only saying what thousands say every day." In calls to exterminate Southerners and their "odious ways," Northerners sounded much like English Puritans who advocated the obliteration of their "barbarian" Celtic neighbors. It may be no coincidence that Irish-born reporter William Howard Russell described Federal Secretary of War Edwin Stanton as "excessively vain, . . . a rude, rough, vigorous Oliver Cromwell sort of man." Typically, Yankees referred to Confederates as dirty and ignorant, just as the English had spoken of the Irish, Welsh, and Scots. A Minnesotan called Confederate soldiers "vagabonds," while another Yank denounced them as "ruffians and desperadoes." Several Federals spoke of Southerners as "savages," and one Connecticut soldier informed his sister that the "Rebels are Barbarians and savages."[30]

In support of these charges of barbarism, several Yanks reported that some Confederates beheaded their enemies. A Massachusetts soldier claimed that in May 1862 he discovered in an abandoned Rebel camp five neatly polished skulls inscribed with the words "Five Zouaves' Coconuts killed at Bull Run by Southern lead." Another Yankee insisted that Confederates had used the skulls of slain Federals as soup bowls, and a Minnesotan reported that he found in an abandoned Confederate campsite the cranium of a Union soldier that had been "used by the Rebs for a soap dish."[31]

Such claims may have been true. Though the practice of decapitating an enemy and saving his head appears to have been uncommon in the Confederacy, it was not unprecedented either in Celtic history or in the Old South. "They cut off the heads of enemies slain in battle and attach them to the necks of their horses," explained Diodorus of the ancient Celts. "The blood-stained spoils they . . . carry off as booty, while striking up a paean and singing a song of victory; and they nail up these first fruits upon their houses." Livy, writing in the third century B.C., mentioned "Gallic horsemen . . . , with heads hanging at their horses' breasts, or fixed on their lances, and singing their customary songs of triumph." He also stated that Celts "cut off the head" of the Roman consul-elect Lucius Postumius,

---

[30]Abner D. Jones, *Illinois and the West* (Boston, 1838), 157; Julian M. Sturtevant, *An Address in Behalf of the Society for the Promotion of Theological Education in the West* (New York, 1853), 468–69; Wiley, *Life of Billy Yank*, 346; William Howard Russell, *My Diary North and South* (2 vols., London, 1863), II, 433; Wiley, *Life of Billy Yank*, 347–49.

[31]Wiley, *Life of Billy Yank*, 347.

"cleaned out the head, . . . and guilded the skull, which thereafter served them . . . as a drinking cup."[32]

Lest these accounts be dismissed as hyperbole, it should be remembered that beheading enemies is a recurring theme in Irish and Welsh literature. Cu Chulainn, the famous folk hero, collected many heads; indeed, he once displayed twelve that he had taken in combat. Furthermore, the Scots often beheaded their enemies, especially those who aroused their hatred, and decapitation was also practiced on occasion in the antebellum South. When Kentuckians captured outlaw Micajah Harpe, for example, they not only cut off his head but Squire Silas McBee rode home with it attached to his saddle and stuck the trophy on a tree "as a warning to other outlaws." The actual beheading was done in a gruesome manner by a man who "took Harpe's own butcher knife, . . . and taking Harpe by the hair of the head, drew the knife slowly across the back of his neck, cutting to the bone." While this was being done, Harpe remarked: "You are a God damned rough butcher, but cut on and be damned." The man proceeded to cut around Harpe's neck, and "then wrung off his head, in the same manner a butcher would of a hog." A few years later the head of Samuel Mason was exhibited in Natchez, and the heads of Wiley Harpe and James May were stuck on poles by a Mississippi roadside as "warnings to highwaymen."[33]

Much of what seemed to their enemies as barbaric—violence, sloth, and mirth—was literally part of the Celtic way of life. The Celts generally were pastoralists who thought that anyone who worked hard was crazy; it was easier to let animals make one's living and to spend time more pleasantly— eating, drinking, hunting, fishing, gambling, racing horses, dancing, and fighting. Polybius noted that the ancient Celts "slept on straw, usually ate meat and did nothing other than fight." Gerald of Wales wrote of the Welsh in the twelfth century: "They pay no attention to commerce, shipping or industry, and their only preoccupation is military training." The eighteenth-century traveler Thomas Pennant pointed out that the Scots were "indolent to a high degree, unless roused to war, or to any animating amusement." So was the white antebellum Southerner, who was "fond of grandeur, luxury, and renown, of gayety, of pleasure, and above all of idleness," observed Alexis de Tocqueville; "nothing obliges him to exert himself in order to

---

[32]Ross, *Everyday Life*, 73; Cunliffe, *Celtic World*, 83–86; Jan Filip, *Celtic Civilization and Its Heritage* (2nd ed., Prague, 1977), 108; Hubert, *Greatness and Decline*, 191–92.

[33]Ross, *Everyday Life*, 72–74; Powell, *Celts*, 108; Cunliffe, *Celtic World*, 82–87; Mary McGarry, *Great Folk Tales of Old Ireland* (New York, 1972), 74, 91; Notestein, *Scots*, 36; James Hall, *Letters from the West; Containing Sketches of Scenery, Manners, and Customs . . .* (reissue, Gainesville, 1967), 265–82; Paul I. Wellman, *Spawn of Evil* (New York, 1965), 80–100, 120–35.

subsist; and as he has no necessary occupations, he gives way to indolence, and does not even attempt what would be useful."[34]

As their enemies were quick to point out, Celts shared certain warlike characteristics. They glorified war, seemed genuinely fond of combat, and usually fought with reckless bravery. "This people have no self-control," said the Roman writer Livy of the Celts. "They tear their banners out of the ground and set off." Strabo insisted that the "whole [Celtic] race is madly fond of war, high-spirited and quick to battle, and on whatever pretext you stir them up, you will have them ready to face danger, even if they have nothing on their side but their own strength and courage."[35]

"In peace they dream of war and prepare themselves for battle," recorded Gerald of Wales in 1188 of the Welsh people, whom he described as "fierce . . . and totally dedicated to the practice of arms." He noted that they "esteem it a disgrace to die in bed, but an honour to be killed in battle. They agree with the words of the poet: 'Turn peace away, For honour perishes with peace.' " And Gerald concluded: "It is a remarkable fact that on many occasions they have not hesitated to fight without any protection at all against men clad in iron, unarmed against those bearing weapons, on foot against mounted cavalry."[36]

The Scots were as combative as the Welsh. Nearly all of the songs of the Western Isles of Scotland praise brave fighting men. "Better men of war," wrote an enemy of the Scots, "were not under the sky." An Englishman claimed that Scots had no fear of death; a Spaniard insisted that they preferred death to defeat, deemed "it glorious and manly to slay or be slain," and considered it a disgrace to die in bed. To them combat was noble and splendid; they considered warfare both worthwhile and necessary, despite their numerous defeats and enormous losses. Nor did defeat prevent a hero from being admired. Two of Scotland's greatest heroes—William Wallace and Robert Bruce—had fought with uncertain success.[37]

A visitor to the Confederacy in 1861 found "revolutionary furor in full sway, . . . an excited mob, . . . flushed faces, wild eyes, screaming mouths, hurrahing for 'Jeff Davis' and 'the Southern Confederacy.' . . . Young men are dying to fight." One Southerner boasted that the Confederates could "beat the Yankees at the ordeal of dying. Fighting," he said, "is a sport our men always have an appetite for." Many Yanks agreed. One announced: "A

---

[34]Powell, *Celts*, 74–100; Ross, *Everyday Life*, 34–53, 87–109; Cunliffe, *Celtic World*, 42–55; Laing, *Celtic Britain*, 19–44, 131–57; Notestein, *Scots*, 22–30, 92–96, 192–201; Gerald of Wales, *The Journey through Wales and the Description of Wales*, trans. Lewis Thorpe (reissue, New York, 1978), 233; Thomas Pennant, *A Tour in Scotland; 1769* (5th edition, London, 1790), 214; Tocqueville, *Republic of the United States*, 427.

[35]Ross, *Everyday Life*, 74–77; Laing, *Celtic Britain*, 19–30; Cunliffe, *Celtic World*, 56–59; Herm, *Celts*, 1–13.

[36]Gerald of Wales, *Journey*, 234–35. See also Laing, *Celtic Britain*, 150.

[37]Notestein, *Scots*, 31–43; Brown, *History of Scotland*, I, 144–69.

Confederate soldier would storm hell with a pen-knife." There is no record of Confederates attacking with only penknives, but General James R. Chalmers's Mississippi Brigade attacked at Murfreesboro with half the men in one regiment armed only with sticks, and those in another regiment carrying rifles that were still too wet from the previous night's rain to fire. "The Rebles . . . fight like Devills," admitted a Union soldier, and another Yank stated that the Confederates "outfight us . . . in every battle. I admire the desperation [with which they attack]." One observer noted that the Confederates "rushed upon the foe with an impetuosity and fearlessness that amazed the old army officers, and caused foreign military men to declare them the best fighters in the world."[38]

The Celtic fondness for combat extended to individual encounters. Ancient Celts, wrote Diodorus, "are wont to advance before the battle-line and to challenge the bravest of their opponents to single combat." Sometimes Celts even fought each other at meals, where it was customary for the bravest man to claim the best piece of meat. If anyone disputed his right to it, he and his challenger might fight to the death. Cu Chulainn, the famous "Hound of Ulster," who once attacked the sea and fought the waves, was devoted to deadly single combat. "It is a wonderful thing," he announced, "if I am but one day and one night in the world, provided that my fame and my deeds live after me." Affairs of honor, either formal or informal, were popular among antebellum Southerners, just as they had been with their Celtic forebears. Diodorus's description of ancient Celts as full of "pride . . . , impatient of affronts, and revengeful of injuries" was equally applicable to Southerners. They usually went about armed even in time of peace and were quick to anger and to fight.[39]

---

[38]Russell, *My Diary*, I, 134–39; John B. Jones, *A Rebel War Clerk's Diary*, ed. Earl S. Miers (reissue, New York, 1958), 32; Bell I. Wiley, "The Common Soldier of the Civil War," *Civil War Times Illustrated*, XII, No. 4 (July 1973), 28; unpublished reports of Major J. O. Thompson, Forty-fourth (Blythe's) Mississippi Infantry, and Lieutenant Colonel T. H. Lyman, Ninth Mississippi Infantry, William P. Palmer Collection of Braxton Bragg Papers, Western Reserve Historical Society, Cleveland; Wiley, *Life of Billy Yank*, 351; Randolph A. Shotwell, *The Papers of Randolph Abbott Shotwell*, ed. J. G. de Roulhac Hamilton (2 vols., Raleigh, 1929), I, 314.

[39]Cunliffe, *Celtic World*, 57; Ross, *Everyday Life*, 54–71; Herm, *Celts*, 53–54. On the violence of Southerners, see, for example, Anon., *A Visit to Texas . . .* (New York, 1834), 211; William Attmore, *Journal of a Tour to North Carolina, . . . 1787* (Chapel Hill, 1922), 39; George H. Coleraine, *The Life, Adventures, and Opinions of Col. George Hanger . . .* (2 vols., London, 1801), II, 404–05; Faux, *Memorable Days*, 45–48, 179, 187, 200; George William Featherstonhaugh, *Excursion Through the Slave States . . .* (2 vols., London, 1844), II, 42–69; Barton Griffith, *The Diary of . . . , 1832–34 . . .* (Crawfordsville, Ind., 1932), 13; J. Hall, *Letters*, 291–92; Matilda C. J. F. Houstoun, *Texas and the Gulf . . .* (Philadelphia, 1845), 191; Joseph Holt Ingraham, *The South-West . . .* (2 vols., New York, 1835), I, 94–95; C. Mackay, *Life and Liberty*, 173; William Charles Macready, *The Diaries of . . .* (2 vols., London, 1912), II, 246; Frederick L. Olmsted, *A Journey Through Texas . . .* (reissue, New York, 1969), 20, 69–70; Johann David Schopf, *Travels in the Confederation . . .* , trans. and ed. Alfred J. Morrison (2 vols., Cincinnati, 1912), II, 123–24; Charles Sealsfield, *America: Glorious and Chaotic Land . . .* , trans. E. L. Jordan (Englewood Cliffs, 1969), 20–22; Whipple, *Southern Diary*, 24–25, 27–30, 32–33, 40, 79, 115–16.

In 1861 Jefferson Davis told an English reporter that people often laughed at Southerners "because of our fondness for military titles and displays. All your travellers . . . have commented on the number of generals, and colonels, and majors all over the [southern] States. But the fact is, we are a military people. . . . We are not less military because we have had no great standing armies. But perhaps we are the only people in the world where gentlemen go to a military academy who do not intend to follow the profession of arms." In contrast, warfare reportedly was repugnant to most Northerners. "The peaceful habits of our citizens tend but little to the cultivation of the military character," stated Union General Henry W. Halleck.[40]

Despite their aggressiveness, a kind of grand carelessness pervaded Celts and their warfare. The ancient Celts, though able to endure hardship and remain loyal to their leaders, suffered from inefficiency and a lack of staying power that often deprived them of total victories. "When they are stirred up they assemble in their bands for battle quite openly and without forethought," observed Strabo, "and so they are easily handled by those who desire to outwit them." He considered the Celts "all naturally fine fighting men" but "better as cavalry than infantry." At Sassoferrato Celtic cavalry charged with "such a mighty rushing of horses" that the Roman horsemen "ran off, stunned." But the Celts often failed. As battle followed battle, Roman soldiers gradually improved their weapons and tactics and were able to meet their enemies on more than even terms. The Celts, on the other hand, did little to improve either their weapons or their tactics. They never prepared for long engagements and consequently they were always short of supplies and equipment; they fought more as individuals than as units, and they rarely followed up and exploited a success. If they failed to achieve early victory, they often became disheartened and went home. Their independence is revealed in their varied battle attire. Many wore bright clothes and what resembled a Scottish tartan about their necks. Some fought in "bronze helmets . . . , which made them look even taller than they already are," reported Diodorus, "while others covered themselves with breast-armour made out of chains. But most content themselves with the weapons nature gave them: they go naked into battle."[41]

Welsh and Scottish combat also emphasized individualism at the expense of endurance and logistics. Hardship and suffering failed to deter either Welshmen or Scots. "They go barefoot," stated Gerald of Wales, "are not troubled by hunger or cold," and "train themselves to keep on the move both day and night." When a spear was driven through the helmet and head of a Highlander, a clansman put his foot on the man's head and pulled out the

[40]Russell, *My Diary*, I, 250; Henry W. Halleck, *Elements of Military Art and Science* (3rd edition, New York, 1863), 324. See also Whipple, *Southern Diary*, 82–83.

[41]Ross, *Everyday Life*, 56, 72; Cunliffe, *Celtic World*, 46–47; Powell, *Celts*, 103–10; Herm, *Celts*, 3, 16, 182–215; Caesar, *War Commentaries*, 66.

spear. Afterwards the wounded man returned to battle. "Lo! stout hearts of men!" exclaimed the English Earl of Derby, who witnessed the event. "They were content of lie down, for a night's rest, among the heather on the hillside, in snow or rain, covered only by their plaid," explained an authority on the Highlanders. When, during a winter campaign, a chieftain of the Mac-Donald clan ordered a snowball to sleep on, his followers responded: "Now we despair of victory, since our leader has become so effeminate he can't sleep without a pillow."[42]

Scots, like ancient Celts and Welshmen, were loyal to their leaders, tending to stand by and to die with their chieftains. Loyalty, as one scholar remarked, "infected all Gaels whether Highland or Lowland." But loyalty had to be reciprocal: leaders were expected to lead in battle and to risk their lives for their supporters. They usually did. When a chieftain was mortally wounded at Otterburn, for example, he ordered that his condition be concealed from his men. The troops, unaware that he was dying, fought on to victory. A fundamental weakness in this code of loyalty, of course, was that men depended heavily upon the presence of their leaders. If a leader fell in battle, his men frequently became discouraged.[43]

Both Scots and Welshmen prepared haphazardly for war and if unsuccessful early in a battle they usually lost their desire to continue fighting. Many were outstanding horsemen, but they were better as raiders than as traditional cavalry. They gathered for battle in various dress and with an assortment of arms; whatever equipment they possessed, they brought along, including their rations. For the most part, "they lived on the country," explained a historian. "They bring no carriages [wagons] with them," wrote an astonished observer; "neither do they carry with them any provisions of bread or wine. . . . They . . . dress the flesh of their cattle in the skins, . . . and, being sure to find plenty of them in the country which they invade, they carry none with them." Such a lack of system characterized Celtic logistics. A quick decision was what the Celts sought; they had little staying power. After a battle or two, Scots "might slip away on a private quarrel or to deposit their booty and provide for their families." Sometimes they simply became tired and would go home whether or not the war was finished. "In war the Welsh are very ferocious when battle is first joined. They shout, glower fiercely at the enemy, and fill the air with fearsome clamour, making a high-pitched screech," wrote Gerald of Wales. "If the enemy resists manfully and they are repulsed, they are immediately thrown into confusion. With further resistance they turn their backs, making no attempt at a counterattack, but seeking safety in flight."[44]

---

[42]Gerald of Wales, *Journey*, 234, 260; Notestein, *Scots*, 32; MacLean, *Scotch Highlanders*, 20.
[43]Notestein, *Scots*, 33, 35.
[44]Ibid., 31–43; Gerald of Wales, *Journey*, 233–35, 259–60.

Confederates acted with equal independence and carelessness. "The Southern army," remembered a volunteer, "was simply a vast mob of rather ill-armed young . . . [men] from the country." They generally wore assorted dress, carried a variety of weapons, and fought when and how they pleased. They were "not used to control of any sort," remarked a contemporary, "and were not disposed to obey anybody except for good and sufficient reason." When General Lee took command in Virginia in 1862 his army was described as "an 'Armed mob' . . . of *undisciplined individuality*, and, as such, correspondingly unreliable and disorganized." After three years of training and combat, Lee was compelled to admit that the situation had scarcely changed: "The great want in our army is firm discipline."[45]

The average Confederate, whom one authority called "an admirable fighting man but a poor soldier," was doubtless at his best on horseback following some daring leader. Some of the Confederacy's greatest as well as most spectacular military successes were achieved by such bold cavalrymen as Nathan B. Forrest, and in the first years of the war—until their horse supply dwindled—Confederate cavalrymen unquestionably were superior to their Yankee opponents. Stonewall Jackson had his footcavalry, but most Southerners, it was noted, were "not good marchers naturally." They were too accustomed to riding wherever they went. A Confederate advised his parents that his younger brother should "by all means . . . Join the Cavalry—and bear in mind that a private in The Infantry is the worse place he can possibly be put into in this war—so if he wants to have a good time Join the Cavalry."[46]

Loyalty to popular leaders was strong, and such commanders as Lee received extravagant support. But of an unpopular officer, a Texan wrote: "I will stay and tuffit out with Col[onel] Young and then he can go to Hell." The Confederacy's code of loyalty, like that of earlier Celts, required officers to lead their men into battle, which meant that sometimes more than half of the officers in a Confederate army were killed or wounded in a single battle. As a result, the Confederacy was always short of experienced officers. Con-

---

[45]George Cary Eggleston, *A Rebel's Recollections* (New York, 1889), 29, 33; Jefferson Davis, *Jefferson Davis, Constitutionalist: His Letters, Papers and Speeches*, ed. Dunbar Rowland (10 vols., Jackson, 1923), VII, 410; *OR*, XLII (pt. 3), 1213.

[46]David Herbert Donald, "The Confederate as a Fighting Man," *Journal of Southern History*, XXV (1959), 193; Fremantle, *Diary*, 90, 181; Bell I. Wiley, *The Life of Johnny Reb: The Common Soldier of the Confederacy* (Indianapolis, 1943), 341. One visitor pointed out that Southerners never walked anywhere that they could ride even "if only to fetch a prise of snuff from across the way." Schopf, *Travels*, II, 65. A Yankee doctor quoted Jefferson Davis as saying after the war that "his people were better horsemen than those of the North. This was due partly to some remnant of Cavalier origin. . . . [Confederate] cavalry had been superior to ours in the commencement of the war . . . , but their stock of horses gave out sooner, and towards the close of the struggle it became difficult to mount a Confederate regiment." John J. Craven, *Prison Life of Jefferson Davis* . . . (reissue, Biloxi, 1979), 320.

federate Colonel George Grenfell told a foreigner "that the only way in which an officer could acquire influence over the Confederate soldier was by his personal conduct under fire. They hold a man in great esteem who in action sets them an example of contempt for danger; but they think nothing of an officer who is not in the habit of *leading* them. In fact such a man could not possibly retain his position. Colonel Grenfell's expression was, 'every atom of authority has to be purchased by a drop of your blood.' "[47]

Accounts of the ability of Confederates to withstand suffering are legion, as are those of barefoot and wounded Rebels continuing to march and to fight. A Georgian reported that he "carried into the fight [at Second Manassas] over 100 men who were barefoot, many of whom left bloody footprints among the thorns and briars through which they rushed." Though Confederates often fought in tatters, no significant number of them went naked into battle, as did some of the ancient Celts. General Stonewall Jackson reportedly proposed a night attack against the disorganized Federals at Fredericksburg, and when asked by General Lee how the men would distinguish friend from foe in the dark, Jackson suggested that the Rebels remove their clothing. Lee allegedly rejected this proposal; he was understandably afraid that the naked Confederates would be damaged more by the cold December weather than by the enemy.[48]

Confederates frequently were without shoes or proper equipment because they could see no purpose in carrying what they did not need at the moment. Rebels, noted a foreign visitor, were "constantly in the habit of throwing away their knapsacks and blankets on a long march." Sometimes after a battle "many would coolly walk off home, under the impression that they had performed their share." In December 1864 more than half the men in the Confederate army were absent without leave. A major reason for their absence was that Southerners, like all Celts, lacked tenacity. Union General Winfield Scott, himself a Virginian, understood this characteristic. He predicted that Southerners were too undisciplined to fight a defensive war. They "will not take care of things, or husband [their] . . . resources," said Scott. "If it could all be done by one wild desperate dash [then Southerners] . . . would do it, but [they cannot] . . . stand the long . . . months between the acts, the waiting."[49]

Rebel soldiers became increasingly discouraged when the enemy refused to be beaten. "I do not know what is getting into me but I am getting more

[47]Wiley, *Life of Johnny Reb*, 140; Fremantle, *Diary*, 127.

[48]Fremantle, *Diary*, 105; George F. R. Henderson, *Stonewall Jackson and the American Civil War* (2 vols., London, 1898), II, 324.

[49]Fremantle, *Diary*, 97; *OR*, Series 4, III, 520; Ella Lonn, *Desertion During the Civil War* (reissue, Gloucester, 1966), 226; Mary B. Chesnut, *A Diary from Dixie*, ed. Ben Ames Williams (reissue, Boston, 1961), 245.

and more scary every fight I go into," a soldier in Lee's army wrote his wife in November 1864. "In the first two or three engagements I shared in, I felt a sort of exultation in moving about unhurt when others about me were shot down, but all that seems to be done away with now & I am getting . . . as nervous about the whistling of bullets as any person I know of & I actually *suffer* when going into a fight." Another Confederate veteran remarked that before the war ended "the spirit of the men became broken. Constant marching and fighting were sufficient . . . to gradually wear out the army," he recalled. Late in the war, after a Confederate assault failed, General Stephen D. Ramseur sorrowfully wrote: "My men behaved shamefully. They ran from the enemy. . . . The entire command stampeded."[50] Such action was typically Celtic.

The continued devotion of Celts to their wild attacks shows that they valued tradition more than success. For more than two thousand years they relied almost exclusively upon a single tactic in warfare—the charge. At Telamon, Culloden, Gettysburg, and in countless lesser battles, they used the same furious assaults with the same disastrous results. Except for changes in weaponry, descriptions of Celtic battles are almost interchangeable. Polybius's account of classical Celtic combat behavior in which the men, inspired "rather by the heat of passion than by cool calculation," rushed "wildly on the enemy" sounds remarkably like both an early eighteenth-century traveler's statement of how Highland Scots "gave a general shout, and then charged the enemy stoutly" as well as a Federal soldier's description of a Confederate assault at Atlanta where it "seemed as if no man of all the host who were attacking us could escape alive; and yet, still yelling, they persisted in their desperate undertaking. Their line was reformed, and again and again they attempted the impossible."[51]

Note that yelling—indeed, a special kind of yelling—was an intrinsic part of the Celtic charge. The "horrible and diverse yelling" by Celts referred to by Romans, the "clan war-cry" of the Scots, and what during the Civil War was called "the Rebel yell" appear to be another example of continuity in Celtic warfare. There is no absolute agreement on what constituted a Rebel yell, though it is often described "as a high-pitched shout and supposed by some to be a variation of the Southern fox hunters' cry, it invariably produced an eerie feeling within the enemy lines." One Union soldier admitted

<hr>

[50]Wiley, "Common Soldiers," 57; Shotwell, *Papers*, I, 316; Stephen D. Ramseur to his wife, August 4, 1864, Stephen Dodson Ramseur Papers, Southern Historical Collection, University of North Carolina, Chapel Hill.

[51]Ross, *Everyday Life*, 70, 74; M. Martin, "A Description of the Western Islands of Scotland [1716]," *A General Collection of the Best and Most Interesting Voyages and Travels in All Parts of the World* . . . , ed. John Pinkerton (10 vols., London, 1809), III, 608; Richard S. Tuthill, "An Artilleryman's Recollections of the Battle of Atlanta," in *Military Essays and Recollections; Papers Read Before the Commandery of the State of Illinois, Military Order of the Loyal Legion of the United States* (Chicago, 1891), 306.

that hearing it "made the hair stand up on his head." Another Yankee remembered "that 'terrible scream and barbarous howling' . . . loud enough to
be heard a mile off." Still another Federal wrote of a Confederate assault:
"they emerged from their concealment in the woods, and yelling as only the
steer-drivers of Texas could yell, charged upon our division." Available
evidence suggests that the Rebel yell was a variation on traditional Celtic
animal calls, especially those used to call cattle and hogs and hunting dogs.
"Woh-who-ey! who-ey! who-ey!" is the way one man remembered it with
"the first syllable 'woh' short and low, and the second 'who' with a very high
and prolonged note deflecting upon the third syllable 'ey.' " One thing is
clear: it was totally different from the Yankee "cheer" that repeated the word
"hurrah," but pronounced it "hoo-ray," with emphasis upon the second
syllable. "The Southern troops, when charging, . . . always yell in a manner
peculiar to themselves," wrote English Colonel James Fremantle. "The
Yankee cheer is much more like ours."[52]

The wild yells were as much a part of the Celtic temperament as the
headlong attacks. Celts, who were neither provident nor tenacious, always
tried to end the action early. Their charges, when successful, either routed or
destroyed the enemy. But too often they did neither, and when their attacks
failed the Celts had little on which to fall back. This too was characteristic.
Theirs was not a culture that planned ahead. Emotional and inveterate gam-
blers, the Celts willingly staked everything on their charges. Time after time
their assaults against overwhelming odds brought them defeat; no matter, the
reckless charge was too deeply ingrained in Celtic warfare to be abandoned.
There was no glory to be gained from fighting out of a hole in the ground.

[52]Herms, *Celts*, 10; MacLean, *Scotch Highlanders*, 22; Mark Mayo Boatner III, *The Civil War
Dictionary* (New York, 1959), 683; Oscar L. Jackson, *The Colonel's Diary; Journals Kept Before and
During the Civil War* . . . (Sharon, Pa., 1922), 74–76; Fitzgerald Ross, *Cities and Camps of the
Confederate States*, ed. Richard B. Harwell (Urbana, 1958), 39–40; Tuthill, "Artilleryman's Re-
collections," 302–06; J. Harvie Dew, "The Yankee and Rebel Yells," *Century Illustrated Maga-
zine*, XLIII (1892), 954–55; Wiley, *Life of Johnny Reb*, 71–72; Fremantle, *Diary*, 207–08.

An Essay on Selected Sources

Neither all of the works consulted nor all of those cited in the footnotes are mentioned in this essay. Readers are advised to examine each chapter's notes for full citations.

Primary Sources

MANUSCRIPTS: Some of the most revealing information on tactics was located in the papers of certain Confederate political leaders and high-ranking generals, particularly in the Jefferson Davis Papers at Duke University, the Library of Congress, the Chicago Historical Society, and the Mississippi Department of Archives and History, Jackson; in the Louis T. Wigfall and Family Papers at the University of Texas, Austin; in the Pierre Gustave Toutant Beauregard Papers at Duke University and at the Library of Congress; in the Braxton Bragg Papers, William P. Palmer Collection, at the Western Reserve Historical Society, Cleveland; in the Robert E. Lee and Custis Lee Papers at the United States Army Military History Institute, Carlisle Barracks, Pennsylvania; in the Thomas J. Jackson Papers at the Library of Congress; and in the Jubal A. Early Papers also at the Library of Congress.

Valuable letters to and from other Confederate generals were found in the Mansfield Lovell Papers at the Henry E. Huntington Library, San Marino, California; in the Benjamin Stoddert Ewell Papers at William and Mary College; in the William Montgomery Gardner Papers, the Stephen Dodson Ramseur Papers, and the Edmund Kirby Smith Papers, all in the Southern Historical Collection at the University of North Carolina, Chapel Hill; and in the Lafayette McLaws Papers, the William Henry Talbot Walker Papers, and the Samuel Wragg Ferguson Papers at Duke University.

Some useful material was found among the papers of Northerners, especially those of Henry W. Halleck and Alfred T. Mahan at the Library of Congress and of Dennis Hart Mahan at the United States Military Academy.

Several diaries contain choice items, including the T. Otis Baker Diary in the T. Otis Baker and Family Papers at the Mississippi Department of Archives and History, Jackson; the George William Brent Diary in the William P. Palmer Collection at the Western Reserve Historical Society, Cleveland; the Thomas Bragg Diary in the Southern Historical Collection at the University of North Carolina, Chapel Hill; the

Abner Doubleday Journal (photostatic copy) at the Manassas National Battlefield Park; the William Preston Diary in the War Department Collection of Confederate Records at the National Archives; and the Silas D. Wesson Diary in the United States Army Military History Institute, Carlisle Barracks, Pennsylvania.

Certain material was found in such miscellaneous collections as the E. John, Thomas C. W. Ellis and Family Papers at Louisiana State University, Baton Rouge; the David B. Harris Papers at Duke University; the Francis Lieber Papers at the Henry E. Huntington Library, San Marino, California; the Lenoir Family Papers in the Southern Historical Collection at the University of North Carolina, Chapel Hill; the George D. Bayard Papers, the George William Cushing Letters, and the James Duncan Papers at the United States Military Academy.

PUBLISHED PAPERS: The best single source for Civil War military tactics is the U.S. War Department, *The War of the Rebellion: A Compilation of the Official Records of the Union and Confederate Armies* (128 vols., Washington, 1880–1901). This enormous compilation includes reports, letters, telegrams, diaries, etc., dealing with every campaign of the war.

Comprehensive collections of the writings of both the Union and Confederate presidents are either available or in preparation. Lincoln's views on tactics can be found in *The Collected Works of Abraham Lincoln*, edited by Roy P. Basler (9 vols., New Brunswick, 1953–1955). Davis's views are revealed in *Jefferson Davis, Constitutionalist: His Letters, Papers and Speeches*, edited by Dunbar Rowland (10 vols., Jackson, 1923); *Jefferson Davis: Private Letters, 1823–1889*, edited by Hudson Strode (New York, 1966); *The Papers of Jefferson Davis*, edited by Haskell M. Monroe, Jr., and James T. McIntosh (2 vols. to date, Baton Rouge, 1971–   ).

The personal papers of few army commanders have been published. Useful collections include Ulysses S. Grant, *The Papers of Ulysses S. Grant*, edited by John Y. Simon (6 vols. to date, Carbondale, 1967–   ); Robert E. Lee, *The Wartime Papers of R. E. Lee*, edited by Clifford Dowdey and Louis H. Manarin (Boston, 1961), which contains personal, official, and family letters; *Lee's Dispatches: Unpublished Letters of General Robert E. Lee, C.S.A., to Jefferson Davis and the War Department of the Confederate States of America, 1862–65*, edited by Douglas S. Freeman and Grady McWhiney (New York, 1957); William T. Sherman, *The Sherman Letters: Correspondence Between General and Senator Sherman from 1837 to 1891*, edited by Rachel Sherman Thorndike (New York, 1894); *Home Letters of General Sherman*, edited by M. A. DeWolfe Howe (New York, 1909); George G. Meade, *The Life and Letters of George Gordon Meade . . .*, edited by George Gordon Meade (2 vols., New York, 1913).

Essential to any understanding of the operations of the Army of the Potomac in the last eighteen months of the war is Theodore Lyman, *Meade's Headquarters, 1863–1865; Letters of Colonel Theodore Lyman from the Wilderness to Appomattox*, edited by George R. Agassiz (Boston, 1922).

The most useful collections of documents on Mexican War tactics are U.S. Congress, *House Document*, 29 Congress, 1 session, No. 209; *Senate Document*, 29 Congress, 2 session, No. 1; *House Executive Documents*, 30 Congress, 1 session, Nos. 8 and 17, which contain reports and correspondence; Zachary Taylor, *Letters of Zachary Taylor from the Battlefields of the Mexican War*, edited by William K. Bixby (Rochester, 1908); and George Winston Smith and Charles Judah, eds., *Chronicles of the Gringos: The U.S. Army in the Mexican War, 1846–1848; Accounts of Eyewitnesses & Combatants* (Albuquerque, 1968).

Diaries that comment on tactics include Robert G. H. Kean, *Inside the Confederate Government: The Diary of Robert Garlick Hill Kean*, edited by Edward Younger (New York, 1957); John B. Jones, *A Rebel War Clerk's Diary at the Confederate States Capital*, edited by Howard Swiggett (2 vols., New York, 1935); John B. Jones, *A Rebel War Clerk's Diary*, edited by Earl S. Miers (reissue, New York, 1958), a condensed version; Mary B. Chesnut, *A Diary from Dixie*, edited by Isabella D. Martin and Myrta Lockett Avary (New York, 1905); Mary B. Chesnut, *A Diary from Dixie*, edited by Ben Ames Williams (reissue, Boston, 1961), includes portions omitted from the earlier version; Arthur J. L. Fremantle, *The Fremantle Diary . . .* , edited by Walter Lord (reissue, Boston, 1954); Bartlett Yancey Malone, *Whipt 'Em Everytime: The Diary of Bartlett Yancey Malone*, edited by William Whatley Pierson, Jr. (Jackson, 1960); Marsena Rudolph Patrick, *Inside Lincoln's Army: The Diary of Marsena Rudolph Patrick*, edited by David S. Sparks (New York, 1964); George B. McClellan, *The Mexican War Diary of George B. McClellan*, edited by William Starr Myers (Princeton, 1917); and Ethan A. Hitchcock, *Fifty Years in Camp and Field; Diary of Major-General Ethan Allan Hitchcock, U.S.A.*, edited by W. A. Croffut (New York, 1909).

Several published memoirs reveal much about their authors as well as about military affairs. The retrospective views of Jefferson Davis can be seen in his *The Rise and Fall of the Confederate Government* (2 vols., reissue, New York, 1958); Varina H. Davis, *Jefferson Davis . . . A Memoir* (2 vols., New York, 1890), written by his wife; and John J. Craven, *Prison Life of Jefferson Davis . . .* (reissue, Biloxi, 1979), written by his physician. Ulysses S. Grant's *Personal Memoirs . . .* (2 vols., New York, 1885) are clear and direct but not without error. Joseph E. Johnston's *Narrative of Military Operations . . .* (reissue, Bloomington, 1959) is a defense of its author; it is strongly anti-Davis and anti-Hood but a useful book nevertheless, and Frank E. Vandiver's introduction to the new edition is a thoughtful evaluation of Johnston. John Bell Hood's *Advance and Retreat: Personal Experiences in the United States & Confederate States Armies*, edited by Richard N. Current (reissue, Bloomington, 1959) is full of bitterness and errors, yet this controversial volume is essential to any understanding of Hood and the army he led. Alfred Roman's *The Military Operations of General Beauregard in the War Between the States, 1861 to 1865; Including a Brief Personal Sketch and a Narrative of His Services in the War With Mexico, 1846–8* (New York, 1884) is for all practical purposes Beauregard's personal memoir. By having his former aide's name on the title page, Beauregard could eulogize himself without appearing immodest; he also could mask his attack on Davis and the Johnstons.

Other important recollections by high-ranking generals include James Longstreet's somewhat ponderous and biased defense of himself, *From Manassas to Appomattox: Memoirs of the Civil War in America*, edited by James I. Robertson, Jr. (reissue, Bloomington, 1960); Richard Taylor's critical and well-written *Destruction and Reconstruction . . .* , edited by Charles P. Roland (reissue, Waltham, 1968); William T. Sherman's *Memoirs of General William T. Sherman By Himself* (2 vols., reissue, Bloomington, 1957), which are admirably clear, colloquial, and usually trustworthy; Philip H. Sheridan's *Personal Memoirs of P. H. Sheridan* (2 vols., New York, 1888); Jacob D. Cox's *Military Reminiscences of the Civil War* (2 vols., New York, 1900); Jubal A. Early's *War Memoirs, Autobiographical Sketch and Narrative of the War Between the States* (reissue, Bloomington, 1960); John B. Gordon's *Reminiscences of the Civil War* (New York, 1903); Lew Wallace's *Lew Wallace, An Autobiography* (2 vols., New York,

1906); James H. Wilson's *Under the Old Flag; Recollections of Military Operations in the War for the Union . . .* (2 vols., New York, 1912); and Oliver O. Howard's *Autobiography of Oliver Otis Howard* (2 vols., New York, 1907).

Of the many memoirs by other officers and by those in the ranks, some of the most useful on tactics are Luther Giddings, *Sketches of the Campaign in Northern Mexico in Eighteen Hundred Forty-six and Seven* (New York, 1853); John R. Kenly, *Memoirs of a Maryland Volunteer* (Philadelphia, 1873); Raphael Semmes, *The Campaign of General Scott, in the Valley of Mexico* (Cincinnati, 1852); Dennis Hart Mahan, "The Cadet Life of Grant and Sherman," *Army and Navy Journal,* IV (March 31, 1866); E. Porter Alexander, *Military Memoirs of a Confederate* (reissue, Bloomington, 1962); John Beatty, *The Citizen-Soldier; or, Memoirs of a Volunteer* (Cincinnati, 1879); Augustus Buell, *"The Cannoneer": Recollections of Service in the Army of the Potomac* (Washington, 1890); Henry Kyd Douglas, *I Rode With Stonewall* (Chapel Hill, 1940); Rufus R. Dawes, *Service With the Sixth Wisconsin Volunteers* (Marietta, Ohio, 1890); Henry O. Dwight, "How We Fight at Atlanta," *Harper's New Monthly Magazine,* XXIX (1864); George Cary Eggleston, *A Rebel's Recollections* (New York, 1889); Henry E. Handerson, *Yankee in Gray: The Civil War Memoirs of Henry E. Handerson, with a Selection of His Wartime Letters,* edited by Clyde Lottridge Cummer (Cleveland, 1962); Richard W. Johnson, *A Soldier's Reminiscences in Peace and War* (Philadelphia, 1886); Randolph H. McKim, *A Soldier's Recollections: Leaves from the Diary of a Young Confederate . . .* (New York, 1910); Heros von Borcke, *Memoirs of the Confederate War for Independence* (2 vols., Edinburgh, 1866); Sam R. Watkins, *"Co. Aytch": A Side Show of the Big Show* (reissue, New York, 1962); John H. Worsham, *One of Jackson's Foot Cavalry* (New York, 1912).

Another significant source is Robert U. Johnson and Clarence C. Buel, eds., *Battles and Leaders of the Civil War* (4 vols., reissue, New York, 1956). Issued originally in serial form in the *Century* magazine and reissued in many forms, this compendium of articles by Union and Confederate officers describing and defending their roles in the various campaigns is uneven and at times inaccurate, but some of the accounts are invaluable.

MANUALS AND CONTEMPORARY WORKS ON TACTICS AND THEORY: General works on tactics and the art of war include Antoine Henri Jomini, *Summary of the Art of War,* translated by O. F. Winship and E. E. McLean (New York, 1854), and a later edition translated by G. H. Mendell and William P. Craighill (Philadelphia, 1862); Dennis Hart Mahan, *An Elementary Treatise on Advanced-Guard, Out-Post, and Detachment Service of Troops, and the Manner of Posting and Handling Them in Presence of an Enemy* (New York, 1847), and other editions in 1853, 1861, 1862, and Mahan's *Advanced-Guard, Out-Post and Detachment Service of Troops, with the Essential Principles of Strategy, and Grand Tactics for the use of Officers of the Militia and Volunteers* (New York, 1864); Henry W. Halleck, *Elements of Military Art and Science* (New York, 1846, and other editions); An Officer, *The Soldier's Guide* (Philadelphia, 1861); William P. Craighill, *The Army Officer's Pocket Companion* (New York, 1862); William W. Duffield, *School of the Brigade, and Evolutions of the Line* (Philadelphia, 1862); G. T. Beauregard, *A Commentary on the Campaign and Battle of Manassas of July, 1861, Together with a Summary of the Art of War* (New York, 1891); Henry D. Grafton, *A Treatise on the Camp and March* (Boston, 1854); Emil Schalk, *Summary of the Art of War: Written Expressly for and Dedicated to the U.S. Volunteer Army* (Philadelphia, 1862); Lem D. Williams, *The American Illustrated Military Text-Book* (Baltimore, 1861); U.S. War Department, *Report of the [1860] Commission to Examine into the Organization, System of Discipline, and Course of Instruction of the United States Military Academy at West Point* (Washington, 1881); U.S. War Department, *Regulations for the Army of the United States, 1857* (New York, 1857), and *Revised Regulations for the Army of the United States* (Philadelphia, 1862, and Washington, 1863); and U.S. War Department, *Report of the Secretary of War and accompanying documents for the year 1854* (Washington, 1854) and a similar report for 1855 (Washington, 1855).

Infantry tactics are treated in Daniel Butterfield, *Camp and Outpost Duty for Infantry* (New York, 1862); John T. Cairns, *The Recruit, A Compilation of Exercises and Movements of Infantry, Light Infantry and Riflemen, According to the Latest Improvements* (New York, 1855); R. Milton Cary, *Skirmishers' Drill and Bayonet Exercise* (Richmond, 1861); Silas Casey, *Infantry Tactics, for the Instruction, Exercise, and Manoeuvers of the Soldier, a Company, Line of Skirmishers, Battalion, Brigade, or Corps D'Armee* (3 vols., New York, 1862, 1865); Henry Coppée, *The Field Manual for Battalion Drill* (Philadelphia, 1862); William Gilham, *Manual of Instruction for the Volunteers and Militia of the Confederate States* (Richmond, 1861, 1862); William J. Hardee, *Rifle and Light Infantry Tactics; for the Exercise and Manoeuvres of Troops when acting as Light Infantry or Riflemen* (2 vols., Philadelphia, 1855, 1860, 1861; Nashville, 1861; Mobile, 1863); Henry Heth, *A System of Target Practice* (New York, 1862); John C. Kelton, *A New Manual of the Bayonet, for the Army and Militia of the United States* (New York, 1861, 1862); George B. McClellan, *Manual of Bayonet Exercise* (Philadelphia, 1852, 1862); George Patten, *United States Infantry Tactics and Bayonet Exercise* (New York, 1861); John H. Richardson, *Infantry Tactics, or, Rules for the Exercise and Manoeuvres of the Confederate States Infantry* (Richmond, 1862); U.S. War Department, *A System of Target Practice* (Washington, 1862); U.S. War Department, *Abstract of Infantry Tactics; Including Exercises and Manoeuvres of Light-Infantry and Riflemen; for the use of the Militia of the United States* (Boston, 1830, 1847; Philadelphia, 1853, 1861); U.S. War Department, *U.S. Infantry Tactics for the Instruction, Exercise, and Manoeuvres, of the Soldier, a Company, Line of Skirmishers, and Battalion; For the Use of The Colored Troops of the United States Infantry* (New York, 1863); U.S. War Department, *U.S. Infantry Tactics for the Instruction, Exercise, and Manoeuvres, of the United States Infantry, and Riflemen* (Philadelphia, 1861, 1862, 1863); Cadmus M. Wilcox, *Rifles and Rifle Practice* (New York, 1859); George L. Willard, *Manual of Target Practice for the United States Army* (Philadelphia, 1862); Winfield Scott, *Infantry-Tactics; Or, Rules for the Exercise and Manoeuvres of the United States Infantry* (3 vols., New York, 1835, 1840, 1842, 1846, 1847, 1848, 1852, 1857, 1860, 1861).

Works on artillery and fortifications include Board of Artillery Officers, *Instruction for Field Artillery* (Philadelphia, 1860, 1861, 1863, 1864, 1867; Washington, 1863); Robert Anderson, *Evolutions of Field Batteries of Artillery* (New York, 1860); Robert Anderson, *Instruction for Field Artillery, Horse and Foot* (Philadelphia, 1839); Board of Artillery Officers, *Instruction for Field Artillery, Horse and Foot* (Baltimore, 1845); Board of Officers, *Instruction for Heavy Artillery* (Washington, 1851, 1862, 1863; Charleston, 1861); Board of Officers, *Manual for Heavy Artillery for the Use of Volunteers* (New York, 1862); John Gibbon, *The Artillerist's Manual* (New York, 1860, 1861, 1863); Charles P. Kingsbury, *An Elementary Treatise on Artillery and Infantry, Adapted to the Service of the United States* (New York, 1856); Dennis Hart Mahan, *A Complete Treatise on Field Fortification* (New York, 1836, 1861, 1862, 1863; Richmond, 1862);

George Patten, *Artillery Drill* (New York, 1861); Joseph Roberts, *The Hand-Book of Artillery for the Service of the United States (Army and Militia)* (New York, 1860, 1861, 1863, 1865, 1875); Egbert L. Viele, *Hand-Book of Field Fortifications and Artillery; also Manual for Light and Heavy Artillery* (Richmond, 1861).

Cavalry tactics are dealt with in Philip St. George Cooke, *Cavalry Tactics or Regulations for the Instruction, Formations, and Movements of the Cavalry of the Army and Volunteers of the United States* (2 parts, Washington, 1861, 1862; Philadelphia, 1864); *Cooper's Cavalry Tactics, For the Use of Volunteers* (New Orleans and Jackson, 1861); J. Lucius Davis, *The Trooper's Manual: Or, Tactics for Light Dragoons and Mounted Riflemen* (Richmond, 1861, 1862); William Gilham, *Authorized Cavalry Tactics, U.S.A., Manual of Instruction for the Volunteers and Militia of the United States* (Philadelphia, 1861); George B. McClellan, *Regulations and Instructions for the Field Service of the U.S. Cavalry in Times of War* (Philadelphia, 1861); George Patten, *Cavalry Drill and Sabre Exercise* (New York, 1862); U.S. War Department, *Cavalry Tactics* (3 parts, Washington, 1841; 2 parts, Philadelphia, 1855, 1856, 1861; 3 parts, Philadelphia, 1862; 3 parts, Washington, 1863, 1864); Joseph Wheeler, *A Revised System of Cavalry Tactics, for the use of the Cavalry and Mounted Infantry, CSA* (3 parts, Mobile, 1863).

CONTEMPORARY OBSERVATIONS AND TRAVELERS' ACCOUNTS: Celts and Southerners and their ways are described by Anon., *Visit to Texas . . .* (New York, 1834); Carl David Arfwedson, *The United States and Canada, in 1832, 1833, and 1834* (2 vols., London, 1834); Thomas Ashe, *Travels in America . . .* (3 vols., London, 1808); William Attmore, *Journal of a Tour to North Carolina, . . . 1787* (Chapel Hill, 1922); [Carlo Barinetti], *A Voyage to Mexico and Havana; including some General Observations on the United States* (New York, 1841); Louis Auguste Felix, Baron de Beaujour, *Sketch of the United States . . .*, translated by William Walton (London, 1814); James Silk Buckingham, *The Slave States of America* (2 vols., London, 1842); Moritz Busch, *Travels Between the Hudson & the Mississippi, 1851–1852*, translated and edited by Norman H. Binger (Lexington, 1971); Julius Caesar, *War Commentaries of Caesar*, translated by Rex Warner (New York, 1960); George William Frederick Howard, Earl of Carlisle, *Travels in America* (New York, 1851); Michel Chevalier, *Society, Manners and Politics in the United States*, translated by Thomas Gamaliel Bradford (Boston, 1839); George H. Coleraine, *The Life, Adventures, and Opinions of Col. George Hanger . . .* (2 vols., London, 1801); Ebenezer Davies, *American Scenes—and Christian Slavery: A Recent Tour of Four Thousand Miles in the United States* (London, 1849); William Faux, *Memorable Days in America; Being a Journal of a Tour of the United States . . .* (London, 1823); George William Featherstonhaugh, *Excursion Through the Slave States . . .* (2 vols., London, 1844); Barton Griffith, *The Diary of . . . , 1832–34 . . .* (Crawfordsville, Ind., 1932); Frederick Hall, *Letters from the East and from the West* (Washington, 1840); James Hall, *Letters from the West; Containing Sketches of Scenery, Manners, and Customs . . .* (reissue, Gainesville, 1967); Catherine C. Hopley, *Life in the South . . .* (2 vols., reissue, New York, 1974); Matilda C. J. F. Houstoun, *Texas and the Gulf . . .* (Philadelphia, 1845); Joseph Holt Ingraham, *The South-West . . .* (2 vols., New York, 1835); William Kingsford, *Impressions of the West and South During a Six Weeks' Holiday* (Toronto, 1858); Charles Joseph Latrobe, *The Rambler in North America . . .* (2 vols., London, 1835); Charles Macready, *The Diaries of . . .* (2 vols., London, 1912); Alexander Mackay, *The Western World; or Travels in the United States in 1846–47 . . .* (3 vols., London, 1849); Charles Mackay, *Life and Liberty in America; or, Sketches of a Tour in the United States and Canada, in 1857–8* (New York, 1859); David W. Mitchell, *Ten Years in the United States; Being an Englishman's View of Men and Things in the North and South* (London, 1862); Frederick L. Olmsted, *A Journey Through Texas* . . . (reissue, New York, 1969); Charles G. Parsons, *Inside View of Slavery: or, A Tour Among the Planters* (Cleveland, 1855); Thomas Pennant, *A Tour in Scotland; 1769* (fifth edition, London, 1790); John Pinkerton, ed., *A General Collection of the Best and Most Interesting Voyages and Travels in All Parts of the World* . . . (10 vols., London, 1809); Fitzgerald Ross, *Cities and Camps of the Confederate States*, edited by Richard B. Harwell (Urbana, 1958); William Howard Russell, *My Diary North and South* (2 vols., London, 1863); Johann David Schopf, *Travels in the Confederation* . . . , translated and edited by Alfred J. Morrison (2 vols., Cincinnati, 1912); Charles Sealsfield, *America: Glorious and Chaotic Land* . . . , translated by E. L. Jordan (Englewood Cliffs, 1969); Alexis de Tocqueville, *The Republic of the United States of America, and Its Political Institutions*, translated by Henry Reeves (New York, 1858); Gerald of Wales, *The Journey through Wales and the Description of Wales*, translated by Lewis Thorpe (reissue, New York, 1978); Henry B. Whipple, *Bishop Whipple's Southern Diary, 1843–1844*, edited by Lester B. Shippee (London, 1937).

Secondary Sources

GENERAL REFERENCES: Essential on men and events are George W. Cullum, ed., *Biographical Registrar of the Officers and Graduates of the United States Military Academy, at West Point* (2 vols., New York, 1868); Francis B. Heitman, *Historical Register and Dictionary of the United States Army* (2 vols., Washington, 1903); Allen Johnson, ed., *Dictionary of American Biography* (20 vols., New York, 1928); Ezra J. Warner, *Generals in Gray: Lives of the Confederate Commanders* (Baton Rouge, 1959); Ezra J. Warner, *Generals in Blue: Lives of the Union Commanders* (Baton Rouge, 1964); E. B. Long and Barbara Long, *The Civil War Day by Day: An Almanac, 1861–1865* (Garden City, 1971); Mark Mayo Boatner III, *The Civil War Dictionary* (New York, 1959). Standard on the number of troops engaged and the casualties are Thomas L. Livermore, *Numbers & Losses in the Civil War in America: 1861–65* (reissue, Bloomington, 1957), and William F. Fox, *Regimental Losses in the American Civil War, 1861–1865* (Albany, 1889). Helpful essays and information on courses and textbooks can be found in U.S. War Department, *The Centennial of the United States Military Academy at West Point, New York, 1802–1902* (2 vols., Washington, 1904).

MEXICAN WAR: Justin H. Smith's *The War With Mexico* (2 vols., New York, 1919) is old but still indispensable on tactics. Also useful are K. Jack Bauer's *The Mexican War, 1846–1848* (New York, 1974); Roswell Ripley's *The War With Mexico* (2 vols., New York, 1849); Cadmus M. Wilcox's *History of the Mexican War* (Washington, 1892); Isaac Ingalls Stevens's *Campaigns of the Rio Grande and of Mexico, with Notices of the Recent Work of Major Ripley* (New York, 1851).

TACTICAL THEORY BEFORE 1861: Helpful on this neglected subject are Russell F. Weigley, *Towards an American Army: Military Thought from Washington to Marshall* (New York, 1962); T. Harry Williams, *Americans at War: The Development of the American Military System* (New York, 1962); Stephen E. Ambrose, *Duty, Honor, Country: A History of West Point* (Baltimore, 1966); James W. Pohl, "The Influence of

Antoine Henri de Jomini on Winfield Scott's Campaign in the Mexican War," *Southwestern Historical Quarterly*, LXXVII (1973).

CIVIL WAR TACTICS: There is no comprehensive treatment of Civil War tactics but various aspects of the subject are covered in Robert V. Bruce, *Lincoln and the Tools of War* (Indianapolis, 1956); David Herbert Donald, "The Confederate as a Fighting Man," *Journal of Southern History*, XXV (1959); David Herbert Donald, *Lincoln Reconsidered: Essays on the Civil War Era* (New York, 1956); David Herbert Donald, ed., *Why the North Won the Civil War* (Baton Rouge, 1960); Thomas L. Connelly and Archer Jones, *The Politics of Command: Factions and Ideas in Confederate Strategy* (Baton Rouge, 1973); J. F. C. Fuller, "The Place of the American Civil War in the Evolution of War," *Army Quarterly*, XXVI (1933); Edward Hagerman, "From Jomini to Dennis Hart Mahan: The Evolution of Trench Warfare and the American Civil War," *Civil War History*, XIII (1967); Edward Hagerman, "The Evolution of Trench Warfare in the American Civil War," (doctoral dissertation, Duke University, 1965); Joseph Harsh, "Battlesword and Rapier: Clausewitz, Jomini, and the American Civil War," *Military Affairs*, XXXVIII (1974); John K. Mahon, "Civil War Infantry Assault Tactics," *Military Affairs*, XXV (1961); Grady McWhiney, "Jefferson Davis and the Art of War," *Civil War History*, XXI (1975); Grady McWhiney, *Southerners and Other Americans* (New York, 1973); Grady McWhiney, "Who Whipped Whom? Confederate Defeat Reexamined," *Civil War History*, XI (1965); Thomas Vernon Moseley, "Evolution of the American Civil War Infantry Tactics," (doctoral dissertation, University of North Carolina, Chapel Hill, 1967); Francis A. Lord, "Strong Right Arm of the Infantry: The '61 Springfield Rifle Musket," *Civil War Times Illustrated*, I (1962); L. Van Loan Naisawald, *Grape and Canister: The Story of the Field Artillery of the Army of the Potomac, 1861–1865* (New York, 1960); Stephen Z. Starr, "Cold Steel: The Saber and the Union Cavalry," *Civil War History*, XI (1965); Roy P. Stonesifer, Jr., "The Union Cavalry Comes of Age," *Civil War History*, XI (1965); Frank E. Vandiver, *Their Tattered Flags* (New York, 1970); Arthur L. Wagner, *Organization and Tactics* (Kansas City, 1894); Jac Weller, "Imported Confederate Shoulder Weapons," *Civil War History*, V (1959); Bell I. Wiley, "The Common Soldier of the Civil War," *Civil War Times Illustrated*, XII, No. 4 (July 1973); Bell I. Wiley, *The Life of Billy Yank: The Common Soldier of the Union* (Indianapolis, 1951); Bell I. Wiley, *The Life of Johnny Reb: The Common Soldier of the Confederacy* (Indianapolis, 1943).

Important studies of campaigns and battles include John Bigelow, *The Campaign of Chancellorsville* (New Haven, 1910); Bruce Catton, *Glory Road* (Garden City, 1952); Bruce Catton, *Mr. Lincoln's Army* (Garden City, 1951); Bruce Catton, *A Stillness at Appomattox* (Garden City, 1953); Edwin B. Coddington, *The Gettysburg Campaign: A Study in Command* (New York, 1968); Thomas L. Connelly, *Army of the Heartland: The Army of Tennessee, 1861–1862* (Baton Rouge, 1967); Thomas L. Connelly, *Autumn of Glory: The Army of Tennessee, 1862–1865* (Baton Rouge, 1971); Jacob D. Cox, *Atlanta* (New York, 1882); William C. Davis, *Battle at Bull Run . . .* (Garden City, 1977); Abner Doubleday, *Chancellorsville and Gettysburg* (New York, 1882); Clifford Dowdey, *Lee's Last Campaign* (Boston, 1960); Anon., "General Lee's Offensive Policy in the Campaign of 1864," *Southern Historical Society Papers*, IX (1881); Andrew A. Humphreys, *The Virginia Campaign of '64 and '65* (New York, 1883); Edward G. Longacre, *Mounted Raids of the Civil War* (New York, 1975); James Pickett Jones, *Yankee Blitz-*

krieg: Wilson's Raid through Alabama and Georgia (Athens, 1976); James Lee McDonough, *Shiloh—In Hell Before Night* (Knoxville, 1977); James Lee McDonough, *Stones River—Bloody Winter in Tennessee* (Knoxville, 1980); Francis Palfrey, *The Antietam and Fredericksburg* (New York, 1897); John C. Ropes, *The Army Under Pope* (New York, 1889); Wiley Sword, *Shiloh: Bloody April* (New York, 1974); George R. Stewart, *Pickett's Charge* (Boston, 1959); Alexander F. Stevenson, *The Battle of Stone's River* (Boston, 1884); Richard J. Sommers, *Richmond Redeemed: The Siege of Petersburg* (Garden City, 1981); Kenneth P. Williams, *Lincoln Finds a General: A Military Study of the Civil War* (5 vols., New York, 1949–1959).

Generalship and tactics are examined in several biographies. Some of the most useful of these are Lenoir Chambers, *Stonewall Jackson* (2 vols., New York, 1959); Douglas S. Freeman, *Lee's Lieutenants: A Study in Command* (3 vols., New York, 1942–1944); Douglas S. Freeman, *R. E. Lee: A Biography* (4 vols., New York, 1934–1935); J. F. C. Fuller, *The Generalship of Ulysses S. Grant* (New York, 1929); Gilbert E. Govan and James W. Livingood, *A Different Valor: The Story of General Joseph E. Johnston, C.S.A.* (Indianapolis, 1956); Herman Hattaway, *General Stephen D. Lee* (Jackson, 1976); Edward Hagerman, "The Professionalization of George B. McClellan and Early Civil War Field Command: An Institutional Perspective," *Civil War History*, XXI (1975); Warren W. Hassler, Jr, *General George B. McClellan, Shield of the Union* (Baton Rouge, 1957); George F. R. Henderson, *Stonewall Jackson and the American Civil War* (2 vols., London, 1898); Nathaniel C. Hughes, Jr., *General William J. Hardee: Old Reliable* (Baton Rouge, 1965); Grady McWhiney, *Braxton Bragg and Confederate Defeat* (New York, 1969); Charles P. Roland, *Albert Sidney Johnston: Soldier of Three Republics* (Austin, 1964); Frank E. Vandiver, *Mighty Stonewall* (New York, 1957); T. Harry Williams, *P. G. T. Beauregard: Napoleon in Gray* (Baton Rouge, 1955).

SOUTHERNERS AND THEIR CELTIC HERITAGE: On the ancient Celts and their characteristics see Anne Ross, *Everyday Life of the Pagan Celts* (London, 1970); Barry Cunliffe, *The Celtic World* (New York, 1979); T. G. E. Powell, *The Celts* (New York, 1958); Gerhard Herm, *The Celts: The People Who Came out of the Darkness* (New York, 1977); Henri Hubert, *The Greatness and Decline of the Celts* (London, 1934); Jan Filip, *Celtic Civilization and Its Heritage* (second edition, Prague, 1977); M. L. Sjoestedt, *Gods and Heroes of the Celts*, translated by Myles Dillon (London, 1949); and E. Hull, "Observations of Classical Writers on the Habits of the Celtic Nations, as Illustrated from Irish Records," *Celtic Review*, III (1907).

The Celts in the British Isles and their traditions are discussed in Lloyd Laing, *Celtic Britain* (New York, 1979); Michael Hechter, *Internal Colonialism: The Celtic Fringe in British National Development, 1536–1966* (Berkeley, 1975); Alwyn Rees and Brinley Rees, *Celtic Heritage: Ancient Tradition in Ireland and Wales* (London, 1961); Nicholas Mansergh, *The Irish Question, 1840–1921* (Toronto, 1966); Mary McGarry, *Great Folk Tales of Old Ireland* (New York, 1972); Peter Hume Brown, *History of Scotland . . .* (3 vols., Cambridge, 1909–1912); Wallace Notestein, *The Scots in History* (reissue, Westport, 1970); William Ferguson, *Scotland, 1689 to the Present* (New York, 1968); J. P. MacLean, *An Historical Account of the Settlement of Scotch Highlanders in America . . .* (reissue, Baltimore, 1978); R. W. Munro, *Highland Clans and Tartans* (London, 1977).

The continuation of Celtic traditions in the South is discussed in Forrest McDonald and Grady McWhiney, "The Antebellum Southern Herdsman: A Reinterpretation,"

Journal of Southern History, XLI (1975); Grady McWhiney, "The Revolution in Nineteenth-Century Alabama Agriculture," *Alabama Review,* XXXI (1978); Forrest McDonald, "The Ethnic Factor in Alabama History: A Neglected Dimension," *Alabama Review,* XXXI (1978); Grady McWhiney, "Saving the Best from the Past," *Alabama Review,* XXXII (1979); Forrest McDonald and Ellen Shapiro McDonald, "The Ethnic Origins of the American People, 1790," *William and Mary Quarterly,* XXXVII (1980); Forrest McDonald and Grady McWhiney, "The South from Self-Sufficiency to Peonage: An Interpretation," *American Historical Review,* LXXXV (1980); and Cleveland Donald, Jr., ed., *When the South was West: The Old Southwest, 1780-1840* (Jackson, 1982).

Index